Books in the series 'The Colonial Economy of NSW 1788-1835'

A Brief Economic History of NSW

The Colonial Economy of NSW 1788-1835–A retrospective

The Government Store is Open for business–
the commissariat operations in NSW 1788-1835

The Enterprising Colonial Economy of NSW 1800-1830–
Government Business Enterprises in operation

Guiding the Colonial Economy–Public Funding in NSW 1800-1835

Financing the Colonial Economy of NSW 1800-1835

Essays on the colonial Economy of NSW 1788-1835

Industries that Formed a Colonial Economy

British Colonial Investment in Colonial N.S.W. 1788-1850

A Population History of Colonial New South Wales

BRITISH COLONIAL INVESTMENT

IN COLONIAL N.S.W.

1788-1850

GORDON W BECKETT

For book orders, email orders@traffordpublishing.com.sg

Most Trafford Singapore titles are also available at major online book retailers.

Printed in Singapore.

ISBN: 978-1-4669-9188-0 (sc)
ISBN: 978-1-4669-9189-7 (hc)
ISBN: 978-1-4669-9190-3 (e)

Trafford rev. 06/13/2013

 www.traffordpublishing.com.sg
Singapore
toll-free: 800 101 2656 (Singapore)
Fax: 800 101 2656 (Singapore)

CONTENTS

CHAPTER 1

ABSTRACT

The traditional reporting of Australian economic history is:

- Britain settled the continent for 'strategic' advantages and as a source of raw materials for its industry, and as an outlet for its trading and the transfer of resources (a takeover) by the new economic managers
- Economic development took place in the new land, beneficial only to British traditional interests (including the use of valuable raw materials, of the British trade, shipping, insurance and investment industries
- The official intention of settling the colony was for peaceful & co-operative economic development of the new land, beneficial to British traditional interests and not intended to undermine or engage in war with the native population, and to share what food resources were naturally available. The gulf between the two societies was too large to be bridged and the British settlement succeeded while the ancient society was destroyed. The destruction of traditional Aboriginal society was recognized by a depopulation from an accepted population of about 1 million in 1788 to 250,000 by 1848 whilst an estimated 50% of Aboriginal resources were absorbed by white settlers between 1788 and 1809
- The traditional recounting of early Australian Economic History is that Britain decided to settle the continent for 'strategic' advantages and as a source of raw materials for its industry, and as

1

an outlet for its trading and the transfer of resources (a takeover) by the new economic managers.

■ This new class of colonial economic manager, in fact, faced much higher costs than expected, in achieving their 'success'. Their target was to be a bloodless change of ownership followed by economic development of the new land, beneficial only to British traditional interests

The revisionist approach is that:

■ Britain planned for a multi-purpose strategic settlement at Botany Bay
■ Britain did not plan to diminish the native population by thinking that it was 'terra nullius' just because there was no signs of 'farming' or other physical improvements, but
■ The settlement led directly to a presumption of British land ownership as well as ownership of all natural resources, and
■ British development (as defined and outlined) led to a penal colony under autocratic governance before moving through a transition phase of free enterprise, semi-planned economy but still providing raw materials and markets for Britain. As Fitzpatrick points out "The phenomenon of British Industrialization and not the enticements of colonization filled the social foreground[1]

Why did the settlement achieve success after its early struggles? What steps did Britain take that led to a successful settlement and colonization process?

Butlin thinks that the early achievements of the settlement are the result of seven major conditions:

(a) The early elimination of threats from Aborigines and their almost immediate depopulation.

---

[1]   Fitzpatrick, Brian *The British Empire in Australia – An Economic History 1834-1939*

(b) The early privatization of the settlement and the firm establishment of private property, private employed labour and market choice in the settlement

(c) The accession of substantial British support in kind, through the authority to issue bills payable by the British Government, and through the presence of substantial quasi-exports

(d) The desire for non-tradables and for goods that could not be readily tradable

(e) The supply of human capital with skills appropriate to a relatively advanced society

(f) The lack of economics of scale in large areas of non-food production, and

(g) The recovery of property rights in labour time by the majority of convicts

CHAPTER 2

BRITISH COLONIAL INVESTMENT

In any study of British Colonial Investment one needs to define terms and establish parameters. Terms such as 'Investment' need a definition and a clarification.

For instance, does the term 'investment' include transportees, free immigrants, and supplies for the Colony? The answer is 'yes' to transportees, 'yes' to free immigrants, and 'no' to supplies. In this writer's opinion, human capital is as important as monetary capital.

The definitions will be expanded shortly after setting some parameters for the study. British investment into the new Colony of New South Wales from 1788 came in many guises. The British Treasury funded the ships, the supplies, the military payroll, and its support; the civil list included the Governor, the clergy, the medical team, the surveyor, and the advocate-general. These people were salaried and supported. The convicts were clothed and fed. Tools were supplied, as were animals/livestock, building materials, and even a portable canvas 'house' for the Governor. This was the First Fleet.

The Second Fleet was little different. It carried badly needed supplies for a starving colony. The remote settlements of Parramatta, Hawkesbury and Norfolk Island, Windsor and Liverpool, all required investment. This was provided from the grant money allocated by the Treasury to support the Colony.

The first steps taken by Phillip at Sydney Cove – clearing the land, erecting tents, planting crops – are all a mechanism of investment. The second step was to make these facilities 'permanent', in a less temporary way. The crops had failed for want of local knowledge, and the earliest attempts to cut trees for structural timbers was again a failure, because of the inadequate tools and the lack of local knowledge of the moisture content of the trees. The results were that the wood, being undried and erected in a 'green' condition, bowed, twisted and cracked as the wood dried in place. These second steps included the assembly of a kiln for making bricks and tiles, and erection of a windmill, observatory, wharf, and a permanent Government House.

From 1802, only 14 years after establishing the colony, and with the colony still without a 'treasury', Governor King, (Hunter's successor) decided that the need for social services towards the growing orphan population in the colony should be met by local revenue. However, without any form of taxation and without a treasury, the Governor was breaking new ground, and decided to raise the first import duties imposed on the colony.

The first form of indirect taxation attempted in the colony was commenced in 1800 by applying a duty or tariff on all imported items of spirits, wine, and beer, for the purpose of providing funds for completing the erection of a Gaol in Sydney, a work which had previously been carried on by a voluntary assessment, levied in the first instance on the inhabitants of Sydney, but afterwards on the community at large. As the produce of these imposts was found inadequate to complete the work, duties on other articles (of luxury) were resorted to which, with some slight modifications, were continued to be collected under Proclamations of successive Governors till the year 1840. When Governor Macquarie assumed the government in 1810 the population was 11,500 and the duties about 8,000 pound a year. On his retirement from office, in 1821, the population had increased to 29,783 and the port duties to nearly 30,000 pound. This Gaol Fund, as it became known, was the first of the private funds, run on behalf of the Governor, but handled by private individuals – Mr. Darcy Wentworth was appointed to be treasurer of the 'Gaol' Fund and then its successor, the Police Fund. He retired from this paid post in 1818 . . . During this time he also continued his work as Assistant Surgeon in the colony and as Police Magistrate. He also fathered William Charles Wentworth, one part of the threesome who crossed the Blue Mountains, trained in England as a lawyer, wrote two volumes of observations on the colony, which writings were slanted in favor of John Macarthur, whose son-in-law he had hoped to become.

The Orphan Fund had appointed the Rev'd Samuel Marsden as treasurer and board member of the Female Orphan Institute.

The parameters of studying British Investment must include an understanding of the source of revenues into the colony. There are three: direct funding by the British Treasury, local colonial revenue, and bills drawn, in the colony, on the Treasury in London.

    a.   The British Treasury funded the

- Civil list (of salaried colonial officials),
- The military personnel
- The commissary (clothing, food, tool and material supplies)
- Convict shipping contracts, and
- Funds for operating the colony.

The attached table shows the funds furnished during this period, by the British Treasury direct and for the Commissary usage, local colonial operations, and the various 'funds'. b. Local Colonial Revenue, as established for the Orphan, Gaol and Police Funds, were dispersed for items ranging from the purchase of Captain Kent's Home in Sydney for use as a temporary orphan residence, to the new building for female orphans in Parramatta, to improvements at the church of St. John in Parramatta to establishing schools in each of the settlements. The Gaol and Police Funds were used for another wide range of building and maintenance works, including:

- Work on new roads and streets
- Maintenance of roads and streets
- Fencing burial grounds

- Gates and fencing for gaols
- Materials for white-washing gaols
- Apprehending runaway convicts
- Purchasing police house in Newcastle
- Hospital supplies

Until 1835, import duties were over 50% of the colonial revenues and most often in the 70% range. By 1824, sales of crown land had commenced and were growing in importance as a source of revenue for the British Treasury, which maintained full control of the usage of those funds, until self-government in 1852, when they were relinquished as an offset to the colony accepting responsibility for the colonial funding and the civil list.

Reference to the Table 'Expenditure by British Treasury 1788-1835, shows classification of expenditures by

- Government Transport (of convicts to the colony)
- Victuals (stores and food)
- Other stores (tools and materials)
- Bills drawn by the colony on the Treasury
- The Civil Establishment (salaries and allowances)
- The Military and Marine personnel and their allowances

The annual expenditure by the Treasury rose from 18008 pound in 1788 to over 100,000 pound by 1792 before falling to 75,000 in 1795.

The Commissariat fund met obligations for local stores, materials, and labor purchased by the Commissary for settlers, convicts, and military personnel, with its source of revenue being bills drawn on the Treasury in London, and bartering of goods for goods and services with the farmers and settlers.

b. Bills drawn against the British Treasury were an important source of capital for the colony. It is difficult to imagine how the bills were accounted for in London with any degree of certainty. The first bill drawn on the Treasury was by Phillip who in 1787 was authorized to buy supplies and livestock in the Cape on his passage with the First Fleet to Botany Bay. Once the colony was under development, bills were drawn for a variety of reasons

- Visiting ships were paid by a bill drawn on London for selling the badly needed provisions for a starving colony
- Importers, such as Robert Campbell were paid by bills for bring goods and materials from India for use in the colony or for resale
- The commissary purchased meat (Kangaroo) and vegetables from settlers and farmers, although the 'store receipts' were becoming a medium of exchange in order to eliminate the high discounting of bills trying to be cashed in the colony.
- Private bills by military officers and traders were becoming of frequent use, except that there was no guarantee of payment upon presentment and some traders and settlers faced bankruptcy and many creditors.

So the parameters of our study are broad and must essentially cover the source and use of funds by the British Treasury, but this leaves two missing elements for our study, so we have to broaden it yet further.

- The private investment by the money market operators in London as well as holders of private investment capital needs to be examined and included in the study.
- There is then the important question of the 'opportunity' cost of the British Government 'investment'. Opportunity in this context is the alternative use that these investment funds could be put to; opportunity is also the alternative investment that may have had to be made if, for instance in this case, the colony had not been developable and become self-supporting to the extent that the approx. 160, 000 convicts had not been able to be fed, clothed, and put to productive work in the colony. Our analysis of this opportunity cost will include statements as to what cost (thus the 'opportunity' cost) the British Treasury would have faced if a suitable colony had not been found to replace the Americas. Such costs would have included
- The cost of building prisons to hold these prisoners, both convicted and held pending trial

- The cost of guarding these men and women; of feeding, clothing and keeping healthy, these people.
- The costs of holding the prisoners in hulks and rotting barges on the English River System
- An important cost is the continuing crime that would follow a release of prisoners from British gaols back into the community, as compared with ticket-of-leave or emancipated convicts being released only into the Australian landscape, usually never to see England again.

But what about the positive gains that are derived from opening the colony as a penal settlement with some free settlers. Again there are many and largely quantifiable.

- The colony was built by convict labour, who were not paid (other than their 'keep') for their services
- The extensive building program of public buildings, wharves, roads, and infrastructure (water, drainage, and sewerage).
- The building program not only provided a useful employment for the convicts but created private industries wanting to supply materials and services for these important public programs.
- Emancipated or ticket-of-leave convicts were returned to colonial society and many made significant contributions to the economic and social life of the colony.

The attached table shows the author's estimates of the 'opportunity' cost which estimate is approx 140 million pound.

The British expected their colonies to pay their way

We know that the British authorities had the choice of building new prisons in Britain and housing, feeding, guarding and clothing these prisoners, or relocate them to a 'penal colony'. The previous penal colony in America was no longer available because of the American Wars of Independence and the British were no longer welcome there. The recommendation of Sir Joseph Banks, after his voyage to the southern oceans with Captain James Cook, was to use the land and resources available in the newly charted East Coast of 'Australia'. The favourable opportunity cost of this arrangement was enormous. Britain was fighting wars in a number of areas and had numerous Colonies to administer, and one more Colony; supposedly rich in potential rewards and able to be converted to self-sufficiency was most attractive. So, the opportunity cost was became one form of savings.

By 1824 the convicts were also paying their way (in opportunity cost terms) by removing coal from the ground in the Maitland area and using it for heating purposes. No value was ever placed on this work, or on the use of convicts as builders of roads, housing, barracks, storage sheds, port wharves, churches, and government buildings. It would appear that the convicts earned their keep whilst the Colony paid its own way very quickly. The 'Blue Book' of 1828 states that there was revenue from the sale of convict produce such as 'coal, wheat, sugar, molasses, and tobacco' but the value of convict labour was to remain unreported. Historians should recognize the value of the convict work as well as the opportunity cost of having transported the prisoners' offshore, when an assessment is made of the 'investment' made, and the benefits gained by Britain in the new Colony of New South Wales.

The original estimate of direct gains by the British authorities from the original and continuing investment in the Colony of New South Wales was based on 5 (five) identifiable and quantifiable events, even though the convicts were assigned jobs on the basis of 'full keep'.

1. The opportunity cost of housing, feeding and guarding the convicts in the Colony compared with the cost of doing the same thing in Britain.

The original estimates, in this category, were based on an estimated differential of ten pound per head—an arbitrary assessment of the differential cost.

However recent and more reliable information has come to hand which gives further validity to a number of 20 pound per head per annum, compared with the original 10 pound per head per annum.

A letter to Under Secretary Nepean dated 23rd August 1783, from James Maria Matra of Shropshire and London assists us in this regard.

It was Matra, who first analyzed the opportunity of using the new Colony as a Penal Colony; only his estimates were incorrect and ill founded. He had advised the Government that it would cost less than 3,000 pound to establish the Colony initially, plus transportation cost at 15 pound per head and annual maintenance of 20 pound per head.

In fact the transportation was contracted for the second fleet at 13 pound 5 shillings per head and Colonial revenues from 1802 offset annual maintenance.

However, Matra made a significant statement in his letter to Nepean, when he pointed out that the prisoners housed, fed, and guarded on the rotting hulks on the Thames River were being contracted for in the annual amount of 26.15.10 per head per annum. He also writes that 'the charge to the public for these convicts has been increasing for the last 7 or 8 years' **(Historical Records of NSW—Vol 1 Part 2 Page 7)**

Adopting this alternative cost (of 26.75 pound) as a base for comparison purposes, it means that the benefit to Britain of the Colony over a twenty-year period increased from 140,000,000 pound to 180,000,000 pound. This calculation assesses the Ground 1 benefit at 84,000,000 pound.

2. Benefit to Britain on Ground Two is put at 70, 000,000 pound (again over a 20-year period) which places the value of a convict's labour at 35 pound per annum. Matra had assessed the value of labour of the Hulk prisoners at 35. 85 pound.
3. The valuation of convict labour in the new Colony should reflect the convicts not only used on building sites, but also on road, bridge and wharf construction. This would add (based on 35 pound per annum) a further 21,000,000-pound.
4. The Molesworth Committee (A House of Commons Committee investigating transportation) concluded that "the surplus food production by the convicts would feed the Military people and this, over a period of 10 years, would save 7,000,000 pound for the British Treasury.
5. The benefits of fringe benefit grants of land to the Military etc can be estimated (based on One pound per acre) at over 5,000,000 before 1810.

6. We learn from Governor King's Report to Earl Camden (which due to a change of office holder, should have been addressed to Viscount Castlereagh as Colonial Secretary) dated 15th March 1806 that the Convicts engaged in widely diverse work. The Report itself is entitled

"Public Labour of Convicts maintained by the Crown at Sydney, Parramatta, Hawkesbury, Toongabbie, and Castle Hill, for the year 1805

Cultivation—Gathering, husking and shelling maize from 200 acres sowed last year—Breaking up ground and planting 1230 acres of wheat, 100 acre of Barley, 250 acres of Maize, 14 acres of Flax, and 3 acres of potatoes—Hoeing the above maize and threshing wheat.

Stock—Taking care of Government stock as herdsmen, watchmen etc

Buildings—

- *At Sydney: Building and constructing of stone, a citadel, a stone house, a brick dwelling for the Judge Advocate, a commodious brick house for the main guard, a brick printing office*
- *At Parramatta: Alterations at the Brewery, a brick house as clergyman's residence*
- *At Hawkesbury: completing a public school*
- *A Gaol House with offices, at the expense of the Colony*
- *Boat and Ship Builders: refitting vessels and building row boats*
- *Wheel and Millwrights: making and repairing carts*

Manufacturing: sawing, preparing and manufacturing hemp, flax and wool, bricks and tiles

Road Gangs: repairing roads, and building new roads

Other Gangs: loading and unloading boats"

(Historical Records of NSW—Vol 6. P43)

Thus the total benefits from these six (6) items of direct gain to the British comes to well over 174 million pound, and this is compared to Professor N. G. Butlin's proposal that the British 'invested' 5.6 million.

However, one item of direct cash cost born by the British was the transportation of the prisoners to the Colony, their initial food and general well being. Although the British chartered the whole boat, some of the expense was offset by authorizing private passengers, 'free settlers' to travel in the same fleet. A second saving was the authorities had approved 'back-loading' by these vessels of tea from China.

Only limited stores and provisions, tools and implements were sent with Captain Arthur Phillip, the appointed first Governor, and his efforts to delay the fleet until additional tools were ready was met with an order to 'commence the trip forthwith'. This turned out to be a mistake as the new Colony could only rely on minimal farming practices to grow a supply of vegetables and without the tools to scratch the land, remove the trees and vegetation, little progress was made. This was a potentially big cost to the fledgling Colony.

i. The 'Blue Book' accounting records as maintained by Governor Macquarie from 1822 includes a reference to 'net revenue and expenses' which suggests an offset of all revenues against all expenses, and would include as revenue certain convict maintenance charges, to be reimbursed by the British Treasury. Such reimbursement was accounted for and reported only once—in 1825, when it is recorded as a 'receipt in aid of revenue' that an amount of £16,617 'the amount of the parliamentary grant for the charge of defraying the civil establishment'. Prior to and since that date, there are only reports of payments and outgoings to the civil establishment, military, and other personnel, without offset from reimbursement.

ii. Other notations in 1825 include revenues from rentals of government assets (Government outsourcing and privatization obviously started back in 1825) such as;

Ferries   1584 pound
Toll gates   6554

Gardens	1835
Mill	1749
Canteen	910
Church pews	1296

The hire of convict 'mechanics' raised 6853.27 pound

Slaughtering dues contributed 975.54 whilst duty on colonial distillation reaped 4901.30 pound.

The biggest revenue earners were duty on imported spirits (178,434 pound) and duty on imported Tobacco (21,817 pound)

i. Even in 1822 the Colony was showing a small operating surplus. This surplus grew through 1828 until, other than for transportation of convicts to the Colony; the charges on account of the British Treasury were less than One Hundred Thousand pounds for protecting, feeding, and housing nearly 5,000 fully maintained convicts. Against this cost, the charge for housing, feeding and guarding this same number of prisoners in Britain would have been substantially higher, since in addition to the 5,000 gully maintained convicts there were a further 20,000 being paid for by free settlers and used as supervised labour. Britain surely had found a cheap source of penal servitude for at least 25,000 of its former prisoners, and found a very worthwhile alternative to the American Colonies as a destination for its prisoners.

j. Revenue from Crown Land sales and rents was used to offset Civil (Crown) salaries and expenses.

The opportunity cost to the British Treasury includes not only the cost savings but also the lateral savings and benefits produced for England and the British Treasury.

Some of the other advantages to Britain include:

a. The build-up of trade by the East-India Company
b. The advantage of a secure, in-house, supply of raw wool, to keep the spinning mills occupied

c. The opportunity cost of housing, feeding and guarding prisoners

d. The use of convict labour in the new Colony, for such as

- Land clearing, farming, food production
- For road construction

Building projects such as:

- Public wharves
- Barracks
- Public Buildings
- Productions of Materials supply e.g. brick & tile production.
- As unpaid day labour for the pastoral & agricultural industry.

e. We can assume that Land grants, in the Colony, to men on the military and civil list was a form of 'fringe benefits' and should be quantified as an alternative to paid remuneration for these people. Even land grants to emancipists were used as an incentive to increase food production.

f. We can quantify items C, D and E into a 'value of direct gain to the British economy of nearly 140,000,000 pound (refer details in 'Statistics'), compared with the publicly recorded expenditure on transportation, supplies, and military personnel of 5,600,000 pound, between 1788 and 1822.

The purposes of trying to quantify these benefits are to challenge to traditional concept that 'the British *invested* millions of pounds in the Colony of New South Wales'.

It is obviously only the case when the outlay is shown and not the on-going benefits for over fifty years, and indeed two hundred years. It is still arguable that the Continent of Australia is, in Captain Arthur Phillip's words 'the best investment Britain will ever make'.

Having established the parameters for studying British (private and public) investment in the Colony of New South Wales, the question must now be one of who else thinks this investment was of interest and relevance.

N.G. Butlin did not complete his manuscript of 'Forming a Colonial Economy' because his death in 1991.

However his notes to that time were edited and assembled into the book form and we can learn a great deal about the British motives for the colony and its economic development.

Butlin writes "Even though, there may have been other imperial motives behind the British settlement of Australia, there is no doubt that the transportation of convicts to the Antipodes was a convenient solution to social, judicial, and budgetary problems in Britain in the 1780s"

Butlin further deduces that "Persons may move between countries (i.e. immigration) when the capitalized value of the differential in expected lifetime earnings abroad as compared with those at home exceeds the transfer and relocation costs." The good news of free immigration and the capital transfer into the colony was that between 1788 and 1800 is that 21,302 'free immigrants' arrived in the colony. There are 9 identified categories of 'immigrants' during this period.

- Military and civil officers and their families
- Former officials returning to the colony
- Convict families
- Indentured labourers
- Assisted immigrants
- Privately supported persons sponsored by colonials
- Free immigrants and their families

Given that Britain provided not only human capital but also fiscal resources to support the people concerned, the volume, nature, and access to those resources became interesting. However, it remains the case that Britain, having put into place extensive levels of capital, certainly succeeded in withdrawing a great deal of its early fiscal support and bringing the Commissariat effectively under military control.

Obviously another form of 'investment' is public debt, and public borrowing, secured by the full faith and credit of the colonial government

The 'works outlay' is another element of 'public investment' and was not fully accounted for until 1810, upon the arrival of Governor Macquarie. From that date, works outlay (i.e. Capital expenditure from the revenue of the local colony) grew annually from £2194 (1810) to £14700 (1821). However this is a small component of total works outlay or capital expenditure, since a Mr. Henry Kitchen, in a submission to Commissioner J.T. Bigge stated that his estimate of building construction under Macquarie was in excess of 900,000 pound.

A table included in Australians Historical Statistics refers to 'Gross Private Capital Formation at current prices do not commence until 1861 and later in this study we will try to accumulate both public and private capital formation from 1800 – based on a separate studies of colonial industrial development and colonial building and construction development. This table is derived from Butlin's 'Australian Domestic Product, Investment & Foreign Borrowing 1861-1938'. It appears that no previous studies have been undertaken of Private or Public Capital Formation between 1788 and 1861.

T.A. Coghlan is generally recognized as a significant contributor to Colonial Economic History and he writes in Volume 1 of 'Labour and Industry in Australia' of another phase of Public Investment, or its encouragement in the colony, by favourable official policies.

Coghlan writes "Under the Governorship of Macquarie the infant town of Sydney grew considerably. King had been the first Governor to grant leases there (Sydney), but as the leases were only for five years the buildings erected were naturally not of a substantial character. Macquarie granted a number of leases also, but gave permanent grants of land in cases where valuable buildings were to be erected, so that at the end of his term of office Sydney had grown considerably, having the appearance, according to W.C. Wentworth in his *Historical and Statistical Account of the Colony*, of a town of 20,000 inhabitants though its population, numbered only 7,000; and while the houses were for the most part small one-storied dwellings, it contained buildings, private and public, excellent both in construction and in design, and many stores where goods of all kinds could be bought. The Government Store continued in existence as a shop open to the public until January 1815, when Macquarie, considering that its purpose had been served as a means towards keeping down prices, closed it to all except the military and the convicts in government employment." So having fixed the short-term land lease, Macquarie actively encouraged public and private investment in building and construction.

Coghlan provides an insight into another Macquarie step to encourage investment. He writes "Until Macquarie arrived, the means of communicating between one part of the settlement and another was difficult, as all roads were poor. Macquarie had a passion for construction, and his roads were excellent. He made a turnpike road from Sydney to the Hawkesbury, completing it in 1811. Now goods and passengers did not have to be carried by boat, as previously was the case. A few years later he constructed the great road over the mountains to the western plains, and also extended his roads in other directions. With the construction of the roads, internal trade and all the industries dependent thereon developed. It took a further time before travelling by road was safe, as many convicts escaped and took to the bush, preying upon defenseless travelers; journeys to any part of the settlement was usually made in company and it was customary to make even the short journey from Sydney to Parramatta about 14 miles in parties."

If we intend to extend our parameters to further analyze the types and amount of public and private British Investment in the colony of New South Wales, we will have to now review certain other matters:

- The development of private industries e.g. boat-building; timber harvesting and processing; agriculture sand pastoral pursuits, whaling and overseas trading – all of which were reasonably capital intensive operations, and which would have attracted both overseas investors and a local breed of entrepreneurs
- The development of building and construction in the colony, including reference to the public buildings completed in the period, how much they would have cost and how they were paid for.
- We will try to assemble a table of public and private overseas (British) investment, and establish the background to debt in the colony from overseas sources.

- We will attempt to recreate the level of Investment in the colony by category by first identifying the various sources of both public and private investment and relating value to each one
- We will endeavor to track bank deposits and advances, which until the 1850s were generally in the negative (i.e. advances exceeded deposits and it fell to the local banks to accept British deposits for fixed terms of 1, 2 or 3 years. Banks advanced money by way of pastoralists' overdrafts, on city land and on stocks and shares. Land banks offered mortgages. Banks liabilities before 1850 by way of term deposits from overseas depositors were almost 40 million pound.
- One gauge of how much money was flowing through the domestic economy is the volume of cheques, bills, and drafts passing through the clearing-house. By the 1860s, this amount had risen to almost 6 million pound each week.
- Coghlan's 'Wealth and Progress of NSW' for 1900 reflects on the source and disposition of Public Capital and can be tabulated as follows

Source of Funds

Treasury bills & debentures	81688554
Transfer from Consolidated Rev.	1668640
Sum Available for Expenditure	**82430777**

Use of Funds

- Railways   40450473
- Tramways   2720338
- Telegraphs   1255600
- Water supply & Sewerage   9878833

CHAPTER 3

THE ECONOMIC THEORY OF 19TH CENTURY BRITISH INVESTMENT

Before we complete our table of identifying capital formation by the British investor (both Public and Private Investment), let us review a piece by Sir T. H. Farrer (Bart) from his 1887 book 'Free *Trade versus Fair Trade*'. The notation on the front-piece of the book shows the Cobden Club emblem with the words 'free trade, peace, goodwill among nations'. We will discuss Cobden a little later when we review the work of the Federation Senator Edward Pulsford – another outspoken supporter and devotee of the Cobden philosophy, and free trade and open immigration.

"The amount of English capital constantly employed abroad in private trade and in permanent investments, including Stock Exchange securities, private advances, property owned abroad by Englishmen, British shipping, British-owned cargoes, and other British earnings abroad, has been estimated by competent statisticians as being between 1,500 and 2,000 million pounds, and is constantly increasing. Taking the lower figure, the interest or profit upon it, at 5 per cent, would be 75 million pounds, and at the higher figure it would be 100 million pound."

Farrer then equates this income figure to the spread of imports over exports and finds that the two compare. But then he argues there is the question of freights. "A very large proportion of the trade of the United Kingdom is carried in English ships, and these ships carry a large proportion of the trade of other countries not coming to England. This shipping is, in fact, an export of highly-skilled English labour and capital which does not appear in the export returns of the 19th century, and considering that it includes not only the interest on capital but also wages, provisions, coal, port expenses, repairs, depreciation and insurance; and that the value of English shipping employed in the foreign trade is estimated at more than 100 million pound per annum, the amount to be added to our exports on account of English shipping, must be very large". But he goes further, "add to this the value of ships built for foreigners amounting to over 70,000 ton per annum, worth together several millions, and all these outgoings, with the profits, must either return to this country in the shape of imports, or be invested abroad—I believe 50 million pound is too low an estimate of the amount of unseen exports. In addition there are the commissions and other charges to agents in this country, connected with the carriage of goods from country to country, but each of these items do not appear in the statistics of exports. I can only assume that we are investing large amounts of our savings in the colonies, such as Australia."

The Farrer argument in favour of 'free trade' then turns to the 'fair trade' objections to foreign investments.

Farrer writes "When we point to the indebtedness of foreign colonies to England as one reason for the excess of imports, they tell us that we have been paying for our imports by the return to us of foreign securities; and at the same time they complain bitterly that, instead of spending our money at home, our rich men are constantly investing their money abroad, and thus robbing English labour of its rights here"

But we know that is not the whole story.

If England investors remit capital to the colonies, it is not only in the form of cash (which would come from savings) but it is more often in the form of capital goods. England sends iron; the shipbuilders who make the ships that carry the goods, and the sailors who navigate them. When they reach the colonies, what happens then? They return with grain, or coal, or wool, or timber, and that makes those commodities cheaper in England. The investor receives the interest or profits on that capital invested which would generally be greater than what could have been earned if the capital had been invested in England. Now that return can be spent on luxury goods, invested locally or re-invested overseas to commence the whole cycle again. That return will be employed in setting to work English labour, earn a return and so on.

It remains true that on the whole, based on the Farrer argument, the transfer of English capital from an English industry that does not pay to a colonial industry which does pay, is no loss to England generally, and causes no diminution in the employment of English labour. There are at least two drawbacks to colonial investment by a maritime power; one, in the event of a war, the returns would be open to greater risk, and two; the investors can more easily evade taxation by the English Government.

Obviously since 1886, when Farrer constructed this argument, the world has changed, investment opportunities have changed, England has fallen from its pinnacle as a world power and international commercial leader, and the improved collection of statistics now recognizes movements of goods and investments on both current account and capital account. But the concept helped put the Australian colony on the map and attracted enormous amounts of private capital into the colony to make it grow and prosper.

Farrer concludes his argument with this observation.

"The desire to make profitable investments, however valuable economically is not the only motive which governs rich men; it's the love of natural beauty; interest in farming and the outdoor life; personal and local attachments; all of which are quite sure to maintain a much larger expenditure on English land than would be dictated by a desire for gain. Let these other motives have their way, as these investors still contribute to the welfare of the toilers and spinners who produce the goods, and make a good return that in the end makes England wealthier"

CHAPTER 4

FACTORS AFFECTING BRITISH INVESTMENT IN THE COLONY

A number of factors affected the level of capital investment into the colony – many were ill informed and relied on delayed newspaper reports on activity in the various settlements.

a. The offer of assisted migration

b. The failing economic conditions in Britain

c. Economic expansion for the pastoral industry due to successful exploration in the colony

d. The settlement at Port Phillip and the eventual separation of Victoria from New South Wales would promote great investment opportunities

e. The rise of the squattocracy

f. The crash of 1827-28 in the colony shakes British Investors

g. The Bigges' Report of 1823 breathed new life into capital formation especially with Macarthur sponsoring the float of the *Australian Agricultural Company*

h. Further along, the good credit rating of the colonies (and there being no defaults on loans) encouraged larger investments and loans into the colonies

i. Shortage of Labour in the colony and the offer of land grants to new settlers became a useful carrot to attract small settlers bringing their own capital by way of cash or goods or livestock with them.

j.   Two other steps had important consequences, one in the colony and the other in Britain. In 1827 Governor Darling began to issue grazing licenses to pastoralists, and the terms were set at 2/6p per hundred acres, with liability to quit on one month's notice. From this movement grew, writes Madgwick in *Immigration into Eastern Australia,* the squatting movement and the great pastoral expansion, and the idea of the earlier Governors that the colony of New South Wales should be a colony of farmers was thus abandoned. The concurrent event was the floating of the Australian Agricultural Company in London. Development by the AAC and by the free settlers brought increasing prosperity. Exports tripled between 1826 and 1831.

k.   There is a connection between availability of factors of production and the level of investment. In the early days of the colony, labour was present—bad labour, convict labour, but still labour. The governors had demanded settlers with capital to employ that labour and develop the land. They proposed to limit land grants in proportion to the means of the settler. Governor Darling declared (HRA ser 1, vol 8) that 'when I am satisfied of the character, respectability and means of the applicant settler in a rural area, he will receive the necessary authority to select a grant of land, proportionate in extent to the means he possesses.'

Let us examine some of these important elements commencing with the Bigge Report into Agriculture and Trade of the Colony.

THE AUSTRALIAN AGRICULTURAL COMPANY

J.F. Campbell wrote about the first decade of the Australian Agricultural Company 1824-1834 in the proceedings of the 1923 RAHS.

"Soon after Commissioner Bigge's report of 1823 became available for public information, several enterprising men concerted with a view to acquire sheep-runs in the interior of this colony, for the production of fine wool.

The success which attended the efforts of John Macarthur and a few other New South Wales pastoralists, in the breeding and rearing of fine woolled sheep and stock generally, as verified by Bigge, gave the incentive and led to the inauguration of proceedings which resulted in the formation of the Australian Agricultural Company.

The first formal meeting of the promoters took place at Lincoln's Inn, London, (at the offices of John Macarthur, junior).

Earl Bathurst, advised Governor Brisbane in 1824 that . . . .

His Majesty has been pleased to approve the formation of the Company, from the impression that it affords every reasonable prospect of securing to that part of His Majesty's dominions the essential advantage of the immediate introduction of large capital, and of agricultural skill, as well as the ultimate benefit of the increase of fine wool as a valuable commodity for export.

The chief proposals of the company are:

i.   The company would be incorporated by Act of Parliament or Letters Patent.
ii. The capital of the company was to be 1 million pound sterling divided into 10,000 shares of 100 pound each
iii. A grant of land of one million acres to be made to the company
iv. That no rival joint stock company to be established in the colony for the next twenty years
v.   That agents of the company would select the situation or the land grants.
vi. The shepherds and labourers would consist of 1,400 convicts, thereby lessening the maintenance of such convicts by an estimated 30,800 pound or 22 pound/per head/ per annum

The Royal Charter of 1824 forming the company provided for payment of quit-rents over a period of twenty years, or the redemption of the same by paying the capital sum of 20 times the amount of the rent so to be redeemed. These quit-rents were to be waived if the full number of convicts were maintained for a period of five years. No land was to be sold during the five-year period from the date of the grant".

Being important that the investment be seen to have the support of strong leaders in Britain, and democratic governance, the company operated with

- A Governor
- 25 directors
- 365 stockholders (proprietors)

Leading stockholders included

- Robert Campbell
- Chief Justice Forbes
- Son of Governor King

- Rev'd Samuel Marsden
- John Macarthur
- Each Macarthur son, John jr, Hannibal, James, Charles, Scott & William

John Oxley, the Colonial-Surveyor had recommended the area of Port Stephens as an eligible spot for the land grant. The local directors inspected and approved the site but John Macarthur was extremely critical of the selection, the management plan and the extravagance of the first buildings.

This venture was the first major investment into the colony and set the scene for later developments. In 1825 the Van Diemen's Land Company was chartered by the British Parliament and granted land on the northwest corner of the territory.

Both the A.A. Coy and the VDL Coy still operate today after nearly 180 years of continuous operation, a record beaten only by the operation of the Hudson Bay Company in Canada.

2. Macquarie's Bank

Nothing quite engenders confidence in an investor like the thought of a new bank opening for business.

Less than three months after his arrival in the colony, Macquarie foreshadowed his plan for a bank on the South African model, as a 'remedy' to 'be speedily applied to this growing evil' of private promissory notes. With some exaggeration he explained that there was 'no other circulating medium in this colony than the notes of hand of private individuals' which, as he said, had 'already been productive of infinite frauds, abuses and litigation'. He accordingly announced his intention to' strongly recommend the adoption here of the same system of banking and circulating medium as is now so successfully and beneficially pursued at the Cape of Good Hope'.

By June 1810 Macquarie had developed his plan for 'The New South Wales Loan Bank' as a government institution 'as nearly as possible on the same system and principles as the Government Loan Bank at the Cape of Good Hope'. There, he explained the government issued notes by way of loan on the security of mortgages at 6 per cent per annum. He also pointed out that in England the government borrowed on exchequer bills at 5 %, so that the Cape was 11% better off. 'It appears to me' was his conclusion, 'the most perfect model in all its parts that could be possibly adopted here' By October 1810, he was willing to accept any alternative form of bank which Liverpool (Secretary for the Colonies) might believe to be 'better calculated to effect the desired object'.

Obviously a Bank would form the foundation for a monetary policy in the colony, and stop the use of Commissary receipt (store receipts) as an exchange mechanism, promote a currency and an official exchange rate for traders and cease to rely on bills drawn on the British Treasury to pay for goods and services.

3. The British Scene

Circumstances in Britain contributed greatly to the climate of 'greener pastures' over the seas.

Conditions were never more favourable for emigration than they were during the 1830s. The decade had opened with rioting in the agricultural districts in the south of England. This was followed by the upheavals of the Reform Bill of 1832, the Factory Act of 1833 and the Corn Laws, which kept wages low and unemployment high. The Poor Law of 1834 withdrew assistance from the poor and re-introduced the workhouse. The Irish rebellion was creating both upheaval and poverty

These conditions were met by the enthusiastic reports coming from Australia of the progress being made in agriculture, commerce and the pastoral industry. The assistance granted to emigrants as a result of Edward Gibbon Wakefield's reforms made possible the emigration of people who had previously been prevented by the expense. It is almost certain that free passage would not have been a sufficient enticement if conditions in Britain had not been unfavourable. It is significant that years of small migration coincided with good conditions in England accompanied by unfavourable reports from the colony.

4. Creating Opportunities in the Colony

Availability of land and labour to yield profit on invested capital is the constant decisive condition and test of material prosperity in any community, and becomes the keystone of an economy as well as defining its national identity.

British Government policy for the Australian colonies was formulated and modified from time to time. Policies for the export of British capital and the supply of labour (both convict and free) were adjusted according to British industrial and demographic and other social situations, as well as the capability and capacity of the various colonial settlements top contribute to solving British problems.

By the 1820s there was official encouragement of British Investment in Australia by adopting policies for large land grants to persons of capital and for the sale of land and assignment of convict labour to those investors. Then followed the reversal of the policy of setting up ex-convicts on small 30 acre plots as small proprietors. The hardship demanded by this policy usually meant these convicts and families remained on the commissary list for support (food and clothing) at a continuing cost to the government. It was much cheaper to assign these convicts to men of property and capital who would support them fully – clothe, house and feed them.

We can ask, what led directly to the crash of 1827?

Firstly, the float of the Australian Agricultural Company raised a large amount of capital, mostly from the City of London investment community, and this contributed to speculation and 'sheep and cattle mania instantly seized on all ranks and classes of the inhabitants' (written by Rev'd John Dunmore Lang) 'and brought many families to poverty and ruin'.

When capital imports cease, the wherewithal to speculate vanished; speculation perforce stopped; inflated prices fell to a more normal level, and wrote E.O. Shann in Economic History of Australia 'because those formerly too optimistic were now too despairing, and people had to sell goods at any price in order to get money; men who had bought at high prices were ruined, and perforce their creditors fell with them'.

a. In 1842, it was the same. The influx of capital from oversees, pastoral extension, and large-scale immigration, caused much speculation. The banks, competing for business, advanced too much credit. Loans were made on the security of land and livestock, which later became almost worthless; too much discounting was done for merchants (Gipps, HRA Vol 23). In the huge central district on the western slopes, along the Murrumbidgee and the Riverina, the squatters triumphed, as was inevitable. He had the financial resources to buy his run – especially after the long period of drought. Four million acres of crown land was sold for nearly 2.5 million pound. The confidence of British investors was waning. A crisis in the Argentine and the near failure of the large clearinghouse of Barings' made them cautious. Stories of rural and industrial strife in the colony were not inducements to invest: and wood and metal prices were still falling Loan applications being raised in London were under-subscribed, at the same time; the banks were increasingly reluctant to lend money for land development, which was so often unsound.

5. Assisted Migration

The dual policy of selling land to people with sufficient capital to cultivate it, and keeping a careful check on the number of free grants was adopted after 1825. 'Yet the Colonial Office', says Madgwick, 'failed to administer land policy with any certainty (R.B. Madgwick 'Immigration into Eastern Australia'). There was no uniform policy adopted to encourage economic development in a systematic and rational way. The Wakefield system found new supporters. The principle had been established that the sale of land was preferred to the old system of grants. The dual system of sales and grants had failed to encourage local (colonial) purchases. They were willing to accept grants or even 'squat' rather than purchase land. Sales to absentee landlords and investors stepped up, and as can be seen from the following table, provided extensive revenue to the British Government to promote free and sponsored migration.

6. Successful exploration promotes new interest in the Colony

A period of rapid expansion followed the change in economic policy. Wool exports by 1831 were 15 times as great as they had been only 10 years earlier (in 1821). The increase in the number of sheep led to a rapid opening of new territories for grazing. It was the search for new land with economic value that underpinned most of the explorations. Settlers and sheep-men quickly followed exploration, and growth fanned out in all directions from Sydney town.

However, exploration was not the only catalyst for growth.

a. The growing determination to exclude other powers from the continent stimulated official interest in long-distance exploration by sea and by land and in the opening of new settlements. For instance, J.M. Ward in his work ' The Triumph of the Pastoral Economy 1821-1851' writes that Melville and Bathurst Islands, were annexed and settled between 1824 and 1827, whilst Westernport and Albany were settled in order to clinch British claims to the whole of Australia

b. When Governor Brisbane opened the settlement at Moreton Bay in 1824, it was to establish a place for punishment of unruly convicts and a step towards further economic development, and of extending the settlements for the sake of attracting new investment

7. Colonial Failures fuel loss of Confidence

The collapse of British Investment can be traced to one or two causes, or indeed both.

I. The British crisis of 1839 reflected the availability of capital for expansion by the Australian banks of that day – The Bank of Australasia and the Union Bank. These banks, three mortgage companies and the Royal Bank went into a slump due to shortage of available funds and deferred the raising of new funds until after the crisis. Stringency in the English Capital market had a serious impact on the capital raising opportunities in the colonies.

II. The second possibility is that the sharp decline was initiated by bad news of returns in the colonies, and that its role accentuated a slump with the dire consequences experienced in 1842-43. Recovery was delayed and made more difficult as there was 'no surplus labour in the colony'

It would be dangerous to imply or decide that every slump in Australia could be explained as being caused by economic events. British investment was independent then, as it is now, and so the more valid explanation of the downturn in British investment in this period is that negative reports from the colonies disappointed and discouraged investors with capital to place.

Most facts about public finance in New South Wales lead to the conclusion that it was disappointed expectations that caused the turn down in the transfer of funds. At this same time Governor Gipps (Sir George Gipps) was being pushed by bankers and merchants to withdraw government deposits from the banks and thus this action caused a contraction in lending by the banks which in turn caused a slowdown of colonial economic activity. The attached statistics of land sales, registered mortgages and liens on wool and livestock reflects the strong downturn in the agricultural economy, which naturally flowed on to the economy as a whole.

CHAPTER 6

SOME LEADING CAPITALISTS
ARE DRAWN TO THE COLONIES

Robert Brooks of whom Frank Broeze has written in 'Mr. Brookes and the Australian Trade' was a 'financier' whose activities were 'wide-ranging, diverse and flexible – he promoted a wide range of commercial business'

Benjamin Boyd used his association with the Royal Bank to influence that bank's policy to channel the capital of small investors into pastoral development in the colonies rather than the earlier policy of chartering the Australian Agricultural Company, whose shareholders were limited in number and based on patronage.

Donald Larnach was an auditor in the Bank of New South Wales, which had managed to survive the crisis of the early 1840s. In the 1830s the banks had fuelled an unhealthy boom by offering discounts to customers and by accepting the bills of substantial landowners and merchants who themselves lent or gave credit to others. When in 1850 the British Government approved the separation of Victoria from New South Wales, the government gave the colonies the power to prepare their own constitutions. Larnbach led the way to establish a new bank in the Colony of Victoria, which area could not continue the services of the Bank of New South Wales whose charter restricted its business to that colony. This created an opportunity for new investment and new investors through the granting of fiscal independence to this settlement. As the London-based director of the Bank of New South Wales, Launach used the excellent credit performance of the colonies to raise further loan funds in London. Launach noted in his submissions to the City capital merchants that 'no Australian government has failed to pay interest on loans or repay on maturity in the nineteenth century'. It was a good record in an informed market with many knowledgeable Australians in London to give first hand views.

Henry Turner was another London banker who immigrated to the colony where he joined the Commercial Bank of Australia (CBA) as accountant. Turner would explain to his directors that 'the colonial practice of lending on security of land had grown out of colonial circumstances and was justified in terms of social and economic growth of the colony. Land selection acts before the mid-1850s had created a demand from squatters wishing to protect their possession of land by the judicious purchase of freehold. Rather than leave idle the deposits of the thrifty and prosperous, banks had met these demands, and later extended their organizations to help finance farmers, selectors, small graziers and storekeepers. Had they not done so, write Margot & Alan Beever in a biography of Henry Giles Turner, local enterprise would have been retarded. Instead there was the prospect of the growth of a class of industrious and enterprising agriculturalists, such as in England that might become one of the main sources of funds for investment.

Robert Nivison (the 1ˢᵗ Lord Glendyne) was active in the City of London. He would argue that 'Australians' live on our loans, they trade on our prestige, they presume on our protection; but they make sport of our interests, and do their best to exclude both our produce and our surplus labour'. These attacks elicited several articles defending Australia's credit, as well as further 'atrabilious and unwarranted onslaughts upon Australian manners, morals and money'. The specialist British financial press further weighed in with negative comments. They claimed that the debts of each colony had risen substantially, and found that such levels of indebtedness both ominous and deplorable. It noted that for expanding the railways network in Victoria, that colony borrowed at 4.21% but only earned 3.8% from its investment. For NSW the comparable figures were 3.91% and 3.5%. Only South

Australia paid its way, returning 5.26% on money that had been borrowed at 4.08%.

Such attacks inevitably led to a decline of interest in investing in the colonies, and did much to slow the growth of the colonies, especially in the lead up to Federation.

CHAPTER 7

COLONIAL ENTREPRENEURS

The chosen entrepreneurs are:

1. John Palmer
2. Robert Brookes
3. Thomas Sutcliffe Mort (1835 –1890)
4. Thomas Coghlan
5. Robert Campbell
6. Edward Pulsford
7. Lachlan Macquarie
8. Samuel Marsden
9. Simeon Lord
10. Francis Greenway
11. John Oxley

These men cover a whole range of economic activities and industries

Pastoral – cattle and sheep
Industry – shipbuilding to refrigeration
Newspaper editing and writing
Politics and policy
Free trade
Statistical gathering and analysis to Federation
Gold discover
Building & construction
Exploration

Commissariat operations, purchasing, trading
Financing, consignment, auctioneering

Our selection of entrepreneurs includes some fascinating backgrounds and specialties.

- A preacher turned pastoralist (Marsden)
- An industrialist (Mort)
- A public servant turned landowner and ship owner (Palmer)
- An explorer (John Oxley)
- Two former convicts – one an architect and the other a successful trader (Francis Greenway & Simeon Lord)
- An aristocratic merchant (Brooks)
- A statistician turned author
- A free settler and successful merchant

These nine men together changed the face of the colony. They made a difference by being in this world. Although not the traditional entrepreneur as we think of that term today, but in their day, the colony would not have been as successful as it was without the contribution from these unique personages.

It was fortunate that the colony was successful for not all of these men ended up with the riches they might have deserved in better or other circumstances . . .

Many survived over adversity and demonstrated major courage. These were the men of the 18th and 19th century, without whom Australia would not be free economy.

Was there a common thread amongst these men? Their will to succeed, their willingness to take risks and their aptitude to use their innate skills and judgment brought them to the fore. The two who were convicts did not indulge in self-pity but strove to release themselves from bondage and make a new life for themselves.

Francis Greenway

Greenway, on the surface, may appear as an unlikely entrepreneur, especially when compared to the likes of Mort and Palmer, or even Marsden, but we can show that he had the technical skills to make an impact, the brashness to force his opinions when necessary and the luck that is essential to successful entrepreneur. But we must then ask does an entrepreneur need to show sound financial results? We know that Greenway went bankrupt as a precursor to his imprisonment and transportation, and we know that he died in great poverty; but an entrepreneur leaves the results of his success in many forms, and Greenway left his in a series of outstanding colonial buildings, few of which have been allowed to survive the years.

Greenway's contribution as an entrepreneur is neither nebulous nor questionable. It is, without doubt, his designs, his watchful eye at a building site and his extensive choice of materials that make Macquarie the giant of Colonial times and led the colonial economy to forge the base, in so many respects, that allowed successive governors and legislatures to build on a firm base and make the colony of New South Wales a burgeoning triumph. Greenway's contribution was essential to all this. A convict, he may have been but his luck changed the day the convict carrier *General Hewitt* arrived at Sydney Cove in February 1814. He was given a ticket of leave, opened up in private practice, became an adviser to Governor Macquarie, and even advertised his service in the *Sydney Gazette* of December 1814. He first drew attention to himself and created a stir with builders and workers by his evaluation of the, in progress, 'rum hospital' on Macquarie Street. His commission from Macquarie had been to 'report on the construction of the hospital then underway for the Government by private contractors and developers. His report was devastating. The builders had to make costly alterations to the work completed and Greenway made the first of a long line of enemies who were to make his life difficult thereafter.

His list of buildings designed and commissions (refer attached) is formidable and impressive. Technically he made two and three story buildings stand erect for the first time in the colony. His key blocks for arches caused much dispute amongst builders and the other occasional designers in the town, but he persisted and won, and his arches stayed in place denying the critics the pleasure of having correctly predicted an impending disaster. By March 1816, only two years after his arrival in the colony on a fourteen year sentence, Greenway, by now married with seven children, had been appointed 'Civil Architect and Assistant Engineer' on 3 shillings per day. He immediately began to plan a large number of buildings that Macquarie had for years been hoping to build. His first official work was the lighthouse on South Head.

Macquarie was so pleased with this '*Macquarie Lighthouse*' that he fully emancipated Greenway and restored him to full citizenship. Then followed a new Government house and a stable block, the female factory at Parramatta, a large barracks and compound for male convicts –*he Hyde Park Convict Barracks*—, St. Matthew's Church at Windsor, and St. Luke's Church at Liverpool, and St. James's Church in King Street, Sydney. This impressive list of valuable gems of Early Australian Colonial architecture stands as a standard for other buildings of that period and became the foundation stone of a thriving economy, and entrepreneurship that led to generations of trading, pastoral growth, inland exploration, gold discoveries, free immigration, and the advent of rail transportation and telegraphic communications. The Macquarie building period was underpinned by Greenway's technical abilities and led to the development of new building techniques – the use of stone, high rise brick structures, the correct use of local timbers, the local manufacture of imported materials, the use of better lime for bonding and plaster works and molding hitherto unknown in the colony.

Although Commissioner Bigge, in his 1823 report to the House of Commons, commented favorably on Greenway's abilities and sought to put the blame for the extravagant building program on Macquarie rather than on the architect, Greenway, not politically astute, was concerned only with the spoiling of his designs by both Bigge and Macquarie (with whom he had by now had a very public falling out).

Greenway's loss of political patronage and the Bigge cancellation of many of Greenway's projects, led to further effrontery to the Governor and Bigge when he presented (as a salaried employee) a bill for 11,000 pound for services performed based on a 5% fee on work completed. The bill was never withdrawn and finally settled by a grant of 800 acres in swampland on the right bank of the Hunter River

His association with Macquarie's successor (Sir Thomas Brisbane) was brief and resulted only in the Supreme Court building in King Street the Liverpool Hospital, a Government Store in Parramatta and a police officer in York Street, Sydney.

Greenway's return to private practice in 1823 (he was dismissed from public service in November 1822) resulted in only one considerable commission – a house, stables and 'appurtenances' for trader Robert Campbell in Bligh Street. A number of small jobs came his way (the mausoleum for George Howe) but his professional life seemed to have ended with the completion of the Campbell house in 1828.

He retired to his grant on the Hunter River and completed some writing for the press.

His legacy is in the 73 buildings he designed and of those whose construction he supervised. The estimated cost (by this author) of those buildings is close to One million pound of which local materials accounted for nearly 450,000 pound. This contribution to the local economy was an amazing boost to the demand for labour in every sector of life. Free immigration was encouraged, traders brought in boatloads of goods from England on which the Government raised substantial duties for the state revenues, and returned to their homeports laden with wool, whale oil, fur seals, timber, and coal. The government put the revenue to good use and encouraged new agricultural and farming ventures; built roads, created improved port facilities and underwrote 'cottage' industries such as boat-building, timber harvesting, and processing, a slaughterhouse and cloth making.

Greenway was indeed an early colonial entrepreneur and produced some of the finest buildings Australia ever had but like so many was failed by his awkward temperament. He could not have produced them alone but then an entrepreneur relies very largely on his personal skills and the support of an assembled team Macquarie's patronage and protection provided the atmosphere in which the architect could give rein to his genius. Alone, he may have crumbled away the attacks of less competent men or remained a convict for his fourteen-year sentence. Technical success, luck, and brashness were his brilliant star and *bête* noir

John Palmer

John Palmer makes another interesting character in our choice of entrepreneurs. A very early start as a seaman at the tender age of only nine, stole his chance of learning the way of the world on dry land but set him, at a very young age, to the ways of survival, travel and learning the ways of a singular way of life – a seaman, naval cadet and adventurer. At the time of entering the navy, he served in the War of American Independence, during which time he was captured.

In 1786 he joined the HMS *Sirius* as purser, and voyaged to New South Wales with the first fleet, and continued to serve until that ship was wrecked on a voyage to open up Norfolk Island. Governor Phillip appointed him Commissary-General for the colony in 1790.

Palmer's entrepreneurial prowess and skills commenced from that time. The military corps was cornering the local market as 'traders'. Palmer at first resisted the beckoned association to throw his lot in with this bunch, but shortly saw the way to have the best of both worlds. As commissary, Palmer was subject to patronage by the military officers and, in turn, could bestow patronage as the buyer of produce and goods for the commissary. He successfully played both sides, and was granted 100 acres of land on the shores of Woolloomooloo Bay. For a 'poor' man, he built a luxurious house for his extended family (his wife and first child had arrived in 1800, together with his two sisters). By 1805 Palmer's pay had increased to One pound per day, whilst his deputy (William Broughton) remained at 5 shillings per day

Palmer's abilities had resulted in his first accumulation of wealth and besides his 'public' duties he engaged in timber milling and coastal trading. By 1804, he owned three vessels voyaging as far south as Bass Strait and north to the Hawkesbury River. By 1807 he also owned farms totaling 2,500 acres – not a bad result for a boy seaman and a poor government servant.

Although he backed the wrong side during the Bligh overthrow, Macquarie re-instated Palmer to his office as Commissary-General, but in 1819 Macquarie became dissatisfied with the whole commissary operation and retired Palmer to half-pay. Bad investments and poor associations had stripped Palmer of all his lands and livestock, and he retired to his Parramatta and Rouse Hill holdings and was appointed a local magistrate. He became one of the Macarthur-Marsden-Blaxland circle, but died in 1833 at the age of 73.

His major contribution to the colony was the buying system for the commissary food holdings from local producers, the encouragement of local industries especially in the timber, metals, and grain storing/milling operations. His keeping of essentially accurate accounts for the British Commissary is notable for its balancing and clarity. Even Commissioner Bigge in his report to the House of Commons in 1823 found the Palmer system of store receipts to be a sound system.

Palmer's beneficial associations continued especially after his sister, Sophia, married Robert Campbell who at one stage was the colony's largest landowner and livestock owner. One of the Palmer daughters, Sophia Susannah, married Edward Close, settler and Churchman in 1821. Close was a pastoralist with a 2,560 acre land grant at Morphett on the Hunter River) and a magistrate appointed by Brisbane. Although removed from his position as magistrate in the case of Lt Lowe's murder of four aboriginals in custody, Brisbane's successor, Governor Darling, appointed Close to the NSW Legislative Council in 1829.

The Close daughter, married Robert Campbell's son George, and thus linked three main families in the colony – the Palmers, the Campbell's, the Closes.

Any man in Palmer's position was open to compromise, and Palmer accepted a role, on occasions, as the recipient of bitter complaints – especially about favoritism towards the local 'nobility' (the Macarthur family) who had been accused of misusing government livestock – a claim which probably had some merit since both Macarthur's livestock and the government livestock often shared the same pastures near Parramatta for grazing. Other areas of favoritism complained of included decisions about how much grain was to be purchased by the Commissary from various farmers and where it was to be delivered. The more influential farmers got the largest orders and could deliver to their local commissary store, whereas the disadvantaged farmers would have a smaller percentage accepted and would be required to deliver their grain to the Sydney store – usually a much greater distance to travel and a much higher cost. But as an entrepreneur Palmer carried out the governor's directions on rationing for all, fairly and equitably and without discrimination or rancor. He bought supplies fairly, engaged in enterprise of timber milling (again supplying the government lumber yard—a conflict of interest which should be overlooked because the quality of timber of higher than other suppliers could provide, and it had been air dried successfully for an average of two years. His boat building and shipping operations created supplies for export and again assisted the growth and development of the colony at a time when government revenue was flagging. Exports allowed a matching value of imports to be made, on which the naval officer could impose duties and tariffs. His agricultural pursuits were short-lived but his son George carried on with the large holdings near Queanbeyan (at Jerrabomberra NSW), Gungahlin (near the Campbell holding of Duntroon in the Monaro).

We know that Woolloomooloo was Sydney's first suburb, being settled in 1793 when Palmer was granted 100 acres and established a farm there. It remained largely undeveloped until 1840 when it was subdivided to satisfy the need for housing close to the rapidly expanding city. Reclamation of the Woolloomooloo Bay began in 1852 and the following decade saw a rapidly expanding population and the establishment of small worker's houses over much of the area. The Plunkett Street Primary School (the first school in the area) was opened in 1878 and named after John Plunkett a Legislative Councilor, Attorney-General, and President of the Board of National Education from 1848 to 1858. When Greenway (*q.v.*) designed and built the government house stables for Macquarie, the land used had previously been leased to Palmer who had constructed a bake house and a windmill (for grinding flour) on the site. Macquarie, when he wanted the site for his own use as the 4th government house and domain, considered these buildings inappropriate and resumed the land.

Palmer, as reported by Timothy Coghlan (*q.v.)* gave evidence to the House of Commons Select Committee on Transportation in 1812 that the lowest weekly wage for which a laborer could be obtained in the colony was 24 shillings. The commonest laborer earned from 5s to 7s per day.

Marjorie Barnard in 'A History of Australia' writes that the Commissary, under Palmer, was the proto-treasury, and when the colonial treasury was established the commissariat returned to being the sole provisioner for the convicts and military but 'withered away at the end of transportation'. The commissary had been regularly reformed – by Macquarie, Darling and Brisbane, although Palmer maintained the greatest amount of services through the commissary whilst in charge and probably maintained the best set of financial and stock records during commissary operations of over 60 years.

Barnard also observes that the Palmer manorial home set on 100 acres at Woolloomooloo Bay had a triple barricade of wall, ditch, and sweetbriar hedge inside of which he set gardens, workshops, orchards and a family vault.

Palmer once again felt no conflict of interest when he sat as magistrate in a case brought by Macarthur against Robert Campbell (Palmer's brother-in-law). On the other hand, Palmer sided with Macarthur in a matter concerning Samuel Marsden's refusal to marry a female convict at the Female Factory at Parramatta to a male convict. The case resulted in Brisbane dismissing the three magistrates (Palmer. Macarthur and Blaxland)

It was Palmer (writes Dr H.V. Evatt in *The Rum Rebellion)* who advised the House of Commons Committee in 1812 of the evils resulting from the traffic of spirits in the colony. Palmer had been entirely loyal to Governor Bligh who (Palmer believed) had been remarkably successful in suppressing the traffic in spirits. This action by Bligh led to the *Rum Rebellion*

Palmer may not been the great entrepreneur that his brother-in-law Robert Campbell became as a trader, but still his contribution is to be acknowledged as a formidable contributor to the colony and without whom the colony may not have prospered and grown as brightly as it did.

Robert Brooks

Brooks is relatively unknown in the Australian context and that is mainly because, in spite of his contribution to the Australian economic scene, he remained a resident of England and saw this country as he was but passing by (usually in one of his fleet of ships). He passed but once on his own ship *Elizabeth* in 1823-24. He invariably conducted his commercial and financial interests from the *City*, whilst his overseas operations were left largely in the hands of ships' masters, agents and other connections. His London office was kept simple – he never employed more than a few clerks in his office, in spite of the large trading business carried out

Frank Boeze, the Professor of History at the University of Western Australia, brought us the life story of Brooks in his competent 1993 work –'**Mr. Brooks and the Australian Trade** – *Imperial Business in the 19th Century'*.

Boeze describes Brooks as "One of the leaders of mid-19th century trade between London and Australia. Brooks' career can stand as a paradigm of the rise of that trade and of the City (of London) itself.

The white British-sponsored settlements (colonies) of Australia and New Zealand remained economically very closely tied to Britain Until 1850 (and the giant step of self-government) their location and the provisions of the British Navigation Acts ensured that virtually no other than British business could operate in Australia and New Zealand. In fact, under well after World War II, Britain was to remain these nations' most important trading partner and provider of shipping and other services."

During the 19th century Britain received virtually all cargoes from the South Seas, mainly because British investment owned or controlled the shipping and much of the large pastoral and manufacturing capability of the colony. Brooks was one of the more significant personages who contributed to this 19th century dominance. Brooks excelled in and extensively supported the concept of 'private merchant financing' (we see the same thoughts being pursued by another of our entrepreneurs – Thomas Mort). Research on this topic, since it is not a traditional or mainstream banking practice has remained relatively obscure – a delving into this subject would involve a close examination between the London-Australia axis and an understanding of the elements of the Australian trade and its dynamic core (the common players; the control, through investment, by London Boards of Australian industry; the control of shipping and ships; and the merchant banking that financed and funded so much of the exports being moved to London. Brooks' career spanned the turbulent times in the growth of each of these factors and in many ways owned and controlled main aspects of each sector.

Using the classic definition of 'entrepreneurial' aims as a basis for comparison, Brooks followed a business strategy of building a complex structure around ac range of mutually supportive operations, 'as well as a combination of personal, entrepreneurial and environmental elements through a mixed chronological and thematic approach.

A remarkable closeness can be traced between the evolution of the Brooks business and the development of the Australian trade in general.

Brookes participated in many ventures. He owned ships. He bought cargo to sale in those ships. He sold that cargo at the point of destination at a profit. For the return voyage, he bought wool or other products on his own account, brought it to London and marketed that product, and then started the cycle all over again. His fleet grew and grew, and his services were much in demand. He reluctantly took product on consignment or as paid cargo to fill his growing fleet. He was invited onto the Board of a number of significant trading and financial institutions in the City. He was active in the United Bank of Australia in its halcyon days. He contracted with the authorities to carry assisted passage settlers from England to Australia.

And like most entrepreneurs he had his times of crisis and despair but enjoyed the challenge of a recovery.

On many occasions, Brooks acted as both a commission agent as well as financier. For instance Boeze in his contribution to *Australian Financiers* records that on an 1827 order from a John Rickards of Sydney, Brooks charged 2 ½% commission and advanced, short-term, the funds at a rate of 5% p.a. At this time Brooks was particularly interested in whaling and a leading Australian based trader, Robert Campbell (another selected entrepreneur) consigned all his colonial exports to Brooks. By late 1832 Campbell owned brooks over 10,000 pound for advances on goods consigned.

It was in 1827 that Brooks introduced the greatest attraction for pastoralists based in Australia but wanting to benefit from the English wool sales. Brooks commenced advancing funds to exporters against shipments of produce. Following his first wool consignments in 1827, pastoralists and merchants, keen to turn their produce as quickly as possible into ready cash, responded actively to the new approach by Brooks which involved agents of London merchants making credits available. Brooks ran the biggest book of the lot. However for Brooks, the most important factor was his role in the founding (in 1837) and working of the Union Bank of Australia.

In 1838-39 Brooks and some associates attempted to gain control of the UBA in London, but these attempts failed. Although this attempt had failed it were the Brook policies that were adopted by the Bank's London (and controlling) Board . . . These policies included

- Refusing to discount bills drawn against exports to the colonies
- Declining to take mortgages on pastoral land
- The Bank Board also agreed to offer broad discounting facilities to directors and their connections.

Brooks benefited greatly from his privileged position and gained great advantage over his competitors, and used his position to assist friends in London and Australia.

In the colony, Brooks' associates used their access to the UBA to discount drafts drawn on Brooks as an almost unlimited line of credit for investment purposes. "The fact is (wrote Brooks to his agent in Sydney) that money is so valuable to people engaged in trade in this place, whether settlers, ship-owners, or other, that anything in the shape of produce must be turned into money or its equivalent as soon as possible".

By 1841-42 the boom of the previous decade was over. Overstocking of colonial markets, collapse of the land and livestock sectors, and the dramatic end of assisted migration, all made a downturn inevitable. Speculation was entrenched as well as greed by the country agents. They had begun the risky practice of advancing money not only against known bales of wool, but also against wool still on the sheep's back. Similarly with whale oil, advances were being made on the future catches of two ships still tied up at the fisheries. Brooks condemned these practices but his Sydney agents had speculated (with Brooks' funds) too heavily and the UBA called in the advances against Brooks as well as the agent (Robert Dacre). Robert Campbell and virtually all major traders (also making advances unwisely) had failed. Brooks survived by retiring from the trade but by taking over consignments from agents who had failed benefited significantly and kept his fleet operating successfully and profitably. Robert Campbell was also making a strong comeback after bankruptcy. With the UBA changing its risky policies, Brooks was partially shut out from his former influential role and took his Sydney banking business to the Bank of New South Wales.

Brooks had survived the colonial downturn and revamped his global operations. He brought his three sons into the business, assigned them control, and in 1872 retired to his country estate.

Brooks had diversified his interests during the 1850s by investing in a fleet of 14 whalers The Brooks plantation on the Logan River near Brisbane successfully grew cotton at a time when the American colonies refused to send their cotton to England for processing, and the Brooks product received a British government bounty. He was offered a directorship of the London Dock Company, as a means of their ensuring his trade would be handled through those London docks rather than Hull, Bristol or Liverpool. Brooks also became a trustee of the Australasian Gold Mining Company, and arranged for the UBA to extend credit facilities to the company at Bathurst.

The Robert Brooks & Co. firm was finally liquidated in Australia in 1967, after over 125 years of service to the London-Australia trade, numerous investments in the colonies and great success as an entrepreneur.

Robert Campbell

Of all the 'entrepreneurs analysed in this section of the 'Colonial Economy', surely Robert Campbell, if not Thomas Mort, compete for the title of best entrepreneur. Their accomplishments are considerable and both men are well deserving of such a mantle. It is not surprising that in a small and closed community like the colony of New South Wales, an association can be found between the prominent citizens of the town. For instance, Palmer's sister married Robert Campbell; Greenway designed Campbell's house and outbuildings; Campbell was the largest trader in the colony and supplied large quantities of goods to the Commissary store of the colony. Palmer was the Commissary-General. Palmer's interest was in timber and sealskin and Campbell wanted to export such commodities to his markets in England.

Campbell left Calcutta in his ship *The Hunter* in 1798 with a full cargo and headed for New South Wales in an attempt to develop a trading connection between his firm Campbell & Co (a successor to Clarke, Campbell & Co)

Apparently it was a successful commission because upon his return with a second cargo in 1800, Campbell received the governor's permission to take up residence on Dawes' Point (on land that he had bought in 1798), where he began to build warehouses and a private wharf. By 1810 another wharf had been built, behind which stood the Campbell house 'furnished in an elegant manner with colonnades and two fronts'.

Campbell was soon heavily engaged in the Australian trade, at one time (in 1804) having over 50,000 pounds worth of goods in the warehouses. Trade became a two way street. Campbell returning to India with cargoes of timber, wool and coal, whilst coming home with cotton, fabrics, Bric-a-brac and many items badly needed in the colony by the growing numbers of free settlers, military personnel and of course, the many civil list employees. Governor King calculated that Campbell had imported over 16,000 of livestock into the colony between 1800 and 1804. Although Campbell imported 'excessive' quantities of spirits against the spirit of the governor's attempts to limit the trading and consumption of spirits in the colony (to the ultimate exploitation of convicts, farmers, workers and the government) his name was synonymous with fair trading, reduced prices and generous credit and was publicly acknowledged by the small settlers, officers and governor alike. Campbell largely initiated the sealing industry and won his challenge (albeit at some extensive personal cost) to the East India Company's sole right to southern oceans trading with England.

Under Bligh, Campbell quickly became involved with public administration, having an intimate knowledge of the colonial economy. In 1807, he was appointed a magistrate and the Naval Officer (the collector of customs revenues, harbour dues and wharfage charges). As Naval Officer Campbell moved to confiscate a still illegally imported by Macarthur, which move ultimately fused the rebellion against Bligh and the disposition of Bligh as Governor. As a fellow diner at government house on the evening of the rebellion, Campbell was arrested by Johnson and dismissed as treasurer, naval officer and collector of taxes. Following the marriage of Palmer's sister, Sophia, to Campbell, Palmer and Campbell had become limited business partners. In 1810 Campbell was reinstated to his former offices by Macquarie.

During his time in London in support of Bligh, his business ventures failed for lack of experienced management and upon his return to the colony Campbell faced some years of bleak operations and frugal living. He continued to pursue public duties and sat on the Court of Civil Jurisdiction, and assisted in establishing the Bank of New South Wales and became an original shareholder. Macquarie made him a grant of 1500 acres in the Bathurst district. Having assisted Macquarie form the Savings Bank in 1819, Campbell's close association with this institution led to it becoming commonly known as 'Campbell's Bank'. By 1820 Campbell's fortunes had begun to revive. He began handling wool to London, wheat shipments from the Derwent market and commissions from the growing Newcastle settlement. By 1825, Campbell was a ship owner again and sent fully laden to Calcutta. In 1826 Campbell's wharf at Sydney Cove became a private concern and the two Campbell sons were admitted to a new Campbell & Co partnership. The entrepreneur was back on his feet. It is not surprising that the personalities of two key colonial governors wrought such different results on the colony and its people. Bligh reigned in a state of terror and brought disrespect to himself and many of his principal associates. His trial in London took key citizens away from the colony for extended periods and placed many at economic risk – Marsden, Macarthur, Campbell, Palmer and Close. Macquarie took a very different approach to his duties and restored the citizens to economic health, and encouraged rather than discouraged free enterprise and entrepreneurship. The economy benefited from his judgments and even England faired well.

10. Coghlan on Public Finance

Sir Timothy Coghlan was the colonial statistician whilst he was involved in preparing the series 'The Wealth and Progress of New South Wales 1900-01'. He was later appointed as Agent-General in London before compiling the 4-volume set of 'Labour and Industry in Australia'.

A review of the Coghlan account of Public Finance includes references to

- Loan expenditure
- Government Services
- Public Debt
- Colonial Debt Rating
- Land Grants versus Sales
- Treasury bills
- Assets of New South Wales
- Private Finance

The Coghlan analysis on each of these points will now be given analysis.

i. Loan Expenditure

The Loan Account was not established until 1853, although the system of raising money by loans commenced as early as 1842. The first ten loans of the colony were raised on the security of the Territorial Revenue, which fund was the proceeds of Land sales and used for the benefit of assisted immigration. Prior to 1842, capital expenditure was made from normal revenue and no differentiation was made between expenditure on capital account and expenditure on current account. All funds flow into and from Consolidated Revenue. From 1853, after the securing of funds through the Loan Account, all proceeds of loans were paid into Consolidated Revenue fund, without being separated into specific capital or current account allocations. So those funds that were raised for specific capital projects had to rely on available surpluses in Consolidated Revenue if the project was to proceed and be fully funded.

The use to which loan funds were generally put was capital works such that the citizens of the settlements would have running water, sewerage, tramways, and telegraphic services. docks, roads and bridges, public works and buildings, fortifications and military works, immigration, public instruction and school buildings, lighthouses and improvements to harbours and rivers.

Coghlan states that 'a vigorous works policy was usually the order of the day'. This, put simply, meant that 'the opportunity engendered the desire, and the open purses of the investors tempted the colonies to undue borrowing and lavish expenditure'. It is Coghlan's opinion that 'the plethora of money has been harmful in many ways, but is most apparent in the construction of a few branch railways in outlying and sparsely-settled districts which do not even pay their working expenses, with the consequence that interest on loan capital has to be paid out of general revenue. Overall, it will be found that the proceeds of loans have been well expended.' The attached loan expenditure table reflects the growing debt per inhabitant. The table shows two interesting facts

a. The annual loan expenditure per inhabitant varies from 18/9 d to 4/4/-, and
b. The accumulated debt per inhabitant grew, in twenty years, from 17/0/6 d to 44/17/6 d

ii. Public Borrowing and Public Debt

It was after 1831, when the system of free land grants was abolished, and the auction system of land disposal was introduced, that it was decided to pay these auction proceeds into the Land Fund. It was from this fund that that charges relating to the assistance for migrants was to be paid. From 1831 to 1841, this fund was adequate, but in 1841 the fund was insufficient and it was decided to borrow on the security of the Land Revenue. Thus on the 28th December 1841, a notice was placed in the Gazette to the effect that 49,000 were to be raised by way of a debenture loan with interest at 5.25%. This was the start of public debt in the colony, and the first ever raised by Australian Government. A further 10 loans between 1842 and 1850 quickly followed, amounting in total to 705,200 pound, the proceeds of which were allocated exclusively to furthering immigration.

At 1850, when responsible government was underway, the public debt was 1,000,800 pound. Of this amount, 640,500 had been raised on the security of land revenue. The balance of 360,300 pound was raised on the security of general revenue.

Of the total, railways accounted for 474,000; water and sewerage 82,900; public works 21,000 and immigration was 423,000. Of the total 1,000,800 only 47,500 was redeemed out of general revenue, the balance being rolled-over into new loans.

The Public Debt balances for this period are shown on the attached table

ii. Government Services

Sources of Revenue for each colony was generally classified under four (4) headings – taxation, land revenue, receipts for government services rendered and miscellaneous revenue. Prior to 1850, the 'Blue Books' were compiled annually for circulation to the Colonial Office in London, the Colonial Governor, Colonial Treasurer and Legislative Council. After self-government a new system of public accounting was introduced which reflected the four headings mentioned above. Annual comparisons are best made on a per inhabitant basis, and whilst 'taxation' remained fairly constant at a rate per head of 1/17/6 d to 2/4/2 d, land revenue and government services ranged widely. Land revenue grew from 1/9/7 d per head to 2/6/0 d; government services naturally grew from 1/11/11 d to 3/15/1 d, obviously reflecting the growing demands for government to provide all manner of assistance to the settlers and growing population. Services included:

Railways
Tramways
Postage

Telegraphs
Money orders
Water supply
Sewerage
Public school fees
Pilotage and harbour fees
Mint fees

Coghlan confirms that 'the income derived by the government from services, has, been steadily increasing; this is only what would naturally be expected in a growing community, but income per head has been fairly well sustained, holding in a 12 year period from 3/9/11 d to 3/17/11 d. This result is in spite of the fact that the railway system rarely made a 'profit' with earnings generally being around 3.81%, with the average interest payable being 3.61%. As the revenue from services naturally depends upon the amount of production, the rate per inhabitant will not only cease to increase, but will ultimately decline.'

Government services were supposedly being conducted on commercial principles; except that in the case of providing most services, receipts are less than expenditure meaning that these services were generally subsidized from general revenue. The gap appears to have increased exponentially year after year.

iii. Treasury Bills

Treasury Bills issued in the capacity to meet accumulated deficiencies in revenue and for loan services were not issued to the public, as they were reserved for various trusts with large investment funds. These 'Deficiency' bills, as they became known, were not released until the 1880s. The earlier class of Treasury Bills was issued for the purpose of raising bridging funds whilst awaiting loan proceeds. The Colony could usually borrow in London on very favourable terms but in the event of delay or seeking an even better discount rate, the T-Bills were used for this bridging purpose.

CHAPTER 8

ASSETS OF NEW SOUTH WALES

An estimate of the value of property in the colony, just prior to Federation was made and came to a total of 356,350,000 pound. This figure was made up of land at UCV, houses and permanent improvements Livestock; Furniture and personal household affects; machinery and implements; merchandise; shipping; mining properties and plant; coin and bullion.

Today, such an assessment would be almost meaningless but the early statisticians wanted a means of comparing wealth between the colonies.

Figures available for the value of estates, 'wills proved', shows that year by year, property is becoming more widely distributed and this conclusion is borne out by figures available for the second half of the 19th century. During those years, the proportion of persons holding property has increased more than 2 ½ times, which means than in 1850 less than 6 persons out of each 100 held property, and by the end of the century over 15 persons in each 100 held property – and as Coghlan concludes, 'a remarkable condition of progress, the equal of which it would be vein to look for in other countries'.

On individual wealth Coghlan has some interesting statistics:

'The possessors of property include 148,315 males and 39,425 females: One-half of the property is in the hands of 2367 persons; 3/ths in the hands of 4736 and 3/ths in the hands of 10815 persons.

Of the estates assessed, 27% were between 200 and 5,000 pound; 22% were between 5 and 25,000 pound; and 48% were over 25,000 pounds'. We might well ask how this degree of 'wealth' was created.

For the same year as the value of property was assessed, the annual income of 301,965 males was 26,924,000 or 89 pound per head. For females the average declined to 36 pound. In addition there were 31,222 incomes of over 200 pound per annum amounting to 17,595,000 pound.

v. Private Finance

Coghlan states that 'money has been freely poured into New South Wales by British investors. In the last 30 years of the 19th century, the sum was 109 million pound. Over half of that sum represented the net amount of loans raised in London by various colonial governments; 8 million pound was the amount of capital brought by people intending to be permanent immigrants; and 51 million was the amount of other investment capital. This latter amount included investments by persons living abroad, advances by banks and finance companies and loans from private persons.

Now Coghlan counters this argument by concluding that 'including capital withdrawn from investments, the total of payments returned to investors, in this same period was 110,982,000, so that there was actually no net transfer of capital in spite of the ending capital indebtedness'.

Coghlan points out that the capital brought into the colony by migrants averaged over 260,000 pound each year and has been a material element in the progress of the colony. The 51 million invested by people not living in the colony, included money derived from the English banks. In addition there is the capital of the Australian banks, and the capital employed by other investment companies, the mining companies, and mortgages, both rural and city.

Coghlan estimates that the total of private capital invested in the colony of New South Wales prior to 1871 is 16 million pound. He does not provide a source or breakdown of these figures. In another sweeping generalization, Coghlan states that the colony was a 'debtor-state' since its indebtedness was greater than its asset value. This is hardly justified and is easily disputed. It is certainly not supported by statistics derived from the other colonies that should show zero on consolidation. Coghlan is generally well regarded for his industry in putting together his voluminous studies on statistics relating to the colony but is questioned widely on the source of much of his information. A lot of it appears to have been contrived to meet his needs, rather than have his writings reflect the statistical information gained.

Real Estate Transactions

The Real Property Act of 1862 was the successor to the Deeds Registration Act of 1843. The new act completely revolutionized the procedure with regard to land transfers and was modelled on the Torrens' Act of South Australia (the Torrens title system). The key feature of the new act was that transfers of real property (i.e. land) were by registration of title instead of by deeds. The act also afforded protection to owners against 'possessory claims, as a title issued under the Act stood good against any length of adverse possession'. From the passing of the new act, all lands sold by the Crown were conveyed to the purchasers under its provisions and the provisions of the old law were restricted to transactions in respect of grants already issued.

All mortgages, except those regulated by the Bills of Sale Act of 1855 are registered at the Registrar-General's Office, and it is a fair assumption that the great majority of mortgages accepted are recorded, although when trying to determine the value of recorded mortgages, it is to be remembered that not all mortgage documents show a precise value. Some are recorded with the notation 'valuable consideration' or 'cash credit' being inserted instead of a specific sum. Prior to 1855, mortgages were recorded under the Deeds Registration Act of 1843

11. The Colonial Building Program

It might be thought that one of the biggest, if the largest elements of public investment in a new colony would be the construction and building program – in other words 'public works'. We know now that this category is, in fact, the second smallest (just ahead of Civil List salaries). We can very this estimate by compiling a list of buildings and works between

1800 and 1825 and costing the labour and material components of the works carried out. We know that for 10 of these 25 years, Macquarie (supported by Francis Greenway) completed an enviable list of buildings, mostly gallant and practical, but all aesthetically attractive.

We will review the list of greenway designed buildings, and the list of Macquarie era buildings, and estimate the construction cost of each building, before reconciling this sum with known estimates provided to Commissioner Bigge, keeping in mind that Bigge was endeavouring to destroy Macquarie's credibility and the witness to Bigge's committee (a Robert Kitchener) was out to destroy the Greenway credibility.

CHAPTER 9

LIST OF GREENWAY BUILDINGS

(With assistance from *Francis Greenway Architect-1997)*

1. General Hospital, Sydney
2. Magazine, Fort Phillip
3. Design of Government House, Sydney
4. St. John's Parsonage, Parramatta
5. Portico, Government House, Parramatta
6. Macquarie Lighthouse, South Head
7. Obelisk, Macquarie Place, Sydney
8. Military Barracks, Sydney
9. Government Wharf, Windsor
10. Parramatta Gaol, Parramatta
11. Hyde Park Convict Barracks
12. St. Matthew's Church, Windsor
13. Chief Justice's House, Sydney
14. Colonial Secretary's House, Macquarie Place, Sydney
15. Judge Advocate's House, Macquarie Place, Sydney
16. Chaplain's House, Spring Street, Sydney
17. Government Stables, Government Domain, Sydney
18. Fort Macquarie, Bennelong Point, Sydney
19. Public Fountain, Macquarie Place, Sydney
20. St. Luke's Church, Liverpool
21. St. Luke's Parsonage, Liverpool
22. Female Factory and Barrack, Parramatta
23. Female Orphan School, Parramatta

24. Government House, Sydney
25. Dawes Point Battery, Dawes Point, Sydney
26. Turnpike Gate & Lodge, Parramatta Road, Sydney
27. St. Andrew's Church (Foundations), King Street, Sydney
28. Supreme court House, King Street, Sydney
29. Lumber Yard, Bridge Street, Sydney
30. Male Orphan School, George Street, Sydney
31. Dockyard, George Street, Sydney
32. Market House, George Street, Sydney
33. Court House, Windsor
34. Charity School, Elizabeth Street, Sydney
35. Police Office, George Street, Sydney
36. Granary & Store, George Street, Parramatta
37. St. Mary's Catholic Chapel, Hyde Park, Sydney
38. Princess Charlotte Memorial
39. Liverpool Hospital, Liverpool.
40. Pigeon House
41. Governor Brisbane's Bath House, Government Domain, Sydney
42. St. Matthews Rectory, Windsor
43. Ultimo House, Ultimo Sydney
44. House for Sarah Howe, Lower George Street, Sydney
45. House for George Howe, Charlotte Place, Sydney
46. Tomb for George Howe, Devonshire Street Cemetery, Sydney
47. House for Sir John Jamieson, Charlotte Place, Sydney
48. House for T.W. Middleton, Macquarie /Hunter Streets, Sydney
49. Work for R.W. Loane
50. Cottage, Parramatta
51. Proposed House, George /Argyle Street, Sydney
52. House for Sir John Wylde, Sydney
53. Bank of New South Wales, George Street, Sydney
54. Wharf House, Lower George Street, Sydney
55. House for Jemima Jenkins
56. Shop for John Macqueen, Lower George Street, Sydney
57. Cleveland House, Bedford Street, Surrey Hills
58. Cottage, Cockle Bay, Sydney
59. Pair of Houses for Sir John Jamison, George Street, Sydney
60. Shop for George Williams, George Street, Sydney
61. House for Robert Campbell Sr, Bunkers Hill, Sydney

62. Shop for Barnett Levy, George Street, Sydney
63. Henrietta Villa, Point Piper
64. House for Thomas Moor, Elizabeth Street, Liverpool
65. Waterloo Warehouse, George /Market Streets, Sydney
66. House for William Cox, O'Connell Street, Sydney
67. Regentville near Penrith
68. Glenlee, Menangle
69. House for Robert Crawford, Lower Fort Street, Sydney
70. House & Store for Robert Campbell Jr, Bligh Street, Sydney
71. Bungarribee, Eastern Creek
72. Hobartville, Richmond
73. Warehouse for John Paul, George Street, Sydney
74. Springfield, Potts Point, Sydney
75. Jerusalem Warehouse, George Street, Sydney
76. Grantham, Potts Point, Sydney-
77. General Hospital, Sydney
78. Magazine, Fort Phillip
79. Design of Government House, Sydney
80. St. John's Parsonage, Parramatta
81. Portico, Government House, Parramatta
82. Macquarie Lighthouse, South Head
83. Obelisk, Macquarie Place, Sydney
84. Military Barracks, Sydney
85. Government Wharf, Windsor
86. Parramatta Gaol, Parramatta
87. Hyde Park Convict Barracks
88. St. Matthew's Church, Windsor
89. Chief Justice's House, Sydney
90. Colonial Secretary's House, Macquarie Place, Sydney
91. Judge Advocate's House, Macquarie Place, Sydney
92. Chaplain's House, Spring Street, Sydney
93. Government Stables, Government Domain, Sydney
94. Fort Macquarie, Bennelong Point, Sydney
95. Public Fountain, Macquarie Place, Sydney
96. St. Luke's Church, Liverpool
97. St. Luke's Parsonage, Liverpool
98. Female Factory and Barrack, Parramatta
99. Female Orphan School, Parramatta

100. Government House, Sydney
101. Dawes Point Battery, Dawes Point, Sydney
102. Turnpike Gate & Lodge, Parramatta Road, Sydney
103. St. Andrew's Church (Foundations), King Street, Sydney
104. Supreme court House, King Street, Sydney
105. Lumber Yard, Bridge Street, Sydney
106. Male Orphan School, George Street, Sydney
107. Dockyard, George Street, Sydney
108. Market House, George Street, Sydney
109. Court House, Windsor
110. Charity School, Elizabeth Street, Sydney
111. Police Office, George Street, Sydney
112. Granary & Store, George Street, Parramatta
113. St. Mary's Catholic Chapel, Hyde Park, Sydney
114. Princess Charlotte Memorial
115. Liverpool Hospital, Liverpool.
116. Pigeon House
117. Governor Brisbane's Bath House, Government Domain, Sydney
118. St. Matthews Rectory, Windsor
119. Ultimo House, Ultimo Sydney
120. House for Sarah Howe, Lower George Street, Sydney
121. House for George Howe, Charlotte Place, Sydney
122. Tomb for George Howe, Devonshire Street Cemetery, Sydney
123. House for Sir John Jamieson, Charlotte Place, Sydney
124. House for T.W. Middleton, Macquarie /Hunter Streets, Sydney
125. Work for R.W. Loane
126. Cottage, Parramatta
127. Proposed House, George /Argyle Street, Sydney
128. House for Sir John Wylde, Sydney
129. Bank of New South Wales, George Street, Sydney
130. Wharf House, Lower George Street, Sydney
131. House for Jemima Jenkins
132. Shop for John Macqueen, Lower George Street, Sydney
133. Cleveland House, Bedford Street, Surrey Hills
134. Cottage, Cockle Bay, Sydney
135. Pair of Houses for Sir John Jamison, George Street, Sydney
136. Shop for George Williams, George Street, Sydney
137. House for Robert Campbell Sr, Bunkers Hill, Sydney

138. Shop for Barnett Levy, George Street, Sydney
139. Henrietta Villa, Point Piper
140. House for Thomas Moor, Elizabeth Street, Liverpool
141. Waterloo Warehouse, George /Market Streets, Sydney
142. House for William Cox, O'Connell Street, Sydney
143. Regentville near Penrith
144. Glenlee, Menangle
145. House for Robert Crawford, Lower Fort Street, Sydney
146. House & Store for Robert Campbell Jr, Bligh Street, Sydney
147. Bungarribee, Eastern Creek
148. Hobartville, Richmond
149. Warehouse for John Paul, George Street, Sydney
150. Springfield, Potts Point, Sydney
151. Jerusalem Warehouse, George Street, Sydney
152. Grantham, Potts Point, Sydney-

CHAPTER 10

RECONSTRUCTING THE MACQUARIE ERA CONSTRUCTION PROGRAM

The Bigge's Report provides a partial list of building work completed by Macquarie. The items, which to Bigge are the most useful buildings on the list, include:

(The numbers refer to references in Greenway's –1822 Map of Sydney)

<u>**Sydney Items**</u>

- The Commissariat (King's) Store at Sydney (8)
- St. Phillips Church at Sydney (12)
- Improvement of Government House at Sydney (1)
- Sydney Gaol (30)
- Clearing of grounds contiguous to the Government Houses (1)
- A Parsonage House at Sydney (30)
- Military Barracks at Sydney—Wynyard Square (13)
- Hospital in Sydney –"Rum" Hospital –Macquarie Street (21)
- Hyde Park Convict Barracks (20)
- Military Hospital in Sydney – Wynyard Square (27)
- Improvements to Lumber-Yard at Sydney (28)
- Improvements to Dockyard at Sydney (29)
- St. James Church (19)

- Colonial Secretary's House & Office (4)
- Sydney Cove-Governor's Wharf (26)
- Water Bailiff—House and landing (31)
- Houses for Judge-Advocate (Judge of Supreme Court) – (4)
- Court-house at Sydney (18)
- School-house at Hyde Park (16)
- Market house at George Street, Sydney (15)
- Government stables at Sydney (2)
- Fountain in Macquarie Place (6)
- Obelisk in Macquarie Place (7)
- The Turnpike Gate—Lower George Street (22)
- Fort (Macquarie) at Bennelong Point (3)
- Battery at Dawes Point (10)
- Greenway's House and office (9)
- Windmill—(built at Public Expense)—at Garrison barracks (23)
- Windmill—(built at Public Expense)—at the Domain. (24)
- Magazine at Fort Phillip (11)
- St.Andrew's Church foundation (15)
- Orphan House in Sydney (25)

Parramatta, Windsor, Liverpool & Outer Sydney Area Items

- Carters Barracks and goal at Windsor
- Female Factory at Parramatta
- St. Matthews Church at Windsor
- Church at Liverpool
- Chapel at Castlereagh
- A Parsonage House at Parramatta
- A Parsonage House at Liverpool
- Hospital at Parramatta
- Hospital at Windsor (a converted brewery formerly owned by Andrew Thompson)
- Hospital at Liverpool
- Convict Barracks at Parramatta
- Improvement of Government House at Parramatta
- An asylum for the aged and infirm near Sydney
- Bridge at Rushcutter's Bay—South Head Road
- Macquarie Light-house at Sydney South Head

(This list accounts for 46 items on Bigge's 63 reference)

Newcastle Items

- Hospital
- Gaol
- Commandant House
- Surgeons Quarter
- Workhouse
- Blacksmiths Forge
- Pier
- Windmill
- Parsonage House "(Bigge Report)

Greenway Items (drawn but under construction)

- Officer Quarters-Hyde Park
- Alterations to Judge Advocate's House
- Alterations to Lumber Yard building
- Alterations to Dawes Battery
- Alterations to Liverpool parsonage
- Portico, Gov House, Parramatta
- Alterations to Orphan School, Sydney
- Alterations to Government House, Sydney
- Judge Field's House –Sydney
- Plans for Mr. Marsden's House at Parramatta
- Survey for the new General (Rum) Hospital
- Plans for the Windsor Church
- Plans for the Liverpool Church
- Plans for Judge Field's house
- Plans for Parramatta Female Factory
- Survey of Parramatta Bridge
- Survey of Sydney Gaol
- Measuring work by contractors at Sydney Gaol
- Plans for Windsor Court-house
- Plans for new toll-gate
- Plans for Obelisk in Macquarie Place
- Plans for fountain in Macquarie Place.

(If we count 'alterations' to buildings, we can account for the whole 63 items stated by Commissioner Bigge to have been undertaken in the Macquarie Era)

The Commissariat (King's) Store at Sydney (8)		7500
St. Phillips Church at Sydney (12)		3250
Improvement of Government House at Sydney (1)	600	
Sydney Gaol (30)	6000	
Clearing of grounds contiguous to the Government Houses (1)		200
A Parsonage House at Sydney (30)		350
Military Barracks at Sydney—Wynyard Square (13)		11000
Hospital in Sydney –"Rum" Hospital –Macquarie Street (21)		0
Military Hospital in Sydney – Wynyard Square (27)		6750
Improvements to Lumber-Yard at Sydney (28)		2000
Improvements to Dockyard at Sydney (29)		1000
St. James Church (19)	6240	
Colonial Secretary's House & Office (4)		875
Sydney Cove-Governor's Wharf (26)		3500
Water Bailiff—House and landing (31)		1250
Houses for Judge-Advocate (Judge of Supreme Court (4)		4800
Court-house at Sydney (18)	6450	
School-house at Hyde Park (16)		3500
Market house at George Street, Sydney (15)	300	
Government stables at Sydney (2)	9000	
Fountain in Macquarie Place (6)		500
Obelisk in Macquarie Place (7)		375
The Turnpike Gate—Lower George Street (22)		2750
Fort (Macquarie) at Bennelong Point (3		21000
Battery at Dawes Point (10)		4675
Greenway's House and office (9)		1695
Windmill—(built at Public Expense)—at Garrison barracks (23)		2250
Windmill—(built at Public Expense)—at the Domain. (24)		2230

Magazine at Fort Phillip (11)	1240	
St.Andrew's Church foundation (15)	2500	
Orphan House in Sydney (25)	2180	
Parramatta, Windsor, Liverpool & Outer Sydney Area		
Carters Barracks and goal at Windsor		9750
Female Factory at Parramatta		278500
St. Matthews Church at Windsor		5600
Church at Liverpool		5250
Chapel at Castlereagh		4750
A Parsonage House at Parramatta		1250
A Parsonage House at Liverpool	520	
Hospital at Parramatta		6500
Hospital at Windsor (a converted brewery formerly owned by Andrew Thompson)		3365
Hospital at Liverpool		5850
Convict Barracks at Parramatta		21500
Improvement of Government House at Parramatta	1120	
An asylum for the aged and infirm near Sydney		8625
Bridge at Rushcutter's Bay—South Head Road		2275
Macquarie Light-house at Sydney South Head	7050	
(This list accounts for 46 items on Bigge's 63 reference)		
Newcastle Items		
Hospital		6693
Gaol		8824
Commandant House		1356
Surgeons Quarter		1569
Workhouse		5228
Blacksmiths Forge		2135
Pier		3556
Windmill		2150
Parsonage House "(Bigge Report)		1189
(We now account for 55 out of the 63)		
Greenway Items (drawn but under construction)		
Officer Quarters-Hyde Park	10600	

Alterations to Judge Advocate's House	600	
Alterations to Lumber Yard building	2000	
Alterations to Dawes Battery	1200	
Alterations to Liverpool parsonage	520	
TOTALS	55600	344865

Kitchen Estimates   922,857.13.11

Since the actual total for the estimated construction work completed in the Macquarie era is less than $500,000, and it is most unlikely that the total could have reached $922,000, then it is safe to assume that Henry Kitchen, in producing this misleading estimate to Commissioner Bigge was provided with the intention of further blackening the names of both Greenway and Macquarie – both of whom disliked and were disliked by Kitchen. This was a deliberately malicious and deceptive piece of disinformation by Kitchen.

There is another possible explanation that stretches credulity somewhat but could be justified as a possibility. It is always assumed that convict labour was essentially 'free', and should therefore not count or contribute to the total cost of the finished construction.

If we make a number of assumptions concerning day rates of equivalent pay, and about the productivity level of the convicts in a major construction job, keeping in mind they were supervised by other convicts, then we may be able to say that the 400,000 pound of cost assembled in the Table above is for materials and that the equivalent value of the convict labour makes the difference of the 522,000 to bring the total estimate up to Kitchen's estimates.

The relevant assumptions are (based on Greenways cost estimates on Page 59 above)

- The number of days of mechanics labour to complete the Government House Stables was 16,686.5
- The average cost per man day was 1 shilling
- Labour reflected a 33% content of the total finished cost.

So applying these assumptions to the construction work in the rest of the table, we find that all projects would have taken 2,683,108 days of mechanics labour or approx 8,450 man years. The convict population increased between 1812 and 1820 by 10,800 men and totaled 19,000 men by 1820, and to suppose that 44% of the male convicts were employed in construction work is not unreasonable. At the minimum rate of 1 s per day, our labour cost total becomes 134155 pound; thus, at an average of 3 shillings (compared with Coghlan's cost for 'free' mechanics at 5s per day, we would achieve the difference of 480,000 pound. Coghlan estimates that a convict would only produce about 60% of a 'free' laborer.

Our conclusion, if we stretch the point, is that Kitchen's estimate of a construction cost for the period of 900,000 is valid if our materials are valued at 402,000 and our labour accounts (at the average rate of 3 shillings per day) to a further 470,000-pound.

12. A Final Word

Two interesting discoveries emerge from the table *–British Investments in to the Colony 1800-1850.*

We have noted above that T.A. Coghlan, that doyenne of all things statistical, especially in relation to the colony, states very strongly and without qualification that 'the private capital invested in the colony prior to 1871 was 16 million pound.

Coghlan provides no supporting evidence to substantiate this statement, but having broken the actual verifiable figures down into components, that Coghlan figure sounds quite plausible. This writer's estimates of private capital invested in the colony between 1800 and 1850 are 14,388,000 pound. The components include Government borrowings overseas; immigrant's capital; foreigner's investment, and I have included the amount of land mortgages recorded under the Deeds Registration Act of 1843. Although land mortgages after 1843 would normally have been recorded, there was provision in the Act for re-registration of earlier mortgages and many lenders, both private and corporate, took advantage of ratifying their previous lien rights. Since my figures relate to the period to 1850, it is more than likely that between 1851 and 1870, a further 1.7 million pound was invested privately. So Coghlan is essentially. Correct.

However it is the N.G. Butlin assumptions that trouble me, and I would like to restate an earlier conclusion that the British accepted an excellent return on their investment in the colony, and this is really what the opening of the colony was all about.

The Table of British Public Investment in the colony shows from the inception of the colony, through to self-government, the British 'invested' nearly 70 million pound in capital works or their equivalent. What this means is that I have included the cost of shipping and transporting the convicts to the colony and the cost of food and provisioning. Professor Butlin, at one point, refers to the level of British investment for this same period as being 74 million, but the components are not described. However, it is a not unreasonable figure to work with. It includes the early grants to the colony from the British Treasury; it includes the transportation of the convicts and their food en route; it includes the treasury bills drawn by the colony on the British Treasury for materials and contract labour, purchases from trading ships coming into the Harbour; it concludes payments made for civil list and military salaries, and it includes the verified public works expenditure. Each of these figures has been drawn from the 'Joint Copying Project of Historical documents' and 'historical statistics'.

The essential point of this assembly of public investment is to put into perspective the original investment by the British Treasury and compare it with the level of 'return' the British, as a whole, were to receive.

So, before we assemble the figures into a table of investment and return, let's review again the elements of what constitutes a 'return'.

Each of the elements of the return, and we might even say the expected return, for it was James Matra's submission to the British Government that first identified that the colony would be self-supporting within two years of commencing and provide advantages to Britain. It was Arthur Phillip in a letter to Lord Sydney in July 1788 who wrote ' . . . nor do I doubt but that this country will prove the most valuable acquisition Great Britain ever made . . . . '

The elements of this 'opportunity cost' include:

a. The opportunity cost of housing, feeding and guarding prisoners in England. This is set at the rate of 20 pound per head per annum, but does not take into account any offset for work undertaken by prisoners.

b. The use of convict labour for construction work on colonial buildings. This is set at 35 pound per annum for 2/3rds of the convicts (Macquarie employed about 70% of the male convicts in this way.

c. The balance of the male convicts were used on road construction, wharves, barracks etc and had an equivalent value, net of support payments, of 35 pound per annum (The James Matra letter of October 1784 stated that the contract price for maintaining prisoners on the hulks was 26/15/0 per annum). In the early years, we can also include in this figure, the convict labour used for land clearing, farming and food production, and the convict labour used for maintaining the supply of building materials, timber, bricks, tiles etc

d. The Molesworth Committee concluded in their Report to the House of Commons that there were significant savings in food costs for these convicts

e. Another benefit to the British by way of opportunity cost is the value of the land grants to the Military officers by way of fringe benefits as civil payments. On average, the land had a value of 1 pound per acre and we know that land grants were in the order of 5228015 acres

f. An as yet economically unquantifiable gain to British industry was the value of the import wool trade, and the export purchases of tobacco and spirits for the colony. In addition timber, coal, whale oil, skins and fur were all important imports by British Industry, and assisted Britain by making them less reliant on Europe.

g. It is assumed that the private investment received a return on capital equivalent to an interest and super profit.

So out Summary Table can now be assembled

TABLE

British Investment & Returns from the Colony of NSW

Public Investment

Treasury grants	23741000
Convict transport/food	6051550
Treasury Bills	5384584
Civil List	888858
Military	9629170
Commissary	8134000
Public Works	1265000
Total Public Investment	69,482,162

Benefits & Gains to the British

Opportunity Costs	-a.	84000000
Convict labour	-b	70000000
Convict labour	-c	21000000
Food savings	-d	7000000
Land grants	-e	5228015
Total estimated Returns		180228015

CHAPTER 11

IMMIGRATION & INVESTMENT

The Economic Theory of 19th Century British Investment

Before we complete our table of identifying capital formation by the British investor (both Public (Government) and Private Investment), let me review a piece by Sir T. H. Farrer (Bart) from his 1887 book 'Free Trade versus Fair Trade'. The notation on the front-piece of the book shows the Cobden Club emblem with the words 'free trade, peace, goodwill among nations'. We will discuss Cobden a little later when we review the work of the Australian Senator Edward Pulsford – another outspoken supporter and devotee of the Cobden philosophy, and free trade and open immigration.

"The amount of English capital constantly employed abroad in private trade and in permanent investments, including Stock Exchange securities, private advances, property owned abroad by Englishmen, British shipping, British-owned cargoes, and other British earnings abroad, has been estimated by competent statisticians as being between 1,500 and 2,000 million pounds, and is constantly increasing. Taking the lower figure, the interest or profit upon it, at 5 per cent, would be 75 million pounds, and at the higher figure it would be 100 million pound."[2]

Farrer then equates this income figure to the spread of imports over exports and finds that the two compare. But then he argues there is the question of freights. "A very large proportion of the trade of the United Kingdom

---

[2]   Farrer, T.H *Free Trade or Fair Trade*

is carried in English ships, and these ships carry a large proportion of the trade of other countries not coming to England. This shipping is, in fact, an export of highly-skilled English labour and capital which does not appear in the export returns of the 19th century, and considering that it includes not only the interest on capital but also wages, provisions, coal, port expenses, repairs, depreciation and insurance; and that the value of English shipping employed in the foreign trade is estimated at more than 100 million pound per annum, the amount to be added to our exports on account of English shipping, must be very large". [3] But he goes further, "add to this the value of ships built for foreigners amounting to over 70,000 ton per annum, worth together several millions, and all these outgoings, with the profits, must either return to this country in the shape of imports, or be invested abroad—I believe 50 million pound is too low an estimate of the amount of unseen exports. In addition there are the commissions and other charges to agents in this country, connected with the carriage of goods from country to country, but each of these items do not appear in the statistics of exports. I can only assume that we are investing large amounts of our savings in the colonies, such as Australia."[4]

The Farrer argument in favour of 'free trade' then turns to the 'fair trade' objections to foreign investments.

Farrer writes "When we point to the indebtedness of foreign colonies to England as one reason for the excess of imports, they tell us that we have been paying for our imports by the return to us of foreign securities; and at the same time they complain bitterly that, instead of spending our money at home, our rich men are constantly investing their money abroad, and thus robbing English labour of its rights here"[5]

But we know that is not the whole story.

When England investors transferred capital to the colonies, it is not only in the form of cash (which would come from savings) but it is more often in the form of capital goods. England sends iron; the shipbuilders

---

[3]   Farrer *ibid*
[4]   Farrer *ibid*
[5]   Farrer *ibid*

who make the ships that carry the goods, and the sailors who navigate them. When they reach the colonies, what happens then? They return with grain, or coal, or wool, or timber, and that makes those commodities cheaper in England. The investor receives the interest or profits on that capital invested which would generally be greater than what could have been earned if the capital had been invested in England. Now that return can be spent on luxury goods, invested locally or re-invested overseas to commence the whole cycle again. That return will be employed in setting to work English labour, earn a return and so on.

It remains true that on the whole, based on the Farrer argument, the transfer of English capital from an English industry that does not pay to a colonial industry which does pay, is no loss to England generally, and causes no diminution in the employment of English labour. There are at least two drawbacks to colonial investment by a maritime power; one, in the event of a war, the returns would be open to greater risk, and two; the investors can more easily evade taxation by the English Government.

Obviously since 1886, when Farrer constructed this argument, the world has changed, investment opportunities have changed, England has fallen from its pinnacle as a world power and international commercial leader and the improved collection of statistics now recognises movements of goods and investments on both current account and capital account. But the concept helped put the Australian colony on the map and attracted enormous amounts of private capital into the colony to make it grow and prosper.

Farrer concludes his argument with this observation.

"The desire to make profitable investments, however valuable economically, is not the only motive which governs rich men; it's the love of natural beauty; interest in farming and the outdoor life; personal and local attachments; all of which are quite sure to maintain a much larger expenditure on English land than would be dictated by a desire for gain. Let these other motives have their way, as these investors still contribute to the welfare of the toilers and spinners who produce the goods, and make a good return that in the end makes England wealthier"[6]

---

[6]   Farrer *ibid*

CHAPTER 12

FACTORS AFFECTING BRITISH INVESTMENT IN THE COLONY

A number of factors affected the level of capital investment into the colony – many were ill informed and relied on delayed newspaper reports on activity in the various settlements.

l. The offer of assisted migration

m. The failing economic conditions in Britain

n. Economic expansion for the pastoral industry due to successful exploration in the colony

o. The settlement at Port Phillip and the eventual separation of Victoria from New South Wales would promote great investment opportunities

p. The rise of the squattocracy

q. The crash of 1827-28 in the colony shakes British Investors

r. The Bigges' Report of 1823 breathed new life into capital formation especially with Macarthur sponsoring the float of the Australian Agricultural Company

s. Further along, the good credit rating of the colonies (and there being no defaults on loans) encouraged larger investments and loans into the colonies

t. Shortage of Labour in the colony and the offer of land grants to new settlers became a useful carrot to attract small settlers bringing their own capital by way of cash or goods or livestock with them.

u. Two other steps had important consequences, one in the colony and the other in Britain. In 1827 Governor Darling began to issue grazing licenses to pastoralists, and the terms were set at 2/6d per hundred acres, with liability to quit on one month's notice. From this movement grew, writes Madgwick in *Immigration into Eastern Australia*, the squatting movement and the great pastoral expansion, and the idea of the earlier Governors that the colony of New South Wales should be a colony of farmers was thus abandoned. The concurrent event was the floating of the Australian Agricultural Company in London. Development by the AAC and by the free settlers brought increasing prosperity. Exports tripled between 1826 and 1831.

v. There is a connection between availability of factors of production and the level of investment. In the early days of the colony, labour was present—bad labour, convict labour, but still labour. The governors had demanded settlers with capital to employ that labour and develop the land. They proposed to limit land grants in proportion to the means of the settler. Governor Darling declared (HRA ser 1, vol 8) that 'when I am satisfied of the character, respectability and means of the applicant settler in a rural area, he will receive the necessary authority to select a grant of land, proportionate in extent to the means he possesses.

Let us examine some of these important elements commencing with the Bigge Report into Agriculture and Trade of the Colony.[7]

1. The Australian Agricultural Company

J.F. Campbell wrote about the first decade of the Australian Agricultural Company 1824-1834 in the proceedings of the 1923 RAHS.

"Soon after Commissioner Bigge's report of 1823 became available for public information, several enterprising men concerted with a view to acquire sheep-runs in the interior of this colony, for the production of fine wool.

---

[7] Bigge, John Thomas *Commissioners' Report into Agriculture & Trade in NSW – Report No. 1 1823*

The success which attended the efforts of John Macarthur and a few other New South Wales pastoralists, in the breeding and rearing of fine woolled sheep and stock generally, as verified by Bigge, gave the incentive and led to the inauguration of proceedings which resulted in the formation of the Australian Agricultural Company.

The first formal meeting of the promoters took place at Lincoln's Inn, London, (at the offices of John Macarthur, junior).

Earl Bathurst, advised Governor Brisbane in 1824 that.

His Majesty has been pleased to approve the formation of the Company, from the impression that it affords every reasonable prospect of securing to that part of His Majesty's dominions the essential advantage of the immediate introduction of large capital, and of agricultural skill, as well as the ultimate benefit of the increase of fine wool as a valuable commodity for export.

The chief proposals of the company are:

vii. The company would be incorporated by Act of Parliament or Letters Patent.

viii. The capital of the company was to be 1 million pound sterling divided into 10,000 shares of 100 pound each

ix. A grant of land of one million acres to be made to the company

x. That no rival joint stock company to be established in the colony for the next twenty years

xi. That the agents of the company would select the situation or the land grants.

xii. The shepherds and labourers would consist of 1,400 convicts, thereby lessening the maintenance of such convicts by an estimated 30,800 pound or 22 pound/per head/ per annum

The Royal Charter of 1824 forming the company provided for payment of quit-rents over a period of twenty years, or the redemption of the same by paying the capital sum of 20 times the amount of the rent so to be redeemed. These quit-rents were to be waived if the full number of convicts were maintained for a period of five years. No land was to be sold during the five-year period from the date of the grant".

Being important that the investment be seen to have the support of strong leaders in Britain, and democratic governance, the company operated with

- A Governor
- 25 directors
- 365 stockholders (proprietors)

Leading stockholders included

- Robert Campbell
- Chief Justice Forbes
- Son of Governor King
- Rev Samuel Marsden
- John Macarthur
- Each Macarthur son, John jr, Hannibal, James, Charles, Scott & William

John Oxley, the Colonial-Surveyor had recommended the area of Port Stephens as an eligible spot for the land grant. The local directors inspected and approved the site but John Macarthur was extremely critical of the selection, the management plan and the extravagance of the first buildings.

This venture was the first major investment into the colony and set the scene for later developments. In 1825 the Van Diemen's Land Company was chartered by the British Parliament and granted land on the northwest corner of the territory.

Both the A.A. Coy and the VDL Coy still operate today after nearly 180 years of continuous operation, a record beaten only by the operation of the Hudson Bay Company in Canada.

CHAPTER 13

MACQUARIE'S BANK

Nothing quite engenders confidence in an investor like the thought of a new bank opening for business.

Less than three months after his arrival in the colony, Macquarie foreshadowed his plan for a bank on the South African model, as a 'remedy' to 'be speedily applied to this growing evil' of private promissory notes. With some exaggeration he explained that there was 'no other circulating medium in this colony than the notes of hand of private individuals' which, as he said, had 'already been productive of infinite frauds, abuses and litigation'. He accordingly announced his intention to' strongly recommend the adoption here of the same system of banking and circulating medium as is now so successfully and beneficially pursued at the Cape of Good Hope'.

By June 1810 Macquarie had developed his plan for 'The New South Wales Loan Bank' as a government institution ' as nearly as possible on the same system and principles as the Government Loan Bank at the Cape of Good Hope'. There, he explained the government issued notes by way of loan on the security of mortgages at 6 per cent per annum. He also pointed out that in England the government borrowed on exchequer bills at 5 %, so that the Cape was 11% better off. 'It appears to me' was his conclusion, ' the most perfect model in all its parts that could be possibly adopted here' By October 1810, he was willing to accept any alternative form of bank which Liverpool (Secretary for the Colonies) might believe to be 'better calculated to effect the desired object'.

Obviously a Bank would form the foundation for a monetary policy in the colony, and stop the use of Commissary receipt (store receipts) as an exchange mechanism, promote a currency and an official exchange rate for traders and cease to rely on bills drawn on the British Treasury to pay for goods and services.

3. The British Scene

Circumstances in Britain contributed greatly to the climate of 'greener pastures' over the seas.

Conditions were never more favourable for emigration than they were during the 1830s. The decade had opened with rioting in the agricultural districts in the south of England. This was followed by the upheavals of the Reform Bill of 1832, the Factory Act of 1833 and the Corn Laws, which kept wages low and unemployment high. The Poor Law of 1834 withdrew assistance from the poor and re-introduced the workhouse. The Irish rebellion was creating both upheaval and poverty

These conditions were met by the enthusiastic reports coming from Australia of the progress being made in agriculture, commerce and the pastoral industry. The assistance granted to emigrants as a result of Edward Gibbon Wakefield's reforms made possible the emigration of people who had previously been prevented by the expense. It is almost certain that free passage would not have been a sufficient enticement if conditions in Britain had not been unfavourable. It is significant that years of small migration coincided with good conditions in England accompanied by unfavourable reports from the colony.

4. Creating Opportunities in the Colony

Availability of land and labour to yield profit on invested capital is the constant decisive condition and test of material prosperity in any community, and becomes the keystone of an economy as well as defining its national identity.

British Government policy for the Australian colonies was formulated and modified from time to time. Policies for the export of British capital and the supply of labour (both convict and free) were adjusted according to British industrial and demographic and other social situations, as well as the capability and capacity of the various colonial settlements top contribute to solving British problems.

By the 1820s there was official encouragement of British Investment in Australia by adopting policies for large land grants to persons of capital and for the sale of land and assignment of convict labour to those investors. Then followed the reversal of the policy of setting up ex-convicts on small 30 acre plots as small proprietors. The hardship demanded by this policy usually meant these convicts and families remained on the commissary list for support (food and clothing) at a continuing cost to the government. It was much cheaper to assign these convicts to men of property and capital who would support them fully – clothe, house and feed them.

6. What led directly to the crash of 1827?

b. Firstly, the float of the Australian Agricultural Company raised a large amount of capital, mostly from the City of London investment community, and this contributed to speculation and 'sheep and cattle mania instantly seized on all ranks and classes of the inhabitants' (written by Rev John Dunmore Lang) 'and brought many families to poverty and ruin'.

c. When capital imports cease, the wherewithal to speculate vanished; speculation perforce stopped; inflated prices fell to a more normal level, and wrote E.O. Shann in Economic History of Australia 'because those formerly too optimistic were now too despairing, and people had to sell goods at any price in order to get money; men who had bought at high prices were ruined, and perforce their creditors fell with them'.

d. In 1842, it was the same. The influx of capital from oversees, pastoral extension, and large-scale immigration, caused much speculation. The banks, competing for business, advanced too much credit. Loans were made on the security of land and livestock, which later became almost worthless; too much discounting was done for merchants (Gipps, HRA Vol 23) In the huge central district on the western slopes, along the Murrumbidgee and the Riverina, the squatters triumphed, as was inevitable. He had the financial resources to buy his run – especially after the long period of drought. Four million acres of crown land was sold for nearly 2.5 million pound. The confidence of British investors was waning. A crisis in the Argentine and the near failure of the large clearinghouse of Baring's made them cautious. Stories of rural and industrial strife in the colony were not inducements to invest: and wood and metal prices were still falling Loan applications being raised in London were under-subscribed, at the same time, the banks were increasingly reluctant to lend money for land development, which was so often unsound.

CHAPTER 14

ASSISTED MIGRATION

The dual policy of selling land to people with sufficient capital to cultivate it, and keeping a careful check on the number of free grants was adopted after 1825. 'Yet the Colonial Office', says Madgwick, 'failed to administer land policy with any certainty (R.B. Madgwick ' Immigration into Eastern Australia'). There was no uniform policy adopted to encourage economic development in a systematic and rational way. The Wakefield system found new supporters. The principle had been established that the sale of land was preferred to the old system of grants. The dual system of sales and grants had failed to encourage local (colonial) purchases. They were willing to accept grants or even 'squat' rather than purchase land. Sales to absentee landlords and investors stepped up, and as can be seen from the following table, provided extensive revenue to the British Government to promote free and sponsored migration.

CHAPTER 15

EXPLORATION

Successful exploration promotes new interest in the Colony

A period of rapid expansion followed the change in economic policy. Wool exports by 1831 were 15 times as great as they had been only 10 years earlier (in 1821). The increase in the number of sheep led to a rapid opening of new territories for grazing. It was the search for new land with economic value that underpinned most of the explorations. Settlers and sheep-men quickly followed exploration, and growth fanned out in all directions from Sydney town.

However, exploration was not the only catalyst for growth.

c. The growing determination to exclude other powers from the continent stimulated official interest in long-distance exploration by sea and by land and in the opening of new settlements. For instance, J.M. Ward in his work ' The Triumph of the Pastoral Economy 1821-1851' writes that Melville and Bathurst Islands, were annexed and settled between 1824 and 1827, whilst Westernport and Albany were settled in order to clinch British claims to the whole of Australia

d. When Governor Brisbane opened the settlement at Moreton Bay in 1824, it was to establish a place for punishment of unruly convicts and a step towards further economic development, and of extending the settlements for the sake of attracting new investment

8. Colonial Failures fuel loss of Confidence

The collapse of British Investment can be traced to one or two causes, or indeed both.

a. The British crisis of 1839 reflected the availability of capital for expansion by the Australian banks of that day – The Bank of Australasia and the Union Bank. These banks, three mortgage companies and the Royal Bank went into a slump due to shortage of available funds and deferred the raising of new funds until after the crisis. Stringency in the English Capital market had a serious impact on the capital raising opportunities in the colonies.

b. The second possibility is that the sharp decline was initiated by bad news of returns in the colonies, and that its role accentuated a slump with the dire consequences experienced in 1842-43. Recovery was delayed and made more difficult as there was 'no surplus labour in the colony'

It would be dangerous to imply or decide that every slump in Australia could be explained as being caused by economic evens. British investment was independent then, as it is now, and so the more valid explanation of the downturn in British investment in this period is that negative reports from the colonies disappointed and discouraged investors with capital to place.

Most facts about public finance in New South Wales lead to the conclusion that it was disappointed expectations that caused the turn down in the transfer of funds. At this same time Governor Gipps (Sir George Gipps) was being pushed by bankers and merchants to withdraw government deposits from the banks and thus this action caused a contraction in lending by the banks which in turn caused a slow down of colonial economic activity. The attached statistics of land sales, registered mortgages and liens on wool and livestock reflects the strong downturn in the agricultural economy, which naturally flowed on to the economy as a whole.

CHAPTER 16

EDUCATION, IMMIGRATION
1788-1838

A.G. Austin in Australian Education 1788-1900 offers an explanation as to the lack of interest in educating the lower classes.

"Nowhere in Phillip's Commissions or instructions was any mention made of the children accompanying the First Fleet, or of the child convicts whom the British Government saw fit to transport, for it was alien to the official mind of the late 18th century to feel any interest in the welfare of these children. By 1809 the War Office had been persuaded to appoint regimental schoolmasters, but in 1788 the education of these children formed no part of the business of any department of state.

The conservative opinion in Britain was convinced that education was exactly the wrong remedy and agreed with the Bishop of London's conviction that it was 'safest for both the Government and the religion of the country to let the lower classes remain in that state of ignorance in which nature has originally placed them'.

In this atmosphere anyone who undertook the education of the poor became an object of suspicion. Even the devout *Hannah Moore* had to defend her schools against charges of Methodism, Calvinism and subversion. Ms. Moore wrote: 'they learn such coarse work as may fit them as servants. I allow no writing for the poor. My object is to train up the lower classes in habits of industry and piety'. Nearly a century later John Stuart Mill still thought it necessary to warn his readers that 'a general state education . . . established a despotism over the mind'.

The Pitt Tory Government resisted those favouring State intervention in education. They saw no reason to meddle in the upbringing of other people's children, and no reason to suppose that the new Governor of NSW would presume to dispute their opinion.

The early governors of NSW soon found it necessary to change their adoption of British policies, especially regarding education in the colony, since Britain was not a fragment of English society transplanted, but a military and penal garrison in which the governors were responsible for every detail of daily life. In a settlement where the maintenance of discipline, the regulation of food production, the rationing of supplies, the employment of labour, and the administration of justice were necessarily committed into one man's hands, there was no room for that *laissez-faire* indifference which characterized the conduct of public affairs in Britain.

Not only were the governors moved by the misery of the convicts' children but also they realized that the future of the colony had to built upon these children. In a colony where there was three times the number of men as there were women, a deplorably high proportion of illegitimate and abandoned children required some measure of protection and supervision. In 1807 on Bligh's testimony, there were 387 married women in the colony, 1,035 concubines, 807 legitimate children and 1,024 illegitimate children.

Phillip had set aside, near every town, an allotment for a church and 400 acres adjacent for the maintenance of a minister and 200 Acres for the schoolmaster. However the governors were not really concerned to assert the supremacy of either Church or State. All their actions were matters of expediency. To finance schools, they made direct grants of land, assigned convicts and issued rations. To staff schools they had used soldiers, convicts, missionaries and other literate person they could find. To accommodate the schools, they used churches, barracks, storehouses and private buildings. It was Macquarie who first set down the staging order of divinity. All clerics would be, for the first time, from 1810, responsible to the principal chaplain.

By the end of the Macquarie era, many changes had been made to the social order in the colony, including education, and most of these changes were in principal accepted by J.T. Bigge in his reports to the British Commissioners. Bigge's reported that ' the flow of immigrants and the increasing number of emancipated convicts has so increased the population of free settlers that the prosperity of the settlement as a colony has proportionately advanced, and hopes may reasonably be entertained of its becoming perhaps at no distant period a valuable possession of the crown. This makes me think that it is no longer fit for its original purpose'.

For public education to be considered as a government responsibility and controlled by a cleric meant that part of the cost could be defrayed by public revenue. The suggestions made by the new Archdeacon of the colony were that public education be controlled by a cleric who was also placed at the head of the Church Establishment. The costs could be defrayed, was the suggestion, by the parents contributing, annually, a ' bushel of good clean sound wheat, or equivalent value in meat, or 1/8th of the colonial import duty could be diverted to education; governments could subdivide its land at Grose Farm, Emu Plains, Rooty Hill and Cabramatta into small farms and apply their rents to the endowment of schools in general'. The last suggestion and the one that attracted Lord Bathurst's ear was that a 'new land reserve of some 25,000 acres should be established near Bathurst or Newcastle'.

The British Government ultimately decided in 1825 to direct Governor Brisbane to form a 'corporation and invest it with clergy and school estates, and from the proceeds it should support the Anglican Church and schools and school masters in connection with the established church' The territory of NSW was to be divided into counties, hundreds, and parishes as a result of a survey of the whole colony. The Corporation was not a success largely because it was never properly funded the way it was expected, nor did it enjoy the high enthusiasm or interest of the governor.

Macquarie 'reported' to Viscount Castlereagh on 30th April 1810 on the progress in carrying out British instructions

'In pursuance to your Lordship's instructions, I lost no time in directing my attention to the principal object pointed out in them, namely, to improve the morals of the colonists, to encourage marriage, to provide for education, to prohibit the use of spirituous liquors, and to increase the agriculture and livestock so as to ensure a certainty of supply to the inhabitants under all circumstances'. In his next dispatch Macquarie reported that 'with a view to the decent education and improvement of the rising generation, I have established several schools at head quarters and the subordinate settlements, which I trust will not fail of being attended with very desirable effects'. He also requested 'a few more chaplains and some additional schoolmasters which are very much required, and it would be very desirable if some should be sent out as soon as possible'.

Alan Barcan in his imaginative work '*History of Australian Education*' notes that, in line with regular military policy the NSW Corps brought their own tutor with them for teaching the children of military personnel. No such luxury was available for the residents of Norfolk Island. In 1793, Lieutenant King (Governor of the island) established an import duty on liquor in order to raise funds for education. King built the first stone schoolhouse in 1794 and a second in 1795. Collins records ('*An Account of the English Colony in NSW*') that 'the first school was for young children, who were instructed by a woman of good character; the second was kept by a man, who taught reading, writing, and arithmetic, for which he was well qualified, and was very attentive'.

King also opened an Orphan Institution in 1795 when by this time there were 75 destitute children. These children were taught, fed, clothed, and given vocational training.

In Sydney Governor Hunter met with the school children each year, and as David Collins records, in 1797, Hunter inspected the children from three schools and 'was gratified with the sight of 102 clean and decently—dressed children, who came with their several masters and mistresses'.

In 1798, the Rev'd Richard Johnson (the first cleric in the colony, who had arrived with the First Fleet) amalgamated the three schools in Sydney and the three joint teachers held classes in the church. They had 150 to 200 children enrolled of 'all descriptions of persons, whether soldiers, settlers, or convicts' (/Johnson's Rules). After the Church was burnt down on 1st October 1798, it moved to the courthouse and then to a disused warehouse, but enrolments halved.

When King arrived to take over as Governor in 1800, he continued his deep interest in education and 'education expanded significantly'. (Barcan). There were three main reasons for this expansion.

a. King himself took a deep interest in education and brought with him the experience gained from his Norfolk Island success
b. Increased colonial prosperity and better financial provision. King imposed an import duty on goods to establish a fund for education. When the Female Orphan Fund opened in August 1801, there were 54 girls aged from 7 to 14 in the school. In August 1804, King gave it an endowment of 13 000 acres to secure its economic stability. Samuel Marsden, its Treasurer and religious guardian commented that the Orphan School is 'the foundation of religion and morality in this colony'
c. The growth of population, which produced both the need for and the ability to sustain schools. By 1800 Sydney was a town of 2 000 and the colony had some 5 000 inhabitants. Significance could be seen in the

  • Growth of a small commercial middle class,
  • The publication of the *Sydney Gazette*, which offered an avenue for expression of opinion
  • A 'distinction' between state-aided 'public schools' and 'private' education

Vocational training was possibly the most important challenge and target of the education system. In 1798, Hunter reported that young male convicts had been assigned to an 'artificer's gang in order that they may be useful mechanics'. In 1805, King developed a system of apprenticeships for boys. In the same year advertisements appeared in the *Sydney Gazette* for apprentice seamen. The Female Orphan School developed some vocational training for the girls by offering 'needlework, reading, spinning and some few writing'. A few of the girls became servants with them being 'bound as apprentices to officer's wives'.

The overall shortage of labour in the colony caused vocational training to make only slow progress.

Immigrants and Free Settlers

Collins records that on the 15th January 1793, the *Bellona* transport ship, arrived in Sydney Harbour with a cargo of stores and provisions, 17 female convicts and five settlers one of whom was a master wheel-wright employed by the governor at a salary of 100 pound per annum. A second was a returning skilled tradesman who had been previously employed as a master blacksmith. All five settlers had brought their families.

Collins conjectures that these first three settlers had received free passage, a promise of a land grant and assistance with farming, as the incentive for becoming the free settlers,

Manning Clark (*A History of* Australia*)* records that in 1806, 'a dozen families from the Scottish border area arrived as free emigrants and each received 100 acres of land on the banks of the Hawkesbury River in a place they called Ebenezer. They were devout Presbyterians, and were allowed to worship in the colony according to their own lights'. However the authorities were not prepared to tolerate the practice of the catholic religion, because they saw it 'as an instrument of mental slavery, a threat to higher civilization, and a threat to liberty' (Clark Vol 1)

Developing Immigration

Even by the census of 1828, NSW had fewer than 5,000 people who had come out voluntarily, in a population of 36 598. The colony had the attractions unavailable in the USA, free land and convict labour. Settlers were given land for agriculture and pasture usage. This meant freehold land, and it only applied to men who had immigrated as private citizens, to military officers who had decided to stay and to pardoned convicts who had been granted land.

In 1831, the British Government, against the opposition of many in the colony decided to stop giving away land grants to settlers and chose instead to 'sell' the land and use some of the proceeds to sponsor migrants to the colony. The initial sales price was 5 shillings an acre. It was a way of inducing poor families to leave the country, but as well of relieving the labour shortage. Between 1831 and 1840 about 50,000 prisoners were transported and about 65,000 free men and women chose to emigrate

The battle of the sexes was more equal amongst emigrants than among convicts: but even South Australia, which was wholly an emigrant's colony, had only 8 females for every 10 males by 1850, and in Australia as a whole there was fewer than 7 in every ten. The resulting challenge was only partially met by Caroline Chisholm who met every convict and emigrant ship to stress the dangers to young unmarried women. Her main accomplishment was to convince the Colonial Office, in 1846, to offer free passage to all families of convicts resident in the colony. Her detractors suggested that the result of her efforts towards convict families and emigrating poor families would be to create an imbalance of Catholics in the colony, who were already twice the proportion of the Australian population as they were in England.

CHAPTER 17

ELEMENTS OF POPULATION INCREASE

a. Sex distribution

Australia has, since the first settlement of the continent in 1788, differed materially from the older countries of the world. Older countries, that are countries having an established civilised population, have, in general, grown by natural increase and their composition usually reflects that fact with the numbers of males and females being approximately equal, with a tendency for females to slightly exceed males. This slight excess arises from a number of causes

- Higher rate of mortality amongst males
- Greater propensity of males to travel
- The effects of war
- Employment of males in the armed forces
- Preponderance of males amongst emigrants

MASCULINITY OF THE NSW POPULATION 1800 to 1855

1800	44.91
1805	40.00
1810	31.16
1815	30.76

1820	41.81
1825	53.00
1830	52.06
1835	45.71
1840	34.25
1845	21.05
1850	16.13
1855	11.14

This compares with other countries in various years, which would create a guide and average for base purposes

Canada	1911	6.07
India	1911	2.24
New Zealand	1919	1.15
Australia	1919	1.00
Poland	1914	0.41
Hungary	1912	-0.94
Ireland	1915	-1.36
England	1917	-16.43

Age Distribution

During the first 80 years of settlement, the age distribution of the colonial population has varied considerably. Prior to 1856, the distribution averaged as follows:

Males >15	31.4
Males 15-65	67.4
Males <65	1.17
Total	100%
Females >15	43.0
Females 15-65	56.2
Females <65	0.77
Total	100%
Persons>15	36.28
Persons 15-65	62.72
Persons <65	1.0
Total	100%

Sources of Race & Nationality

The primary distribution is between the aboriginal natives and the immigrants, who since 1788 have made the colony their home. Under immigrants would come not only the direct immigrants but also their descendants. For the first 60 years after settlement, the Aboriginal population was in decline (refer also to Chapter 3 of this study – The Aboriginal Economy of 1788). It is of interest to note that in the first census of the aboriginal population in 1911, the Commonwealth statistician made the following reference.[8] " At the census of 1911 the number of full-blood aboriginals who were employed by whites or who lived on the fringe of white settlement was stated to be only 19,939. In Queensland, Western Australia and the Northern Territory, there are considerable numbers of natives still in the 'savage' state, numerical information concerning whom is of a most unreliable nature and can be regarded as little more than the result of guessing".

"The academic studies by Dr. Roth, formerly Chief Protector of Aborigines in Queensland puts the number of full-blood aborigines in the 6 colonies at 80,000 in 1919"[9] As a matter of Commonwealth census policy no count was attempted of 'half-castes' as 'no authoritative definition has yet been given.

The predominant race of immigrants and their descendants is British. However, by 1900, the local born population had reached 83%. The figure in 1856 was calculated to be in the 52.5% vicinity. The other main birthplaces included Germany, China, Scandinavia, Polynesia, British India and Japan

Natural Increase

The two factors, which contribute to the growth of a population, are the 'natural increase' by excess of births over deaths and the 'net migration', being the excess of arrivals over departures. In a new country such as the colony of NSW between 1788 and 1856, the 'net migration' occupies an

---

8   *Commonwealth Year Book 1901-1919* (1920) p.88
9   CYB *ibid* p.89

important position as a source of increase of population especially as the early imbalance of sexes and the shortage of females in the colony, allowed for only a relatively small natural increase.

Net Immigration

The quinquennial period in which the greatest net migration to the Colonies occurred is outside our study period but was that of 1881-85 with a total of 224,040, whilst the period 1901-05 departures exceeded arrivals by 16,793

Total Increase

The total increase of the population is found by the combination of the natural increase with the net immigration

Rate of Increase

The rate of increase in the early colony rose quickly but then steadied as migration took on a smaller 'net ' effect. After 1830 the average rate was only 4% but then declined steadily until by 1901, the rate was only 1.38. NSW always enjoyed the highest rate of increase and averaged over 5% before 1850 declining to 4.83 from 1860. The 1850s were a period of low natural increase and high net migration with the gold fields being the main catalyst.

Density of Population

From one aspect the total population may be less significant than in respect of the absolute amount than in respect of the density of its distribution. The total land area of the country is 2,974,581 square miles, and at the time of the Constitution of 1901, the country only had a population of 5,347,018 persons, with a density of 1.80. Even today that density is only a little less than 7. The comparative densities are, for the earliest period of statistics maintained (1919 – Statesman's Yearbook), Europe at 122.98, Asia 54.45. Americas 16.87 and Australasia 2.38

Urban Population

One of the key features of the distribution of population in Australia is the tendency to accumulate in the capital cities. In every colony the capital city had a greater population than any other town in the colony. It was the hub and as such it carried certain features. The main population area was a port for international shipping. There were adequate fresh water sources servicing the population. In the early days of the colony of NSW the 'urban' population would have been close top 100%, but as Macquarie developed and serviced his regional towns, the urban percentage declined until by 1900, Sydney had only 41.38 % of the colonial population

Aboriginal population

The Commonwealth Year Book of 1901 reminds us that "The Commonwealth Constitution Act makes provision for aboriginal natives top"be excluded for all purposes for which statistics of population are made use but the opinion has been given by the Commonwealth Attorney-General that 'in reckoning the population of the Commonwealth, half-castes Are not aboriginal natives within the meaning of Section 127 of the Constitution', and should therefore be included in any census count."[10] Thids is one reason that the ABS (Australian Bureau of Statistics had so much doubt over the number of aborigines in the country – they had not been counted and would not be counted at any time until 1966. The ABS records guesses ranging from 150,000 to as low as 61,705 in 1925[11]

Enumeration

In colonial NSW, the system of 'musters' was the way chosen to count the free settlers. The governor would 'gazette' or announce the date and place of the next muster, and usually commissariat officers would officiate at the count. The basis of the count was often widened to include a record of the number and type of livestock, of acres cultivated and would be

---

[10]   Commonwealth Year Book #3– W. Ramsey-Smith ' *Special Characteristics of Commonwealth Population*' P.89

[11]   4The count in each state is estimated at 30th April 1915 by Ramsey Smith as NSW-6,580;Victoria 283; Qld 15,000; SA 4,842; WA 32,000; NT 3,000 for a total of 61,705

used to verify the rations receivable by that family 'off the store'. In 1828 the muster system was replaced by the first 'census' where a more detailed record was made of the population demographics including ages, sex and birthplace of each inhabitant and whether 'free' or 'convict'.

CHAPTER 18

MUSTERS

The Excitement of the Muster

J.C. Caldwell writes in the introduction to the Chapter on 'Population'[12] "For the first 40 years of the Australian colonies, our knowledge of population numbers is derived from the musters. Their major deficiencies are that of the omission of the native peoples. Even in 1800 the musters perhaps account for only 1 or 2 percent of the actual population".

Official musters were held in 1799,1805,1810,1817,1820 and1821. The first full-scale census was held in November 1828.

Most announcements of intentions to account for all persons were generally signed by the Governor of the day and the task assigned to the Commissary officials. Governor John Hunter issued the following General Order on the 23rd September 1795[13].

A general muster will be held on Saturday next, the 26th instant at Sydney; on Thursday, the 1st October, at Parramatta and Toongabbie; and on Saturday, the 3rd October, at the settlement at the Hawkesbury – at which places the Commissary will attend for the purpose of obtaining a correct amount of the numbers and distribution of all persons (the military excepted) in the different

---

12   Australians: Historical Statistics
13   HRNSW – Governors Despatches 1795

aforementioned settlements, whether victualled or not (victualled) from the public stores.

Notice is hereby given to all persons concerned to attend, so that every man be accounted for; and such as neglect complying with this order will be sought after and be either confined in the cells, put to hard labour, or corporally punished.

The sick may be accounted for by the Principal Surgeon, and officers' servants by their masters

CHAPTER 19

REVISIONISM

Overview

There is a traditional viewpoint on Australian Colonial Economic History as espoused by Shann, Fitzpatrick & Fletcher and repeated by Butlin (N.G Butlin) to the effect that Australia was an area of very ancient settlement, within which the Aboriginal economy was a stable ordered system of decision-making that satisfied the needs of its people. British occupation (without any apparent deliberate intent) soon destroyed the Aboriginal economy and society with the accompanying decimation of its population[14]

We may not need to yet re-write our economic history but it does help to understand the economic setting that gave rise to the rapidly expanding British society in the new settlement of Botany Bay, with its rapidly declining native population and a developing economy that met the needs of Britain as being a valuable source of raw materials for its industry, as an outlet for its trading and the resulting transfer of resources (a takeover) by the new economic managers (the British autocratic governors). These new managers, in fact, faced much higher costs than expected, in achieving 'success'. Their 'success' was to be measured by being able to commandeer these natural resources and transfer them from an ancient society to the new society. This takeover was never the apparent original intent, but rather the official intention was to seek a type of merger rather than a

---

[14] Butlin uses some of these expressions in '*Economics and the Dreamtime*' p.184

takeover. However, the gulf between the two societies was too large to be bridged and British settlement succeeded while the ancient society was destroyed.

Butlin finds a similarity between the 'economic' invasion of Britain by the Romans and the 'takeover' of economic interests in the Great South Land.[15] It is quite a stretch of the imagination but there are certain similarities that given the 1600-year time-span can be identified. Similar strategies learnt from history are probably what Butlin is offering.

"Rome had the essential springboard from Italy to develop a vast network of imperial control[16] extending over much of Europe and the Mediterranean. For 500 years these traditions were injected into England. On one hand Rome delivered a military market, a money economy, organised administration, a villa system of agriculture married to the Celtic farming of Britain, improved agricultural productivity, urban centres, transport systems and extended trade contacts with Europe. On the other hand, it was military control and reflected the hierarchical organisation and exploitation of unfree labour on which the ancient world depended. Butlin acknowledges that these thoughts are derived from Salway in *Roman Britain*.

One can see the similarities between the Roman takeover of early Britain, and the British takeover of New Holland. G. Arnold Wood in his prehistory of Australia makes a similar point but concludes, "It is scarcely conceivable that a transfer of influences corresponding to those of Rome on Britain could have been spread by Asians to Australia".[17]

For all the attribution that we can validly extend to the British for the takeover of Aboriginal economy, many questions remain unanswered. For instance,

- What were the economics of the 'takeover'?
- What were the legalities of the 'takeover'?

---

[15] Butlin *Economics and the Dreamtime* p.187
[16] Butlin uses the word 'imperial' often and probably means 'British' rather than royal or monarchist
[17] G.A. Wood *The Discovery of Australia*

- Who were the major players?
- Was disease the main or only component of the Aboriginal depopulation?
- What were the real intentions of Britain in the 'takeover'?

One must ask if the success of establishing the colonial settlement by the use of the seven conditions referred to below were a result of a tightly planned economy or a mixture of planned or under-regulated, penal or free. It would seem that many of the elements of success had to have been part of an integrated planning process. For instance, the instruction for Bills to be drawn on the Treasury in London was a better alternative for a penal settlement not having an exchequer and any means of exchange, by way of coinage; the competition with and elimination of Aborigines may not have been British government policy but it was a consensual (by British Colonial Office policy) internal struggle for land and hunting rights; whilst the early privatisation of the settlement came about by the failure of government to produce sufficient food locally. The resulting issuance of land grants to the military officers and emancipists gave this new land-owning class the opportunity to either make money or feed themselves and their families adequately; the privatisation of the treasury by King and Macquarie was both a convenience and a display of not really wanting to get involved or know the details of local expenditures. It was both cheaper and less onerous to the governor not having to account for every penny of this discretionary and illegal revenue to the British Government; British financial support and legal and administrative oversight was necessary because it was a penal settlement rather than a 'slave' market, where convicts were sold to settlers and taken off the hands and the 'books' of the British government – this again was a deliberate policy decision by the British authorities; the supply of human capital with skills appropriate to a relatively advanced society may or may not have been deliberate—it is still a matter of conjecture as to whether convicts were selectively chosen in Britain (at the court or even the prison level) for transportation as Phillip and his successors had requested – but, at least we know from the records that Macquarie attended each arriving ship to select the skilled mechanics that he most needed for government service; the lack of economies of scale was a matter of transition from commissariat policy to import replace and make what could be made locally (and on a timely basis) and then turn it over to private enterprise for convenience. Butlin properly identifies 7 early achievements as if they were 'manor from heaven', but most appear to be deliberated policy ideas whose time had come.

A Revisionist Theory of the Colonial Origins

It is probably not surprising that an Economic Historian, more so than an Historian, would ask for a more rational explanation of the reasons for the formation of the Colony of New South Wales in 1788. Although not traditionally a matter of Australian economic history, this study has grown into one where the regular understanding is clarified and revised by an interpretation and understanding of events that cross over the boundary from history into historical economics. It would seem that the authorities in the British Treasury would have raised consideration, if not in the Home Office, as to what impact another British Colony would have on the Treasury funds. The economic argument would have been more than the mere 'opportunity' cost of not having a penal colony as a repository. The first question becomes, is it wise or proper to question the traditional understanding and theories of history? If schoolchildren have been taught for at least 50 years (I can verify from 1950) that Australia was selected as a penal colony and for the transportation of prisoners from British prisons, then why do we raise doubts in 2001?

A.G.L. Shaw introduces '*Great Britain and the Colonies 1815-1865*' with this rather exculpatory comment

"The fate of any historical interpretation about a problem or a period is to become itself re-interpreted. Not infrequently when a reigning hypothesis gets unseated, clarity and simplicity gives place to complexity, conflicting evidence, a melange of contributory causes. And, as the inexact science which history will undoubtedly remain, introducing 'multi-variables' is to lose at once that sense of certainty and intellectual satisfaction. Many major themes in the explanation of 19th century British history are currently in need of re-examination."

In this study we are revisiting the traditionalist theory that the only reason for the colony of New South Wales was as a penal settlement. It was carefully planned and discussed at all levels based on the simple submission by Sir Joseph Banks in evidence before the House of Commons Select Committee on Penitentiaries in 1774.

The traditionalist argument is, in its most simplistic structure:

Upon Cook's news that he had taken possession of a great country (New South Wales), England did not immediately decide to colonise it. She already had a huge empire, and wanted no more for the present, for colonies were expensive to govern, and they oftentimes caused wars. With the American Colonies in mind, it seemed that colonies brought no profit while they were struggling and expensive, and that when they became prosperous they rebelled.

Even though Cook and Bank's journals were doctored by Hawkesworth before publishing to make NSW sound better than it was, the choice of a new colony would have been (in the opinion of F. Hawke) New Zealand or the Friendly Islands before Botany Bay was selected.

However the need was different now with the revolt by the Americas and the accumulation of over 1,000 prisoners each year in Britain. They were being kept in prison and in hulks tethered together in mid-stream, and soon became over-full. It was Banks that suggested Botany Bay as a new penal colony, which is surprising when we remember what Banks said about NSW. He now seemed to think it was just the right place. It was far away and no danger of prisoners escaping. Thus the colony was simply to be used as a jail for prisoners and a repository for the poor of England! Russel Ward in *Australia* puts it simply "In 1788 the Australian nation was founded by and for Great Britain's surplus of convicted criminals, a fact which used to give many respectable Australians pain and which threatened a few with schizophrenia."

But this is over-simplistic, for Ward implies that Britain was blinded to all other considerations other than the placement of prisoners somewhere else than in Britain. As any economic Historian would know, if nothing else the economic considerations of adding another colony to the British Empire was just extra expense. But there was something else! Foreign policy issues, trade and industry issues, ridding the homeland of the poor and unemployed, following the Industrial revolution were all considered and the penal colony idea was the icing on the cake, and not the sole determinant.

Why does the traditional view need reviewing?

The record needs setting straight for future generations and at least for the next 50 years!

The answer to the question 'what are the reasons for the settlement' once seemed obvious. In the 1780s England was facing an urgent problem – jails were overflowing, crime was increasing; the solution was transportation – but to where? Botany Bay was selected!

This is the traditional copybook answer repeated for the past half-century!

In 1888, a British historian, Gonner, suggested a larger story – Botany Bay was settled for economic reasons, to compensate Britain for the loss of her American Colonies. This theory found no support in Australia until K.M. Dallas (a Tasmanian historian) discussed it in 1952. Dallas asked – Why would a nation of merchants go so far and pay so much money, if it were merely to dump convicts? It was Dallas that even set Geoffrey Blainey to rethinking the rational explanation.

Lord Sydney, as Secretary of State, had stated the problem and the government's position in 1780: The traditionalists bought this explanation without much question or even concern.

"The several gaols and places for the confinement of felons in this Kingdom, being in so crowded a state that the greatest danger is to be apprehended not only from their escape, but from infectious distempers which may hourly be expected to break out among them".

However these were the reasons for the policy of 'transportation' and not for settling the colony!

Some Background to Events leading to the Government 1786 decision

In the 18th Century, England was in the throes of domestic upheaval. She was going through the Industrial Revolution. The country was being transformed from a rural-based economy to an industrial one. Farms were closing. Factories were opening. People were relocating from the country to the city. The results were overcrowding, primitive sewerage, disease and an increase in crime, mostly due to higher levels of poverty. On top of that there was no police force, only a collection of corrupt wardens. The English penal code was to be made even more severe than it already was! Gaol was to be no more of a rehabilitation or preventative strike then, than it is now. The gaols were overflowing and short-term (7 years or less) convicted persons were placed on 'hulks' tied together in mid-stream of the Thames

Men were escaping from the hulks in growing numbers and there was a real fear that the situation would get out of hand. Crime, cost and prisoners were increasing – finance, accommodation and patience with the problem were not.

Building more prisons (made permissible by the Penitentiary Houses Act of 1779) was one solution, where convicts could be employed in hard labour. The scheme foundered because of wrangles over location and cost. By 1784, the authorities moved again to transportation and a 1784 Act to resume transportation was passed but without a specified location. Parliamentary Committees investigated Africa, but the unhealthiness of the climate, the infertile soil and a fear of hostile natives combined to rule out the region. A disastrous experiment at Cape Coast Castle resulted in a 45% death rate amongst convicts in a single year.

Even in 1785 and 1786, sites in Canada and the West Indies were under consideration, but by 1779 Joseph Banks had proposed Botany Bay just before Matra wrote his report to the Admiralty in 1883. Matra emphasised the great commercial advantages of Botany Bay, based on his having been a midshipman under Cook during his 7-day stay on the East Coast of new Holland. The colony could serve as a base for trade with China (tea), with

Nootka Sound (furs) and the Moluccas (spices) and for the cultivation of flax.

Sir John Young, another adviser to the Peel government, submitted a plan in 1785 for a settlement suitable for convicts and commercial gain. The Beauchamp Committee of the House of Commons rejected both schemes. The cost of transportation was the main objection. The evidence suggested a passage cost of about 30 pound, which was 6 times the cost of passage to America. Although Botany Bay was rejected in 1785 as too expensive, just one year later, on 18th August1786, it was chosen as the site. Botany Bay was selected as the last resort, almost in desperate circumstances. Circumstances pressuring the decision included the debts of the Prince of Wales, negotiations for a treaty with France, and growing agitation against the 'slave trade'. The convict problem appeared small, in comparison, but deserved and got a rapid solution. The government's aim was mercantilist – colonies or settlements were only useful if they benefited the mother country. England was a trading nation with imperial ambitions. Botany Bay was selected for the general advantages it offered as well as being a place suitable for transportation.

These general advantages included:

- Botany Bay was useful as a naval base and a refitting port in the South Seas.
- England's interest in the Pacific had increased, especially after the loss of the American colonies.
- Rivalry with the French in the East became a foundation for a base.
- The colony of NSW had important commercial attractions; flax and timber, essential for naval supplies could be grown there. Convicts were not dumped at Botany Bay; they were sent as the first settlers for a naval base and refitting port.
- That is why the early emphasis on rehabilitation. From that base, the vital trade routes could be tapped—tea from China, fur from North America, the whaling industry, and South American loot carried on Spanish ships.

After 1785, when the French, and Dutch alliance was renewed, the French revived their-own East India Company into the Pacific. In 1786 the British annexed Penang and Botany Bay was settled as a useful base for trade. The official documents do give us the profit motive, which the English needed to undertake the venture. These official documents included

- Cook's report of Norfolk Island having superior quality of the 'spruce pines and flax'; and the 'greatest consequence to us as a naval power'—Matra.
- Phillip was instructed to cultivate flax, which Phillip did within one month of arriving at Botany Bay. The flax and pine timber were as important in 1788 as steel and oil are today.
- However, the traditionalists still argue that Botany Bay was settled *at a certain point in time* because the government needed to solve its convict problem. The revisionists argue – why that place and not another? The pressure groups won the day in 1786 – the politicians saw the disgraceful and frightening state of the hulks; the 'opposition' in parliament needled the government for its failure to find a solution; powerful economic groups (of merchants) were well represented in the discussions for protecting trade against competition from national rivals.

The government made a sudden, but not hasty, decision in the face of all this pressure.

Revising the Interpretation

A revisionist theory draws a very different analysis whereby there were numerous basic determinants (other than the penal colony) of the formation of the colony and that it became only a means to an end to send convicts from the overflowing British prisons to the early colony.

For a start, the fact was that no British government in the past had been directly responsible for initiating the permanent settlement of any territory. The American colonial enterprises, dating back to the early seventeenth century, had been the work of individuals seeking a better life, or of companies acting with the general support of the government or under Royal charter, but none had been directly fostered by the government.

With no private or commercial interests likely to set up a pioneering enterprise in the newly chartered territories, emigration from the British Isles to various American colonies went on free from any thought of the more distant places as alternatives. 'Not only remoteness but the very nature of the lands observed by members of Cook's expedition inhibited serious interest', writes Younger in *Australia and the Australians* 'whilst New Zealand's ferocious tribesmen inspired fear, and Sir Joseph Banks wrote of New South Wales that "a soil so barren and at the same time entirely void of the helps derived from cultivation could not be supposed to yield much towards the support of man" '.

The British government supported privatisation of colonisation, but the settlement of such remote and unproductive places did not appeal to any private group, and the British government saw no reason for action. A readiness to take possession (as Cook had done in the name of King George III) did not imply a readiness to follow such action with occupation; nor did the mere declaration of possession in itself confer any substantial right or obligation on the British government.

These basic determinants of whether or not to settle the area of *New Holland* included:

- Foreign Policy considerations
- Military (in particular, naval) considerations
- Scientific & technical considerations
- The tyranny of the distance
- Economic (in particular, trade) considerations

Only after quantifying the strategic criteria within these five categories did the rationale of the colony being developed at government expense but being made to pay its own way, as rapidly as possible, did the formation of a penal settlement come about as a means to underpin the economics of the future colony.

Foreign Policy Considerations

Commodore John Byron sailed from Plymouth in 1764 with orders, that in order to avoid arousing Spanish jealousies and retaliation were kept secret. After passing through the Straits of Magellan he sailed on the familiar north-westerly course over the Pacific, making few discoveries; he sighted only outlying islands of minor groups, and after visiting Tinian he went on to Batavia and returned home, completing the circumnavigation in the record time of twenty-two months. On his return to England in 1766 his ship, the frigate *Dolphin*, was placed under Captain Samuel Wallis who, with Captain Philip Carteret in the *Swallow*, set off on another circumnavigation. The two ships were separated soon after passing through the Straits of Magellan. Wallis reached Tahiti (Naming it King George Island), the Society Islands, and the Wallis Archipelago, sailing home by way of Batavia. Carteret discovered Pitcairn Island and sailed through St George's Channel, so proving that New Ireland and New Britain were separated.

For much of the eighteenth century there was a distinct possibility that naval warfare (between France and Britain) would be extended into the Pacific. Both the French and English were doing their share of voyaging in these waters, sometimes no more than a few months, or a few leagues, apart. England's victory in the Seven Years war, acknowledged at the Treaty of Paris in 1763, resulted in England's supremacy over the French in India, and the loss of France's North American colonies to England. (France, however, retained some possessions in India and the best of her sugar-islands.) In the long run the English victory also decided the future of the Pacific.

Scientific & technical consideration

During the years of struggle, increasing attention was given to scientific inquiry and geographical speculation, both in England and France. Now that practically all the remainder of the world was charted, the Great South Land – Terra Australis or Terra Incognita – had become a matter of immediate concern. Books about voyages in the Pacific and southern seas, proposing further exploration or the founding of settlements, and speculating about unknown parts, contributed to the growing interest.

It was also an era of scientific exploration, undertaken against a background of great expansion in scientific thought. Significant advance in the theoretical sciences of mathematics and astronomy had been made in the 17th century; now these new principles were being applied to navigation. The invention of the sextant in England in 1730 and the subsequent development of the chronometer, made it possible to take exact celestial measurements, and so to chart a ship's position with accuracy. These inventions, with modifications in ship-design resulting in greatly strengthened vessels, opened the way for new geographical discoveries.

Economic & trade considerations

With the founding in 1711 of the South Sea Company, one of London's joint-stock ventures to seize public imagination, the distant Pacific became a region for more than literary fantasy. The South Sea Company was to trade with Spanish America and concessions were gained for it for that purpose, but its great appeal to the speculator lay in its hoped-for trade with the rich lands thought to await discovery in the Pacific. Expectations of dazzling wealth were conjured up, although operations never became profitable. The fraudulent booming of the company's shares were followed by a collapse of the so-called South Sea Bubble in 1720, causing disillusionment as well as great scandal. The collapse brought to a sudden and calamitous end, all speculative interest in nebulous plans for trade in the Pacific. Nevertheless, the English period of discovery had begun.

Distance personified

Between 1744 and 1748, a handsome new edition was published in London of the *Complete Collection of Voyages and Travels* (which had originally appeared in 1705 edited by John Harris) urging further discoveries. As well as narratives of navigators, the book contained prefaces and notations by John Campbell, who sought to draw attention to opportunities for new enterprise believed to exist for enterprising Englishmen. Pointing to the value of commerce, Campbell explained the narratives of travel in the South Sea in terms of the new challenge that awaited those with foresight and courage to act:

'It is most evident from Tasman's voyages that New Guinea, Carpentaria (i.e. Cape York Peninsula), New Holland, Van Diemen's Land and the country discovered by Quiros make all one continent, from which New

Zealand seems to be separated by a strait, and perhaps is part of another continent'.

Campbell went on to suggest that there were great prospects for Britain if settlements (or, as he termed them, plantations) were established there. Convinced of the immense value of the southern continent, which he termed Terra Australis, he was opposed to a monopoly being granted to the East India Company to trade there. He made a strong plea that the South Sea Company should have rights there 'as a point of high importance,' and wrote that if Britain wished to make the greatest gain 'it may, indeed be requisite to remove ill judged prohibitions, and to break down illegal exclusions'.

He urged that New Guinea should be settled at once, 'and with competent force, since without doubt the Spaniards would leave no means unattempted to dispossess them.' In the space of a very few years, he believed settlement of New Guinea (and a trade in slaves from there) would prove of great consequence to the South Sea Company. He also recommended the formation of a settlement on the southern coast of Terra Australis. This, he believed, would lead the way to the opening of a new trade route 'which must carry a great quantity of our goods and manufactures.' Such a settlement would also be attended by other advantages. 'There is in all probability,' Campbell wrote, 'another Southern continent which is still to be discovered.'

'Perhaps it was the aura of unreality associated with the southern lands as much as the British preoccupation with European wars, that held back further exploration for so long' writes Marjorie Barnard in *A History of Australia*. Dampier had returned to London in 1701, hinting at prospects in lands still untouched. Yet, apart from the wartime expedition of Captain George Anson in 1739, it was not until 1764 that the British government sent another ship into the Pacific area.

Investigating the New World

These voyages were all undertaken by Britain to advance 'the honour of this nation as a maritime power – and the trade and navigation thereof' (Lord Sydney). The English ships each followed a course through the Straits of

Magellan and then struck northwest, finally reaching the coast of New Guinea. Close behind them were the French, who had the same objectives and who directed their efforts to the same area. Captain Louis Antoine de Bougainville reached the Society Islands and Tahiti a year after Wallis, and continued westward, making some new discoveries in the Samoa group. His next landfall was an archipelago that he decided – correctly – was Quiros's long lost and long-sought Australia del Espiritu Santo. Here, he told himself, was the opportunity to solve the old riddle of the Southern Continent.

'So Bougainville sailed away from the Great Barrier Reef. He still believed he had been close to land, but consoled himself with the reflection that it could easily have been 'a cluster of islands' not the east coast of New Holland. His subsequent course took him through the hazardous waters of the Louisiade Archipelago, through the Solomons and New Britain, and north of New Ireland to the Moluccas and eventually to Europe' (Younger).

An English geographer, Alexander Dalrymple, had written a book, in 1769, in which he explained how easy it would be move into what he imagined to be the great, rich, populous continent of the south – a land 'sufficient to maintain the power, dominion, and sovereignty of Britain by employing all its manufacturers and ships.' Dalrymple, who had spent many years in the employ of the East India Company, had returned to London in 1765 and set about a study of material available on the South Seas. He secured a copy of a memorial printed in 1640 – discovered by the English expedition that captured Manila in 1762 – and from this long-hidden document he deduced the existence of a strait to the south of New Guinea. In a little book, *Discoveries in the South Pacific to 1764*, which was written in 1767 but not published until 1769, Dalrymple included a map in which the strait was marked, as well as the routes of Tasman and Torres. In this booklet he recapitulated all the discoveries that had been made in the South Pacific, including Juan Fernandez Islands off the coast of the Chile, the discoveries of Quiros and Tasman, and those of Le Naire to the north of New Guinea. He drew the conclusion that all these widely separated fragments were probably parts of the same great continent – a continent possibly extending over a hundred degrees of longitude in latitude 40°S, so that it was larger than the whole of Asia from Turkey to the extremity of China!

Cook had no idea of the importance of his discovery of and claim over the East coast of New South Wales. He and his superiors were much more interested in the Great South Land, whose whereabouts were such a puzzle. His second and third voyages were spent in searching between NZ and South America, and between Alaska and northeastern Asia, but did nothing more in 'our' part of the world. Haskell records that 'England then joined the loyalists in fighting 'our' cousins, the Americans; in the end 'we' were defeated but it set men thinking of the new land in the southern seas. James Matra, a midshipman on the *Endeavour,* drew up a scheme by which loyalists should be set down in NSW to found a colony there, with labourers brought from China and the South Sea Islands to do all the hard work for them. The great difficulty was that the French were also interested in exploring the South Seas, and if Matra's suggestion had been formed as Matra proposed, a strong French fleet would come down upon it and seize the country. Matra asked the Government for help on the grounds that if the scheme were carried out under the direct orders of the Government, there would be no fear of a French attack'. (*Australia and the Australians* – Haskell)

The recent war in the Americas served another argument in favour of Matra's suggestion:

- England had been fighting Spain as well as France; so, if England had to fight them again, NSW would be an admirable centre from which to attack the Dutch and Spanish Islands in the Malay Archipelago. But the argument that prevailed in the end was much more persuasive than that. It was that NSW would be a most suitable place to which to send prisoners.

The Goals of the Transportation Program

The aims of the British authorities in transporting criminals can be deduced from instructions to their representatives, the governors, from Westminster debates and from official regulations. The colonial office made one such statement, in 1789:

"Transportation seeks three ends – the prevention of crime in Britain, the moral reformation of the convicts themselves and the welfare of the colonies to which they are removed". To these should be added a fourth aim: that Britain would simply be rid of an unwanted element in the society. But would it be the deterrent in Britain and become an integral part of the penal system of the time. The assumption behind the penal system was that the individual broke the law of his own free will. He must then pay for his crime and be an example for others. Transportation as a major punishment was supposed to serve this end. As an aim, rehabilitation was observed to be a failure. In the colonial experience, the prisoners would not accept that they should contribute to the 'welfare of the colony'. This concept had been incorporated into the laws of Britain. If prisoners were to be punished then it should be undertaken in the most useful way possible. The colony should be sufficiently remote to prevent fleeing. No prisoner was to return to England, even as an emancipist. The penal colony was to become self-sufficient and self-supporting as soon as possible. This meant that the system was to operate with as little expense to the mother country as possible. England's welfare was not to be forgotten.

There were many contradictions in the transportation system. Punishment by transportation was different to each individual involved. For some, the release from the hulks was a blessing. For others, separation from family was a giant burden. The punishment was meant to be severe, consistent and considered by the public to be so. This was supposedly the deterrent. Communication meant that the details of colonial life had to be shared with the public over 12,000 miles away. With social policy being so paramount, at least in theory, it is enigmatic that between 1788 and 1850, all but four governors were drawn from the navy and the military ranks, to which control and discipline, not reformation, were the keynotes to the system

The element of chance determined the treatment, response and attitude of the prisoners. Convicts were subject to meeting officials, directly under the governor – the surgeon, the ship's captain, the military officers, overseers and the free settlers to whom the prisoner would be assigned. Many of these officials would be hard and tireless in their intentions to extract the last pound of flesh from the 'free labour'. A convict's actions alone did not determine his, or her, treatment by the system. Typical was the treatment of the women – they were 'damned whores, beyond redemption, worthy only of punishment'. They did however have another use. They were to ensure the normalcy of the penal settlement by being sexual partners for the men of the colony and mothers of their children.

There was a wide diversity of opinion in Britain and the colony on what benefits accrued to the colony as a result of transportation, which suggests that we cannot arrive at a definitive answer.

The simplistic answer that transportation provided the colony with a population really begs the question.

Would there have even been a colony had it not been needed for a transportation program?

That there was need for a transportation program therefore ensured that the capital requirements for creating a secure penal colony were provided. This funding assisted with infrastructure, buildings for housing, barracks, stores, offices, roads, wharves, and bridges all in the name of gainful employment of these transportees. So, from the colonial viewpoint, the supply of capital led to employment, local industries, free enterprise, farming opportunities, trade, local revenue, a growth population, a sinecure for the military officers. Self-sufficiency at the lowest possible cost was always the goal. Arthur Phillip questioned the value of convicts as workers. He claimed, as did his successors, that 'they were used to lives of indolence and thievery, and were poor workers'

Summary

As Marjorie Barnard points out:

"It is difficult to conceive of a plan that is based on a colony of social misfits on a coast that all reports had described as barren, waterless and dangerous. James Matra put a more credible plan forward in 1783. He had at least seen the east coast of the continent and Joseph Banks supported his scheme. Matra wrote

The climate and soil are so happily adapted to produce evert various and valuable production of Europe that with good management and a few settlers, in twenty or thirty years they might cause a revolution in the whole system of European commerce and secure to England a monopoly of some part of it, and a very large share in the whole."

These schemes, however credible the source would have fallen on stony ground but for an uncomfortable by-product of the American War of Independence. In the days of the Old Dominion, England had got rid of her felons very easily and inexpensively by shipping them off to the plantations of Virginia. At first the government paid contractors 5 pound a head to carry them across the Atlantic. Later it became a better bargain. The contractors made their profit at the American end. The services of a skilled man for the term of his punishment were sold for between 15 to 20 pound. Women brought from 8 to 10 pound each. This showed a good profit although deaths were usually heavy. The convicts were slaves in all but name. Once handed over the government took no more notice of them.

Our revisionist theory is much more complex than the simplistic traditional opinion.

It would seem that foreign policy, trade and economic policy, scientific and technical opportunities, and supplying the military (mainly the naval stores) were the fundamental considerations in determining to occupy the colony, following which the answer to the question – how are we going to pay for any settlement, especially since this excursion will be government sponsored – was answered with the suggestion that the prisons are overflowing in Britain; it is costing the government upwards of 32 pound per convict per year; why don't we transport the overflow of convicts and the poor and unemployed people to the new colony as fodder for its economic development and divert some, if not all of the funds used to support them in Britain to the support of these people in a new colony; it will only be the original shipment that will be degenerates; their successors will be free peoples able to look after themselves both financially and economically, and Britain will not only have rid itself of these drains on the economy of Britain but have created the basis for future trade with the mother country and its colonies.

CHAPTER 20

THE ECONOMICS OF TRANSPORTATION IN THE COLONY

Matra's Figures of the Cost of Establishing the Colony

From the HRNSW we find that "Mr. Matra's proposal was placed before the Coalition Government of Fox and Lord North but they left office before full consideration. The Pitt Ministry considered the Matra suggestions to send out the convict population from England to New South Wales. The proposal had the support of Admiral Sir George Young, and eventually appeared in a paper circulated in January 1785 entitled 'Heads of a Plan for effectually disposing of convicts by the establishing of a Colony in New South Wales'. This plan (set out in full in Appendix B) includes a proposal for a penal settlement, the use of ships and marines, the immediate and forward provisioning requirements, including livestock and seed, and sundry matters such as guards for the ships and transports, surgeons, trade in flax and timber and tropical products. The estimate of expenditure was given as being 1,497.10.0 per annum for staff, and a clothing allowance of 2/19/6 for each convict per annum. The cost of supplies, including tools, was estimated to be in excess of 1,300 pounds, to which Matra would have added the transportation and food cost per head of ' a sum not to exceed 3,000 pound'. Matra observed in his proposal that "most of the tools, saws, axes etc for the use of the party left may be drawn from the ordnance and other public stores, where at present they are useless; and the vessels also, being part of the peace establishment can, nor ought to be, fairly reckoned in the expenditure. The Matra Proposal is attached at Appendix A.

CHAPTER 21

SUMMARY AND CONCLUSION

Does logical thinking apply in these circumstances? If we were planning on settling a newly discovered land, having just lost access to another, would there be only one consideration? I think not! The best report to the authorities would be one that set down the present circumstances in 'our' region, and in 'our' sphere of influence, and then list all the benefits that would accrue to 'our' country, upon making the move to settle or colonise on that new land. It would be a stepping-stone, and not an end in itself.

There would be expenditures associated with the establishment, and thus a cost-benefit analysis would be set down. Even if the costs were to be diverted from another government outlet for expenditure, there would be benefits and the support for that first step would be stronger if the 'opportunity' cost in favour of the new colony was stronger and more favourable than the cost under the former expenditure.

And so it was with Cook's discovery, except the British neglected for 'cost' reasons, the most fundamental of steps – that of reconnoitring the colony before despatching the First fleet. Matra, Phillip and others had strongly suggested a 'forward party' to select the best sight, to commence preparing the sight, commence a basic building program and ensure fresh water and appropriate crops were available when the main party arrived. The authorities refused to go along with this commonsense approach and the consequences were enormous for Phillip. Cook and Banks believed, in an untested theory, that pockets of soil near the coast could support small colonies of Europeans – so long as the colonists imported their seeds, plants and livestock. Blainey concludes that Cook and Banks arrived at a good time (both month and year – 1st May, 1770) for witnessing 'vast quantities of grass and vegetation'. But he suggests that they could 'not possibly assess the soil and climate during such a brief (7 day) visit. Here was a new land, lying on the opposite side of the equator and growing exotic plants; a land occupied by people whose way of life offered few clues about the land itself'.

It was on the misconception of 'rich and fertile soils' that Britain was to locate their first settlement on the new land. The choice would have been very different if the Endeavour had landed during a hot dry spell.

This analysis we mentioned being completed for the authorities listing the costs and the benefits as well As the strategic value of the land, would also have included a statement on the integral value of the land itself. However, the conclusion would and must have been that thew country, by the standards of the age, was valueless.

We know now that the stony plains and hillsides conceal minerals and oils of immense value, and that pipelines and railways can move huge resources quickly and efficiently from remote and isolated areas to the nearest port. But the 17th and 18th century decision-makers did not have that knowledge. They knew the limitations of the world and sensibly ignored the new land. There seemed to be no riches near the coastline, and it did not appear to offer (as did most other colonies) energetic, docile labourers. There were no apparent new timbers, spices, vegetables or fibres. What the British desperately hoped for was access to tall pines, to flax and hemp or at least soil which could grow such crops, but it was the prospect only that caused excitement. And that excitement turned out to be badly misplaced. The new land appeared to explorers before Cook, not to even provide a port of call for refitting, restocking and refreshment.

Was this land really worth claiming, let alone settling? Blainey acknowledges in his source notes to 'A Land Half Won' a different perspective from the one he submitted ten years earlier in The Tyranny of Distance. By 1980 he was able to write "my view now is that Botany Bay was settled for four distinct reasons: the search for new naval supplies, the need for a half-way house on new trade routes, the convict problem, and not least the over optimistic assumptions held about the climate and soils of Botany Bay". Blainey goes on to admit that 'further re-reading of the Cook and Banks Journals has convinced me that their mistaken deductions about the climate and soil of Botany Bay were vital prerequisites for the English settlement in Australia.

So to our conclusions about foreign policy, defence, trade and law and order considerations we should add misstatement about and misunderstanding of the new land as a significant factor in determining the final outcome.

Although the House of Commons passed the first Transportation legislation in 1717 (4 Geo I, c.11), it remained high on the agenda in Britain as both a social policy as well as an economic policy through the rest of the 18th century. It surely was a neat policy to implement and administer. Convicted felons, who had done little to deserve a 7-year transportation sentence, were handed over to contractors, who without charge to the government would ship these offenders to North America and sell them to the plantation owners in the Carolinas, Maryland and Virginia. It was a winning answer for everyone involved except the prisoner, who was being sold into virtual, if not actual, slavery. The contractor made money, the government had a monetary obligation as well as a future commitment taken off its hands, and the plantation owner, for a small sum of between ten and twenty-five pound (the British government was adding a bounty of 5 pound until 1772) got a worker for life.

It was when the Americans of more independent mind saw the better opportunity came with the huge number of black slaves from Africa than the white trash and waste from England, that the Loyalists came under challenge and the War of Independence threw out the English from the colony. So Britain now needed a colony for the American Loyalists as well as the growing number of human waste being processed through the courts.

But how could the authorities locate a refuge that was under way and would offer the same benefits as the North American colony had offered. The obvious places were Canada and Africa. So the answer to the question of a transportation destination was simple. However the better answer was to locate a destination that cold assist in solving other challenges.

A naval supply base, a transit base for traders, a base from which to launch interference against the Spanish, Dutch and French, who growing presence in the southern hemisphere was causing strategic concerns; these were questions awaiting an answer. When one combined with these the question of a transportation destination, the answer was a new colony in the Pacific with convicts being the icing on the cake. This is when the convict system became, in essence, a form of compulsory, assisted migration. The colony's main economic activities would be suckled by the convict system.

As a revisionist theory of the colonial origins, it is not new or even original it is commonsense and logical. It made sense to the merchant pressure group in London; it made sense to the Colonial, Home and Foreign Offices within the government, and the general population who were affronted by the hulks and overcrowded prisons, the growing poverty and social disorder. The only group not enamoured with the decision were the contractors who had carted so many prisoners to the North American colonies and had no wish to travel twice the distance and through unchartered waters to an unknown destination.

It took little enough time (12 years) for the naysayers in London to complain that the colony was leaning towards being a waste of money.

The 1798 Report of the House of Commons Committee on Finance included this reference to the colony of New South Wales." The labour of the whole number of persons sent to these colonies, whether as convicts or settlers, *is entirely lost to the Country*, nor can any return, to compensate such a loss, be expected till that very distant day, when the improved state of the colony may, by possibility, begin to repay a part of the advance, by the benefits of its trade". The attitude of the committee was simple; 'the more thriving the settlement the more frequented: The more frequented the less difficulty of return – The more thriving too the less terrible'.

CHAPTER 22

THE REASONS FOR THE COLONY

The purpose of this study is to examine the various theories by historians for the U.K. creating the colony under the British flag.

Some of these writers being examined include:

a. Haskell (The Australians)—1943
b. Mellor et al (Australian History – the Occupation of a continent) 1978
c. Blainey (The Tyranny of Distance) 1966
d. Barnard (A History of Australia) 1962
e. Coghlan (Labour & Industry in Australia) 1902
f. Younger (Australia & the Australians) 1970
g. Jose, A (History of Australasia) 1897
h. Wood, F.L.W. (A Concise History of Australia) 1935
i. Clark, C.M.H. (A History of Australia) 1962
j. Shaw The Economic Development of Australia 1944
k. Shann The Economic History of Australia 1930
l. Butlin, S Foundations of the Australian Monetary System 1953
m. Butlin, N Forming A Colonial Economy 1993
n. Beckett (An Economic History of Colonial Australia) 2000

F.L.W. Wood says

Upon Cook's news that he had taken possession of a great country (new South Wales), England did not immediately decide to colonise it. She already had a huge empire, and wanted no more for the present, for colonies were expensive to govern, and they oftentimes caused wars. With the American Colonies in mind, it seemed that colonies brought no profit while they were struggling and expensive, and that when they became prosperous they rebelled.

Even though Cook and Bank's journals were doctored by Hawkesworth before publishing to make NSW sound better than it was, the choice of a new colony would have been New Zealand or the friendly Islands before Botany Bay was selected.

However the need was different now with the revolt by the Americas and the accumulation of over 1,000 prisoners each year in Britain. They were being kept in prison and in hulks tethered together in mid-stream, and soon became over-full. It was Banks that suggested Botany Bay As a new penal colony, which is surprising when we remember what Banks said about NSW. He seemed to think it was just the right place. It was far away and no danger of prisoners escaping.

Arthur Jose says

Cook had no idea of the importance of his discovery. He and his superiors were much more interested in the Great South Land, whose whereabouts were such a puzzle. His second and third voyages were spent in searching between NZ and South America, and between Alaska and northeastern Asia, but did nothing more in 'our' part of the world. England then joined the Loyalists in fighting our cousins, the Americans; in the end we were defeated but it set men thinking of the new land in the southern seas. James Matra, a midshipman on the *Endeavour*, drew up a scheme by which loyalists should be set down in NSW to found a colony there, with labourers brought from China and the South Sea Islands to do all the hard work for them. The great difficulty was that the French were also interested in exploring the South Seas, and if Matra's suggestion had been formed as Matra proposed, a strong French fleet would come down upon it and seize the country. Matra asked the Government for help on the grounds that if the scheme were carried out under the direct orders of the Government, there would be no fear of a French attack.

The recent war in the Americas served another argument in favour of Matra's suggestion. England had been fighting Spain as well as France; if England had to fight them again, NSW would be an admirable centre from which to attack the Dutch and Spanish Islands in the Malay Archipelago. But the argument that prevailed in the end was much more persuasive than that. It was that NSW would be a most suitable place to which to send prisoners.

Arnold Haskell says

In 1783, through a wilful ignorance of their way of life, we lost the American colonies. In 1788 the settlement of Australia began. There never was the slightest intention of compensating ourselves for the loss of the old colonies. There was scarcely a trace of idealism in the scheme. The very discovery of the east coast of New Holland left the greater thinker of the age (Samuel Johnson) completely indifferent. The only reason that a settlement was agreed upon was that, now that North America was no longer available, some answer had to be found to the question, What to do with our convicts? But there was a greater consideration; the convicts came from England as a result of English social conditions. Through this incredible muddle, misunderstanding and inhumanity, and working in a medium that had been condemned in the Old World as rotten, a band of exceptional men was to carve out a Dominion, men who risked more, gave more and created more than many of the more spectacular creators of our history – Phillip, Flinders, Macarthur, Macquarie, worthies whose deeds should be familiar in every British Schoolroom.

Suzanne Mellon, as editor, says

The answer to the question 'what are the reasons for the settlement' once seemed obvious. In the 1780s England was facing an urgent problem – jails were overflowing, crime was increasing; the solution was transportation – but to where? Botany Bay was selected!

This is the traditional copybook answer repeated for the past half-century!

In 1888, a British historian, Gonner, suggested a larger story – Botany Bay was settled for economic reasons, to compensate Britain for the loss of her American Colonies. This theory found no support in Australia until K.M. Dallas (a Tasmanian historian) in 1952. Dallas asked – Why would a nation of merchants go so far and pay so much money, if it were merely to dump convicts?

Lord Sydney, as Secretary of State, stated the problem in 1780:

The several gaols and places for the confinement of felons in this Kingdom being in so crowded a state that the greatest danger is to be apprehended not only from their escape, but from infectious distempers which may hourly be expected to break out among the.

However these were the reasons for 'transportation' not for settling the colony!

In the 18th Century, England was in the throes of domestic upheaval. She was going through the Industrial Revolution. The country was being transformed from a rural-based economy to an industrial one. Farms were closing. Factories were opening. People were relocating from the country to the city. The results were overcrowding, primitive sewerage, disease and an increase in crime. On top of that there was no police force, only a collection of corrupt wardens. The English penal code was made even more severe!

Men were escaping from the hulks in growing numbers and there was a real fear that the situation would get out of hand. Crime, cost and prisoners were increasing – finance, accommodation and patience were not.

Building more prisons (made permissible by the Penitentiary Houses Act of 1779) was one solution, where convicts could be employed on hard labour. The scheme foundered because of wrangles over location and cost. By 1784, the authorities moved again to transportation and a 1784 Act to resume transportation was passed but without a specified location. Parliamentary Committees investigated Africa, but the unhealthiness of the climate, the infertile soil and a fear of hostile natives combined to rule out the region. A disastrous experiment at Cape Coast Castle resulted in a 45% death rate in a single year.

Even in 1785 and 1786, sites in Canada and the West Indies were under consideration, but in 1779 Joseph Banks had proposed Botany Bay, before Matra wrote his report in 1883. Matra emphasised the great commercial advantages of Botany Bay. It could serve as a base for trade with China (tea), with Nootka Sound (furs) and the Moluccas (spices) and for cultivation of flax.

Sir John Young submitted a plan in 1785 for a settlement suitable for convicts and commercial gain. The Beauchamp Committee of the House of Commons rejected both schemes. The cost of transportation was the main objection. The evidence suggested a passage cost of less than 30 pound, which was 6 times the cost of passage to America. Although Botany Bay was rejected in 1785 as too expensive, just one year later, on 18th August1786, it was chosen as the site. Botany Bay was selected as the last resort, almost in desperate circumstances. Circumstances pressuring the decision included the debts of the Prince of Wales, negotiations for a treaty with France, agitation against the 'slave trade'. The convict problem appeared small and deserved and got a rapid solution. The government's aim was mercantilist – colonies or settlements were only useful if they benefited the mother country. England was a trading nation with imperial ambitions. Botany Bay was selected for the advantages it offered as well as being a place suitable for transportation. Botany Bay was useful as a naval base and a refitting port in the South Seas. England's interest in the Pacific had increased, especially after the loss of the American colonies. Rivalry with the French in the East became a foundation for a base. The colony of NSW had important commercial attractions; flax and timber, essential for naval supplies could be grown there. Convicts were not dumped at Botany Bay; they were sent as the first settlers for a naval base and refitting port. That is why the early emphasis on rehabilitation. From that base, the vital trade routes could be tapped—tea from China, fur from North America, the whaling industry and South American loot carried on Spanish ships.

After 1785, when the French, Dutch alliance was renewed, the French revived their own East India Company into the Pacific. In 1786 the British annexed Penang and Botany Bay was settled as a useful base for trade.

The official documents do give us the profit motive, which the English needed to undertake the venture. These documents included Cook's report of Norfolk Island having superior quality of the 'spruce pines and flax'; and the 'greatest consequence to us as a naval power'—Matra. Phillip was instructed to cultivate flax, which Phillip did within one month of arriving at Botany Bay. The flax and pine timber were as important in 1788 as steel and oil are today.

The traditionalists still argue that Botany Bay was settled *at a certain point in time* because the government needed to solve its convict problem. The revisionists argue – why that place and not another? The pressure groups won the day – the politicians saw the disgraceful and frightening state of the hulks; the 'opposition' in parliament needled the government for its failure to find a solution; powerful economic groups (of merchants) were well represented in the discussions for protecting trade against competition from national rivals. The government made a sudden decision in the face of all this pressure.

Marjorie Barnard says

It is difficult to conceive of a plan that is based on a colony of social misfits on a coast that all reports had described as barren, waterless and dangerous. James Matra put a more credible plan forward in 1783. He had at least seen the east coast of the continent and Joseph Banks supported his scheme. Matra wrote

The climate and soil are so happily adapted to produce evert various and valuable production of Europe that with good management and a few settlers, in twenty or thirty years they might cause a revolution in the whole system of European commerce and secure to England a monopoly of some part of it, and a very large share in the whole.

These schemes, however credible the source would have fallen on stony ground but for an uncomfortable by-product of the American War of Independence. In the days of the Old Dominion, England had got rid of her felons very easily and inexpensively by shipping them off to the plantations of Virginia. At first the government paid contractors 5 pnd a head to carry them across the Atlantic. Later it became a better bargain.

The contractors made their profit at the American end. The services of a skilled man for the term of his punishment were sold for between 15 to 20 pound. Women brought from 8 to 10 pound each. This showed a good profit although deaths were usually heavy. The convicts were slaves in all but name. Once handed over the government took no more notice of them.

William Eden, Lord Auckland, in his scholarly *Discourse on Banishment (1787)* enunciated the legal principles behind transportation and revealed the general societal attitude towards the criminal. The convict was an outlaw, and, having offended society, could expect no mercy. Punishment was a mixture of vengeance with a forlorn hope of deterring other potential criminals. Any idea of reform was only a pious gesture. He (Lord Auckland) was not in favour of transportation. He thought felons could be more useful at home, in the salt works and in the mines, on dangerous enterprises when it would be wasteful to expend a valuable citizen, for experiments involving risk or to exchange them in Tunis and Algiers for the redemption of Christian slaves. He wrote also of banishment but gave no clues as to where, other than the Riviera. It could not have been NSW – he had not been there.

There was actually nowhere left, unpossessed, distant, and reasonably healthy except in the Pacific.

All the schemes for colonization of NSW have a neat, often unreasonably reasonable, profit motif, supported by deductions that smack of medieval dialectic. Joseph Banks offered the thought as to whether England could derive any advantage from settlement in Australia, answered, If the people formed themselves a civil government, they would necessarily increase, and New Holland, being larger than Europe, would furnish an advantageous return.

There were originally three reasons for considering a new colony in the Pacific

i.   For the use of resettling the American Loyalists
ii. The persistent suspicion of the French and the Dutch
iii. The superabundance of convicts

Banks gave reasons for supporting Botany Bay before the 1779 Parliamentary Committee into locating a new penal colony.

a. He had spent 8 days there in 1770
b. There was water and timber, the climate was good
c. It was not the ideal home for Englishmen but for convicts, men and women who had forfeited all privileges, it was ideal.
d. He suggested an advance party be sent to plant crops and erect buildings (as had Matra and Phillip)

Timothy Coghlan says:

Joseph Banks and others holding influential positions advocated the establishment of a colony in NSW, the beautiful and, it was thought, fertile territory discovered in 1770 by James Cook, and some point was given to these representations by urgent demand made on the King to provide new homes for those American loyalists who preferred quitting the land of their birth to living under the rule of the successful republicans. It is fruitless now to enquire how much or how little the English Ministry were moved by sentimental considerations in founding a colony in Australia; the fact remains that the scheme of settlement actually carried out was purely penal and military. In truth the authorities saw clearly that the idea of a penal settlement and a free colony at the same place and under the same government was an impossible one. When the First Fleet set out, it carried no one that was not connected with the penal colony—the authorities were much opposed to free settlers entering the colony, and did not desire them in any way. They (the authorities) did not consider they were founding a mere gaol, but an industrial colony; from which would arise in due season a new home for British people. This foresight is evident from several contemporary writers but how the colony was to be evolved out of the penal settlement is not entirely clear. Indeed it is probable that it was a pious hope rather than a real expectation. Botany Bay had been selected by the English Government as a suitable place at which to establish a colony, and when Phillip set sail from England in May1787 it was thither he directed his course.

R.M. Younger says

With the founding in 1711 of the South Sea Company, one of London's joint-stock ventures to seize public imagination, the distant Pacific became a region for more than literary fantasy. The South Sea Company was to trade with Spanish America and concessions were gained for it for that purpose, but its great appeal to the speculator lay in its hoped-for trade with the rich lands thought to await discovery in the Pacific. Expectations of dazzling wealth were conjured up, although operations never became profitable. The fraudulent booming of the company's shares ere followed by a collapse of the so-called South Sea Bubble in 1720,m causing disillusionment as well as great scandal. The collapse brought to a sudden and calamitous end all speculative interest in nebulous plans for trade in the Pacific. Nevertheless, the English period of discovery had begun. It was an era of scientific exploration, undertaken against a background of great expansion in scientific thought. Significant advance in the theoretical sciences of mathematics and astronomy had been made in the 17th century; now these new principles were being applied to navigation. The invention of the sextant in England in 1730 and the subsequent development of the chronometer, made it possible to take exact celestial measurements, and so to chart a ship's position with accuracy. These inventions, with modifications in ship-design resulting in greatly strengthened vessels, opened the way for new geographical discoveries.

Perhaps it was the aura of unreality associated with the southern lands as much as the British preoccupation with European wars, that held back further exploration for so long. Dampier had returned to London, hinting at prospects in lands still untouched, in 1701. Yet, apart from the wartime expedition of Captain George Anson in 1739, it was not until 1764 that the British government sent another ship into the area.

For much of the eighteenth century there was a distinct possibility that this naval warfare would be extended into the Pacific. Both French and English were doing their share of voyaging in these waters, sometimes no more than a few months, or a few leagues, apart. England's victory in the Seven Years war, acknowledged at the Treaty of Paris in 1763, resulted in England's supremacy over the French in India, and the loss of France's North American colonies to England. (France, however, retained some possessions in India and the best of her sugar-islands.) In the long run the English victory also decided the future of the Pacific.

During the years of struggle, increasing attention was given to scientific inquiry and geographical speculation, both in England and France. Now that practically all the remainder of the world was charted, the Great South Land – Terra Australis or Terra Incognita – had become a matter of immediate concern. Books about voyages in the Pacific and southern seas, proposing further exploration or the founding of settlements, and speculating about unknown parts, contributed to the growing interest.

Between 1977 and 1748, a handsome new edition was published in London of the *Complete Collection of Voyages and Travels* (which has originally . appeared in 1705, edited by John Harris) urging further discoveries. As well as narratives of navigators, the book contained prefaces and notations by John Campbell, who sought to draw attention to opportunities for new enterprise believed to exist for enterprising Englishmen. Pointing to the value of commerce, Campbell explained the narratives of travel in the South Sea in terms of the new challenge that awaited those with foresight and courage to act:

It is most evident from Tasman's voyages that New Guinea, Carpentaria (i.e. Cape York Peninsula), New Holland, Van Diemen's Land and the country discovered by Quiros make all one continent, from which New Zealand seems to be separated by a strait, and perhaps is part of another continent.

Campbell went on to suggest that there were great prospects for Britain if settlements (or, as he termed them, plantations) were established there. Convinced of the immense value of the southern continent, which he termed Terra Australis, he was opposed to a monopoly being granted to the East India Company to trade there. He made a strong plea that the South Sea Company should have rights there 'as a point of high importance,' and wrote that if Britain wished to make the greatest gain 'it may, indeed be requisite to remove ill judged prohibitions, and to break down illegal exclusions'.

He urged that New Guinea should be settled at once, 'and with competent force, since without doubt the Spaniards would leave no means unattempted to dispossess them.' In the space of a very few years, he believed settlement of New Guinea (and a trade in slaves from there) would prove of great consequence to the South Sea Company. He also recommended the formation of a settlement on the southern coast of Terra Australis. This, he believed, would lead the way to the opening of a new trade route 'which must carry a great quantity of our goods and manufactures.' Such a settlement would also be attended by other advantages. 'There is in all probability,' he wrote, 'another Southern continent which is still to be discovered.'

The Seven Years War began in the year that de Brosses's book was published. The future of the Pacific was decided in the water of Quiberon Bay in 1759. This naval victory began a long period of English naval supremacy, not to be reversed except during the War of American Independence. England's maritime supremacy made it certain that in the long run the visions of John Campbell should prevail over those of Charles de Brosses. In ironical commentary on this, three years after the end of the Seven Years War there appeared in London the first three volumes of John Callender's *Terra Australis Cognita*. In this book the whole of the arguments put forward by de Brosses, including the details of his idea for settlement, were appropriated by Callender. The only difference was that these arguments were now advanced to urge Britain's discovery and settlement of the Great South Land!

Callender's book was timely. The British Admiralty had no intention of allowing the French to forestall them in the race to new lands, and after 1763 a number of expeditions to the far South Pacific were organized.

Commodore John Byron sailed from Plymouth in 1764 with orders that in order to avoid arousing Spanish jealousies and retaliation, were kept secret. After passing through the Straits of Magellan he sailed on the familiar north-westerly course over the Pacific, making few discoveries; he sighted only outlying islands of minor groups, and after visiting Tinian he went on to Batavia and returned home, completing the circumnavigation in the record time of twenty-two months. On his return to England in 1766 his ship, the frigate *Dolphin*, was placed under Captain Samuel

Wallis who, with Captain Philip Carteret in the *Swallow*, set off on another circumnavigation. The two ships were separated soon after passing through the Straits of Magellan. Wallis reached Tahiti (Naming it King George Island), the Society Islands, and the Wallis Archipelago, sailing home by way of Batavia. Carteret discovered Pitcairn Island and sailed through St George's Channel, so proving that New Ireland and New Britain were separated.

These voyages were all undertaken by Britain to advance 'the honour of this nation as a maritime power – and the trade and navigation thereof.' The English ships each followed a course through the Straits of Magellan and then struck northwest, finally coasting New Guinea. Close behind them were the French, who had the same objectives and who directed their efforts to the same area. Captain Louis Antoine de Bougainville reached the Society Islands and Tahiti a year after Wallis, and continued westward, making some new discoveries in the Samoa group. His next landfall was an archipelago that he decided – correctly – was Quiros's long lost long-sought Australia del Espiritu Santo. Here, he told himself, was the opportunity to solve the old riddle of the Southern Continent.

And so Bougainville sailed away from the Great Barrier Reef. He still believed he had been close to land, but consoled himself with the reflection that it could easily have been 'a cluster of islands' not the east coast of New Holland. His subsequent course took him through the hazardous waters of the Louisiade Archipelago, through the Solomons and New Britain, and north of New Ireland to the Moluccas and eventually to Europe.

Meanwhile, an English geographer, Alexander Dalrymple, had written a book in which he explained how easy it would be move into what he imagined to be the great, rich, populous continent of the south – a land 'sufficient to maintain the power, dominion, and sovereignty of Britain by employing all its manufacturers and ships.' Dalrymple, who had spent many years in the employ of the East India Company, returned to London in 1765 and set about a study of material available on the South Seas. He secured a copy of a memorial printed in 1640 – discovered by the English expedition that captured Manila in 1762 – and from this long-hidden document he deduced the existence of a strait to the south of New Guinea. In a little book, *Discoveries in the South Pacific to 1764*, which was written in 1767 but not published until 1769, Dalrymple included a map in which the strait was marked, as well as the routes of Tasman and Torres. In this booklet he recapitulated all the discoveries that had been made in the South Pacific, including Juan Fernandez Islands off the coast of the Chile, the discoveries of Quiros and Tasman, and those of Le Naire to the north of New Guinea. He drew the conclusion that all these widely separated fragments were probably parts of the same great continent – a continent possibly extending over a hundred degrees of longitude in latitude 40°S, so that it was larger than the whole of Asia from Turkey to the extremity of China!

CHAPTER 23

ECONOMIC HIGHLIGHTS OF
THE BRITISH COLONIAL RULE

Any volume of economic history for Australia must acknowledge the master works by Butlin, Clark, Buxton and others who have covered each topic in such great detail, and with such authority, knowledge and skill. It is presumptuous for any non-academic to question or 'profane' the methodology or conclusions of these giants, especially when one's criticism is somewhat pre-empted and answered in advance by an author's statement and then counter-claim such as 'Buxton (P285—The Riverina 1961-1891)

"It could be argued that the influx of population during the gold-rush years would, as a result of natural increase, have generated pressure on existing resources, including land, and that this may have inevitably led to a struggle for redistribution of wealth."

But then he goes on to say " Recently N. G. Butlin has suggested in *'Investment in Australian Economic Development"* that the selector-squatter struggle has been over-emphasised by historians, but an adequate knowledge of this struggle is necessary for any real understanding of the coarse of pastoral investment in New South Wales and the development of Australian rural society and its politics."

In preparing a work such as this one must set the goals and select the events to be analysed. One goal must be to explain to the reader that one man's opinion of 'key' events would be but one of hundreds of selections by learned men. However in this case, the rise of the Colony from nothing to a self-contained, self-sufficient member of the world economic community must be considered a starting point.

That the British overlorded the Colony for the first 112 years and imposed their own ways, standards and conditions, might well be considered another significant step in our economic history, and then the growth of the rural economy and the definite boost thereto from the coming of the railway system should be another . The great contribution of the wool industry and the coal industry , added to the growth and strengths of the wool and pastoral industries are all significant, and an admirable lead into the economic considerations for the federationists.

There is little controversial about all these subjects, or is there?

Our starting point is the 'economic prologue' of the Colony in New South Wales from the first fleet to Federation; the Federation story accounts for the outline of the Financial aspect of the Federation debates and introduces a prime mover in the Federation movement, Edward Pulsford, the leader of the Free Trade Association. The last section covers that most basic of a state's right, that of regional development, the successor by name change to decentralization.

Each article issues a challenge to the reader—the conclusion in the Development of Public Accounts is that the 'traditional' view of historians that 'Britain invested millions of pounds in the Colony' is disproved; the Pulsford story is one of supporting 'White Australia' for election purposes—he became a Senator in 1901—and is disproved by his frenzied support of firstly, free trade within the Empire and then unrestricted Asian migration; the financial aspects of Federation reveal that insufficient attention was given in the Constitution to long term protection of the states and successive High Court challenges and Commonwealth manipulation have left the State's as mere pawns in a 'Federal' system. A new concept in Regional development should be used to turn the state governments against old policies and platforms.

CHAPTER 24

DEVELOPING THE COLONY

Introduction

Imagine the opportunity of starting a new colony. The possibilities are endless. The opportunity to plan a new town; lay out the streets, design the new buildings; put the people to work; protect the people from foreign adversaries; design the roads; plan what the farmers will grow.

Life should be that simple!

Phillip had these opportunities and spent two years planning before the event. But natural events and other unplanned circumstances thwarted his plans. The weather was not conducive to growing neither the vegetable seeds nor plants he had brought with him, and so the crops in the first year failed. The construction and building program he had so carefully planned out, was delayed from taking place, mainly due to the failure of Phillip to acknowledge that the convicts would not be willing pawns in his grand plan. It was a prison and penal colony, and even the Marines (the military) rejected Phillip's policy that the military should guard and supervise the convicts. This task, they declared, was for independent contractors, and since there weren't any available, convicts supervised convicts, and the building plan suffered accordingly.

The military waited for a surprise invasion that never came, and spent their time learning to take advantage of the convicts by becoming traders and commercial schemers. Who needed a town plan when there were no houses, no means of transport and thus no need for roads other than to guide the convict hauliers to their destination along basic 'goat' tracks. The only people that needed to work were the convicts—the penal settlement had no free citizens other than Government officials. For the first three months, the settlement was a 'tent city'.

Slowly the tents were replaced with crude wooden buildings. But, there was little knowledge of how to work with this new timber. The trees were axe cut, but then the saws could not easily cut the hard, moist logs. The stumps were extremely difficult to remove from this shale and shall soil ground. There was much rock around Sydney Cove and although Phillip had spent quite some days scouting for a good location, he couldn't have foreseen the disadvantages of settling around the Cove. The benefits of magnificent sheltered harboured and fresh running water couldn't offset the disadvantages of the site. Phillip had set a building schedule, which was planned to be finished in a fraction of the time actually taken. The convicts would be housed; the military would be housed, and then the officials; and finally the precious stores sufficient only for 2 years, if properly rationed, and supplemental food was located.

The pressure of finishing any form of cover for both the residents and the stores resulted in 'green' timber was used in construction, and as the planks and poles dried, they cracked and split and fell over. There was no roofing material so 'rushes' from Rushcutters Bay were used as a thatching. The stores were filled with the food supply, but two challenges had been ignored. The threat of fire was nearly as big a threat as the rat plague that enjoyed the stored food.

Lieutenant Collins recorded daily, in his diary, the growth of the small colony. He writes in his 'Account of the English Colony in New South Wales', and sets out a list of the earliest buildings as they were completed.

The Collins diary is an important record of those early days, as the dispatches from the Governor back to England were spasmodic due to the irregular shipping. Collins kept a commentary of the atmosphere and the physical environment, frequently noting the lack of incentive to the convicts to carry out assigned duties and the effect the continuos shortage of food was having on all the residents. He commented that although Phillip's official line was to be friendly to the natives, neither the military nor the convicts abided by Phillip's directions.

In spite of the times being very tough, and far different to those originally envisaged by Phillip when he would sit in front of his cosy fireplace in his cottage in England, great progress was made, and Collins maintained his list of changes and especially buildings under construction. After a few false starts caused by the misuse of tools and timber, the colony took shape. The first house used by Governor Phillip was prefabricated in England and brought out in sections in the First Fleet. The first permanent house commenced in November 1788 was built using bricks made at Darling Harbour. The brickworks were shortly afterwards moved to Brickfield Hill, but the product was inferior because of a change of clay and the inefficient kiln. Later, new brickworks were started at St.Peters, Granville and Gore Hill, before a distant opening of a new kiln at Rose Hill, near Parramatta, where a fresh, quality seam of clay had been found.

The Earliest Progress toward Town Planning

It is fortunate that Lt. David Collins, an officer with the first fleet, kept a diary of both the journey and the early days in the colony

The Collins list of building and development work undertaken includes such items as

- Barracks—prisoners
- Barracks – military
- Storehouses
- Observatory
- Hospital & dispensary
- Government House
- Senior officers & official houses—Ross, Collins, Johnson, Alt, Arndell and Irving
- A hut for Bennelong
- A Magazine at Dawes Point
- A Gun Placement on today's Bennelong Point
- Church

- Mills
- Cells
- Court-house
- Basic Roads

Phillip planned for all these items but lack of rapid or expected progress made him reach only to the Gun Placement at Bennelong Point, which Macquarie found to be so run down that he replaced this item with the Fort Macquarie on the same spot.

Before we take a look at the details of the constructions listed above, let us review the origins of town planning, keeping in mind that Phillip had a vision for the new colony, which had far from reflected the actual circumstances found on arrival in 1788.

It is the story of building and development progress in the colony that we shall review from the history and from the Records. The 'history' comes from the Collins, Tench, Hunter, King, Phillip diaries, and from the Macquarie and Greenway collected papers.

a. Our intent in relating this story is to allow us to trace and follow the building construction sequence and the town planning policy for the colony between 1788 and 1820, estimate the cost, location, dimensions and construction type of each asset and locate an early sketch of each building. We will follow a guided path through official records and mostly convict sketches of the day.

CHAPTER 25

AREAS FOR CONSIDERATION

1. The origins of the Building Program
2. 'Servicing' the needs of the residents
3. What did it all cost
4. The Portfolio of Improvements
5. Infrastructure Development
6. Future Development Plans

a. The origins of the Building Program
b. The need for a prison colony

- The British Government had gone to war in the American colonies and the outcome was to abandon their sale of prisoners to American colonists as encumbered workers. A new source of moving prisoners from overflowing jails and hulks was needed. A House of Commons Committee reviewed Africa and a few other possibilities, but Sir Joseph Banks recommended Botany Bay.

c. The influx of convicts

- The first fleet of prisoners left England in 1787 and arrived at Botany Bay in early January 1788. A week of surveying alternatives sites found that Sydney Cove, with safe mooring conditions, level land and fresh water was much better than Botany Bay and the fleet moved and arrived for settlement on 26th January 1788. Phillip had not considered the disadvantages of the site, being shallow soli, rock and shale and unfriendly natives on whose land Phillip had encroached.

d. Bringing a portable building to the colony

- Captain Arthur Phillip R.N. had been appointed to lead the military officers, head up the Government and form a settlement, which was to be self-supporting within 2 years – for 2 years of provisions was all that had been carried to the new settlement, along with a few head of livestock, some plants, a portable house for the 'Governor' and lots of hope for a successful transformation.

e. Creating a new British outpost

- The reality of the challenge was far greater than Phillip had realised. The land was not the deep rich soil, they had expected, so the plants would not grow; the natives became a problem; there were no free settlers so no free enterprise; the convicts were not in the mind to work hard, so productivity and morale was low. Food was in short supply and Phillip regularly trimmed rations until the prisoners claimed they couldn't work at all on such low rations

f. Establishing a new social order

- With the new colony came a new order – the old English laws had to be amended to deal with the new circumstances. The colony commenced as a pure 'penal' colony without a treasury, without coins or any means of exchange; everything needed in the colony had to be 'imported', and the early shipping delay was seven months of sailing

g. Servicing the needs of the inhabitants

h. The Legal Authority for the Colony.

- The establishment of a colony in New Holland at Botany Bay was authorised by letters from the British Home Secretary, Lord Sydney, in the last weeks of August 1786. These letters were addressed to the Treasury and to the Admiralty and ordered that "you do forthwith take such measures as may be necessary for providing a proper number of vessels for the conveyance of seven hundred and fifty convicts to Botany Bay, together with such provisions, necessaries and implements for agriculture as may be necessary for their use after their arrival." The commission to Captain Arthur Phillip was dated 12th October 1786 and signed by the King. The fleet, at the appointed time of its departure consisted of two naval vessels, six transports and three store ships.

i. The role of the commissary

- The commissary was the 'storehouse' of the colony. It provided rations for every person on the military and civil list. It provided rations, clothing and tools for every convict worker. It held a store of food, grain, tools and material supplies. Every request for a product in the colony passed through the commissary. It was responsible for projecting ahead the rations required and ordering supplies from local farmers or, as was the general case in those early years, from overseas suppliers. It paid for its purchases by a bill drawn on the Treasury in England. Payment to the commissary could be by way of barter items, for instance, grain or other rural commodities, sometimes in the barter of labour to perform certain approved tasks, but because there was no currency in the colony, there was no payment, other than 'in kind'. In the early 1800s the currency became rum or spirits. The commissary traded heavily in this commodity. The commissary kept 'accounts' of what was owed by residents, other than convicts, and would carry these accounts for an extended period in the trust that the account would one day be settled by produce or in another for. However, many ' bad debts' were incurred and had to be either pursued vigorously by the Governor's staff or written off.

j. Working for the 'Civil List'

- Until free settlers were encouraged into the colony – the first free settlers arrived in the Second Fleet – all 'free' residents were employed on the civil list. This list was of people employed by and paid by the British Government and included the chaplain, medical specialists, the Governor, lieutenant-governor, judges and the commissary-general. From year to year the list grew as the demand for government services expanded and soon the list included surveyors, engineers, architects and building supervisors.

k. Town Planning for the early stages

- Phillip arrived in the colony with a 'plan' for controlled development and growth for the colony, in his mind. But circumstances rendered it in tatters. The shortage of food, the lack of understanding of the soils and the climate generally, the unusual terrain encountered, the inability to use and understand the timber available, the unrest among the natives and the attitude of both the convicts and military, all made Phillip struggle with his administration of the Colony. He had planned a town centre with wide streets, a residential area, a military and convict area, and a 'farming' area. His town plan had to be shelved for the reasons set out above, and even after Phillip returned to England and the colony became self-supporting and self sufficient, it was not until Macquarie wrote a Plan for Development, that town planning and construction control became part of the government operations.

l. The need for exploration

- The town of Sydney grew quickly with the arrival of more and more convicts. Phillip had encouraged the satellite towns of Rose Hill, Parramatta and the Hawkesbury. The grazing area known as the 'cow pastures' became too small, and the need for more and fertile farming and grazing land became number 1 priority for the Governors. The Governor encouraged 'exploration ' and decentralisation. Windsor, Liverpool and Castlereagh became new settlements, but in 1813 the great success of Blaxland. Lawson and Wentworth of crossing the Blue Mountains opened up the western pastoral plains to livestock grazing. Macquarie built a road traversing the mountain range and set up the first inland town of Bathurst.

m. Growth, decentralisation and creating small towns

- If the need for new grazing lands became the catalyst for decentralisation, then the mechanics of growth were led by the surge of inland exploration – the story of the inland New South Wales rivers was unfolding, whilst many moves were being made to discover the inland routes to Port Phillip and northern areas, north of the established Newcastle. Small towns sprung up, as trading posts, stops for the Cobb & Co coaches and along livestock routes. It would not be until the discovery of Gold in 1851 that a population surge would follow new industry in regional type centres.

n. Roads and infrastructure

- Macquarie quickly followed the crossing of the Blue Mountains and the opening up of huge pastoral runs with roads and bridges leading inland and along which, coaches and livestock could travel. His plan to make most of the main roads into toll roads, from which revenue for maintenance could be derived. This scheme was promoted and supported by the British Treasury and Macquarie tried to implement the proposal. but with limited success. Toll bridges at Windsor and across the Hawkesbury had not raised the level of revenue expected. The toll road between Sydney Town and Parramatta was the exception, and Greenway designed flamboyant style tollgates for the corner of George and Pitt Streets, and at the other end, just east of the Parramatta River crossing. The Governor had arranged for tenders to collect these tolls but this arrangement became the source of great irritation to stock movers and residents living adjacent to the tollgates, with their need to regularly cross through the gate or bridge system.

o. The continuing needs of the new settlement

- Law and order, government building and buildings, importing goods, wealth creation (traders, spirit merchants)

p. What did it all cost

q. How the public funding system work

- There is some disagreement over the actual funding of the new colony. The colony raised funds on its own account from duties, harbour and port charges, lighthouse charges, and wharfage as well as for the freshwater taken on by visiting sailing ships. In addition to locally raised revenues the British Treasury remitted funds for the civil list salaries and made payment for all supplies and provisions sent to the colony. As well as paying bills of Exchange drawn by the Commissary and Governor in the colony, the Treasury paid for the contracts to transport the convicts, provision the ships, clothe the prisoners and meet the freight charges for provisions being moved to the colony. These revenues and expenses are contained in a number of documents. The Treasury kept the accounts from 1788 to 1802 when the 'Gaol' Fund was established by Governor Hunter to try and replace the burnt out Sydney Jail through public subscription. There was a short fall in th4e fund and so the Governor advanced the required funds to finish the building and simultaneously appointed the Reverend Samuel Marsden to be Treasurer of the Orphan Fund, the purpose of which was to support the growing number of abandoned orphans roaming the streets of the town. The Female Orphan Fund was given a share of the revenue raised in the colony and charged with expending those funds on equipping the orphan school, housing feeding and clothing the orphans selected for support and then of educating them. The second fund set up was the 'Police' Fund – a successor by name change to the Gaol Fund. The appointed Treasurer of the Police fund was Darcy Wentworth. The gross revenue coming into the colony was shared between these two funds, which became the de facto treasury of the colony and the treasurers became the official recorders of the finances of the colony. This situation was confirmed again by Macquarie who left the arrangement in place until 1822 when the British Treasury designated an official office and a new recording and reporting system to operate the finances of the colony. Thus the 'Blue book ' era came into being, and continued in practice until self-government in 1855.

151

r.   The Growth of Public Finance

- Public Finance grew from these first two 'funds' in a penal colony without a treasury into a self-supporting colony without Treasury support by 1817, at which time Macquarie sponsored, firstly, coinage as a medium of exchange instead of 'bills' and a barter system including the 'rum' system as an exchange medium, and secondly he sponsored the Bank of New South Wales. By the end of the Macquarie era and the commencement of the 'Blue book' period, Britain no longer put its hand in its pocket all the time and in fact made the colonial treasury pay for free immigration to the colony. The first sale of crown land was the means of raising extra finance to operate the colony and pay for shipping convicts to the colony. As part of self-government Britain even made the colonial treasurer pay for the Civil List, if it was to keep all local revenues under its control.

s.   The early Treasury functions (coins)

- The first coins came in the pockets of seamen, the military officers and merchant traders, thus the coinage in the colony prior to 1810 was a mixed bag, with the Governor trying to apply an official exchange rate. Hunter tried to extend the usage of coins by punching the centrepiece out of the dollar thus making it the 'holy' dollar and when the Treasury finally sent a large quantity of coins to the colony, the residents found the means of hording the coins and really defeating the purpose of the exercise. The result was a return to using spirits as a medium of exchange.

t.   Sources of revenue funds

- The sources and use of funds are derived from a number of sources between 1788 and 1828. Between 1788 and 1802, the British Treasury paid for all payments in and on behalf of the colony. These direct payments included:

- From 1802 the colony commenced to raise its own revenues by way of 'import' duties, harbour duties, lighthouse and wharfage fees, purchase of services from local residents, trading in government livestock and purchase of free labour for construction. These items of revenue are identified through the 'Orphan & Police Funds) between 1802 and 1822. During these years, the British Treasury 'topped' up the general revenue by meeting the on-going obligations for the convicts, the military, and the civil list. From 1822 the 'Blue Books' recorded the revenue and expenditure for the colony and took the Treasury functions out of the hands of the two private individuals previously operating the Orphan and Police Funds accounts. The Governor in Council (the Governor had appointed a select panel of advisers in the form of a Legislative Council) was always seeking new ways of raising revenue, the demand for which just grew and grew. A significant Part of the British Treasury contribution was being raised from the sale and lease of Crown Lands, which the British had reserved exclusively for their own use, until 1856 when they released this revenue to the NSW Legislature in exchange for the Legislature accepting responsibility for paying the 'Civil ' list.

u. Use of Treasury Funds

• The use of funds ranged from supporting exploration trips, to employing surveyors, architects, and public works supervisors for local purposes, outside the approved scope of British Treasury work. The commissary drew bills for supplies and provisions, purchased locally or from visiting ships, on the British Treasury, and sold provisions to local residents on a barter system until 1813. The locally raised revenue was used to pay for road and infrastructure maintenance including bridges, ferry services between Sydney and Parramatta, and the tolls raised were treated as general revenues rather than being reserved in a specific fund. From 1825, and the successful operation of the Bank of New South Wales, the Colonial Treasurer opened numerous 'funds' as a means of partitioning and isolating funds. For instance there was the Colonial Fund; the Aboriginal Welfare Fund; the Church & School Fund; The Civil Service Superannuation Fund; The 'scab in sheep' fund; The Orphan, Police and Gaol Funds

CHAPTER 26

THE OPPORTUNITY COST
TO BRITAIN

It is still a matter for great academic debate as to what the real cost of establishing the colony was to Britain. On one hand, the argument runs that it cost the British Treasury over $127 million pound sterling to set up and operate the colony (Professor N.G.Butlin). On the other hand, it is argued that there was an opportunity cost attached to the settlement that saved England much, much more than it cost. The As would be expected Philips first priority was to get shelter for traditionalists versus the rationalists. The opportunity costs are easily accounted for:

The savings in operating traditional prisonsThe savings from paying contractors to feed and house the prisoners on the hulks and in the prisons

The savings from using convict labour to build up the colony (assuming Britain wanted another overseas colony)

The benefits from traders using British manufacturers to source materials and supplies for the colony.

The benefit to British textile manufacturers to have a reliable and cheap source of quality raw material (wool) for value adding and re-exporting throughout Europe and Asia.

The benefits of having the colony be the source of food and naval supplies (the navy wanted Norfolk Island as a source of flax –for sail-making, and pine trunks for masts)

w. The Portfolio of Improvements
x. The early years of building

The convicts, the military, him and the stores. By good planning, Phillip had brought with him a prefabricated house for himself, costing the Treasury 125 pound. The other buildings were slow to erect. Step one was to clear the ground, and the convicts were set to this task but were ill equipped with poor and inadequate tools against the harsh terrain. Phillip had not anticipated the shallow soil over rock and shale; nor had he anticipated the very different types of timber to that commonly found in Britain or Europe. The Australian 'Gum' or Eucalyptus is very high in moisture content and very slow to dry. In normal open air rack drying, it takes almost two years to dry sufficiently so that with nailing it does not crack, split, warp or bow. With Phillip in a great hurry to show progress with establishing the settlement, he decided not to wait two years whilst the timber was drying before use. He ordered the trees to be cut, split and used immediately. Within months the buildings constructed from 'green' timber had twisted and split, and the buildings collapsed. Phillip set up a Lumber Yard as part of the Commissary Store, and directed that they be responsible for forestry operations, especially storing and stacking on drying racks all timber designated for construction work. The commissary decided to sub-contract this work and was within four years able to negotiate supply contracts with reputable timber cutters, for dried, quality-sawn timber. When the Sydney area could no longer supply the quantity required, especially during the Macquarie era, regular supply was found from the Newcastle area.

• The early buildings were constructed to British standard design. Barracks, both military and convict were generally 100 feet long and 24 feet wide. This conformed to the configuration specified by the British military throughout the Empire. In addition to barracks, the governor ordered, storehouses, wharfs, a hospital, houses for senior civil list personnel and finally administration offices, and a new house for the Governor.

y. Inventory of the First Fleet

- An inventory of goods shipped with the first fleet was assembled by John Cobley in his work ' Sydney Cove 1788'. Contents included:

z. Resources of the colony e.g. timber, bricks, tiles, tools

- Phillip obviously planned for a reliable supply of natural and local resources to build his colony with and on. But many expected resources were not available. His food supply dwindled without ability to be replenished; his worker resource fell far short of expectations and the productivity per head was a fraction of what was expected; the military refused to supervise the convicts at work and so convicts were to be supervised by convicts; the available timber supply was unsuitable for immediate use; the tools he had brought with him were largely inappropriate, unreliable, scarce and easily stolen by the convicts and the natives. Phillip had a brick making operation set up in the Domain area within months of arrival and he located a small supply of second quality clay nearby. By mid-1789 this operation had been transferred to a new place at Brickfield Hill and a second better supply of clay had been located at Rose Hill, thus making this second small settlement area a staging toward Parramatta. The failure of the timber supply to fill the needs of the construction plans meant there was a growing reliance on and importance to the regular and reliable supply of bricks and tiles. Within months the new facility at Rose Hill was turning out 25,000 bricks each week.

aa. Shortage of skills

- Tools and materials were not the only items missing and missed in the colony. There were few, if any, skills amongst the convicts that could be used or relied upon to assist in forming the colony along the lines Phillip had envisioned. He needed brick makers (and had only one man experienced in this trade; he needed carpenters and mechanics; he needed engineers, surveyor, clerical assistance, but none of these trades was readily available. His appeals to the

British Colonial Office for supervisors were ignored, as were his calls for more and better tools and general building materials.

bb. Designing by default

- Each governor had his own ideas on town development. Phillip had to set the basis for future development by clearing land, laying out streets, giving some intention of future sites for key government buildings such as government house, courts, military bases, convict barracks etc. Governors King and Hunter, both associates of Phillip during his term of office were happy to just keep Phillip's work moving ahead without appearing to strike out into new territory. Bligh, on his arrival had few supporters and did little to improve the settlement other than make a few land grants and some controversial appointments, most of which Macquarie reversed upon his term commencing in 1810. It was left to Macquarie to re-assess the whole future direction and development of the town and its various satellites and try to meet more of the objectives of the colonial office in London. The colonial office wanted expansion for more convicts to be transported and put to gainful work – all such activity to be with minimal cost to the Treasury.

cc. Paying in Kind – a Barter economy—'The Colony has no Treasury (1788-1802)'

- Being a penal colony, the first Governors – Phillip, King and Hunter, did not worry about coinage or the development of a monetary system as a means of exchange. The commissary coped by drawing 'bills of exchange' in favor of visiting traders, shippers and local purchasers, on the British Treasury in London. The barter system became established as the means by which freemen could sell their labor, settlers could sell produce to the commissary, and settlers could trade between each other. It was Professor S. J. Butlin who coined the phrase 'the country has no treasury in his work "Foundations of the Australian Monetary System." He writes that the commissary store receipts were, for many the means of exchange on the streets of Sydney town. The medium of exchange for the military officers was the Paymaster's Bills, again drawn on the Treasury in London. There were a few 'scanty' coins, says Butlin, and a few private bills. Those who had credit balances or credit in London that is mainly the military and civil officers could only draw private bills. In 1799 a 'few tons' of copper coins was shipped to the colony and Hunter decided to assign varying exchange rates to the various coins rather than their face value of farthings ¼ penny, halfpenny 1/2 penny and the penny

dd. Traders set the pace

- Each new colony attracts those traders seeking new outlets for their goods or new markets to supply their wares or new sources of supply to ship back to the primary locations. Robert Campbell was no exception. An English trader, who had moved to India to further his career and success, arrived in Sydney in 1793 with the intention of building a trading relationship between India and the new colony. From the time of its establishment in 1788, writes Margaret Steven in "Merchant Campbell 1769-1846 – A study in colonial trade", the colony's immediate and spontaneous links were with India. Bengal was British and prosperous, and the colony of Botany Bay figured spasmodically in the affairs of Calcutta, which for the first twenty years, played the part of general store to the penal establishment." Campbell's business flourished and this led to convicts and early release convicts being used as 'front' men for firstly the military officers who engaged in trade, and then becoming traders in their own right. For instance Simeon Lord, not long after finishing his sentence became a very wealthy and respectable trader, magistrate and government confidante. Being so isolated, and with a surge of growth from both convicts and free settlers, there was no shortage of those willing to take risks as a trader. Even John Palmer the commissary-general engaged in questionable trade practices whilst still the operator of the commissary, and the ignoble Robert Brookes of London, became one of the largest traders and encouraged the shipping of wool to the English auction houses before the trend was to sell the wool in Sydney sales houses.

ee. Wharves, harbours & navigation

- The need for wharves is obvious in any port town. The fleets (both first and second) could not get close to the shore, and so required unloading facilities, row boats etc to transport convicts, military personnel and stores to dry land. However, even in 1811, there existed only three landing places around Sydney Cove. The Governor's Wharf on the east side of the cove, the Hospital Wharf adjacent to the market house and store house, and Robert Campbell's wharf further north on the west side of the cove. Phillip had built the Dawes Point observatory and the magazine on Bennelong Point, and when a sailing vessel was expected, lit fires on South Head. It took until Macquarie's era to have a lighthouse built on the South Head (Macquarie lighthouse) and Fort Macquarie replaced the old magazine on Bennelong Point.

ff. Military accommodation

- The first military accommodation was on the shore of Sydney Cove in tents, whilst they awaited the building of barracks. Most of the officers remained in tents until mid-1789 (records the diary of Lt David Collins). The priority set by Phillip was for him and the senior civilians to be houses, the convicts to be placed in Barracks, a hospital to be built and storehouses. The military was then to have their barracks built. The whole process was delayed by the use of green wood, which soon twisted and split in the drying process, causing the huts and houses to fall over.

gg. City beautification

- I took until the arrival of Macquarie for any Governor to show or take any interest in aesthetics. Macquarie built Macquarie Square and incorporated an obelisk and fountain into the landscape. He instructed Greenway, as his official architect to design attractive (if not ornate) toll-gates in both Sydney and Parramatta, and ordered the Government Stables in the Domain area next to Government House to become a magnificent edifice to inspire the colonists and demonstrate how attractive buildings would improve the

landscape and the quality of life in the town. He broadened the
streets and planted trees along those streets.

hh. Road and Bridge Development

- 'Roads' were little more than cart tracks before Macquarie
  brick-paved the first road – George Street—in 1814. The first
  bridge was built over the Tank Stream in July 1788, with a bridge
  built over the Parramatta River in 1794. Macquarie introduced
  the 'turnpike' or toll road in 1810. The Windsor Bridge of 65 m
  in three spans was completed in 1813 and by March 1814 the
  Sydney to Liverpool road was completed. The crossing of the Blue
  Mountains in 1813 gave Macquarie reason to build an inexpensive
  road from Parramatta to Bathurst using convict labour with the
  incentive of freedom upon completion.

ii. Expansion of the settlements – Liverpool, Windsor, Castlereagh &
Parramatta

- It was Phillip and his earliest successors who, in their search for
  food production decided to make grants of land to freed convicts,
  military people and free settlers. In the effort to find better
  grazing and farming country, they set up in Rose Hill, Parramatta,
  Toongabbie, Windsor and Hawkesbury (Castlereagh). The results
  were immediate. Food production and grazing too place and by
  1792 the colony was moving steadily to self-sufficiency. Phillip
  distributed breeding livestock to selected farmers in an effort to
  grow the animal numbers to a point where the salt pork could be
  replaced by fresh meat, and fresh vegetables were available to all.

jj. Development Plans for the Future

kk. The rise of the Banks

- It was the Macquarie observation to Lord Bathurst that " . . . the
  colony had no provision for public credit . . ." that becomes the
  first indication that Macquarie was mindful of the need for a bank
  in the colony (Banks, or credit and discount houses had been

operating in England for many years). However it took until 1817 for Macquarie to sponsor and indeed 'charter' a bank – the first bank being 'The Bank of New South Wales'.

Crowley in Colonial Australia –Volume 1 writes " Private banks played a leading role in the development of the New South Wales economy in the 1820s and 1830s. The first was the Bank of New South Wales, which opened for business in Macquarie Place, Sydney on 8th April 1817. Governor Macquarie had granted to the President and Directors of the new bank a special charter for their incorporation as a limited liability company, and had therefore legalised thew institution pending final approval from London. In fact, Macquarie had no legal authority to issue such a charter, and this was later made clear to him and to his successors; it was not until seven years after the bank had opened that it received official approval. It was established to meet the need for a stable local currency and to establish credit facilities for trade, commerce, manufacturing and land settlement. Crowley quotes from the rules and regulations which were adopted for the bank's conduct."

ll. Gold Discoveries

- The last few days of May 1851 saw Sydney town in a flurry of excitement, after the reports of 'The Gold Fever' reached the town on 20th May, 1851 and were published in the Sydney Morning Herald, and followed with hundreds of men walking the road over the Blue Mountains; the shops were crowed with buyers of suitable clothes and tools, appropriate to a 'digger'. The immediate effects of the gold discovery were a sudden increase in the size of the population in eastern Australia and the export to Britain of large quantities of gold bullion. Crowley points out that "at first, wool growing and cattle raising suffered from the loss of workmen, but the squatters quickly adapted to the new situation, mainly because of the new increased demand for meat and grain, and the higher prices brought for these items. Freight costs were also reduced to Britain by the new keen competition between ship owners, at a time when wool prices were also rising."

Rising wages for the manufacturing industry was held partly in check by the constant arrivals of new immigrants in ships with their holds full of pots, pans, tools, clothing, lanterns and cheap furniture. The commercial boom in Sydney and Melbourne led to a land boom and the inevitable speculation in building in the two capital cities as well as the central gold towns, such as Ballarat, Bathurst, Orange and Goulburn.

mm.   Traders in Control

• During the 1820s the colony changed from a 'paternally administered jail into a free—market capitalist economy' (Crowley) in which the everyday use of money increased in importance, private banks increased in number, privately arranged foreign exchange became important, share deals and bill-broking became common, and pastoral expansion was financed by bank overdraft and imported capital. 'Pastoral settlement in the Hunter, Bathurst and Goulburn districts was rapid, and the colony's population increased from 24,000 in 18250 to 36,100 in 1825 and 41,000 in 1829. Wool exports to Britain increased from 175,000 lb in 1821 to 1,106,000 in 1826, and then doubled in the next four years. New settlers brought in capital and in July 1826, the new Bank of Australia opened in competition to the Bank of New South Wales. The dominance, once again, of the traders and great pastoral houses was entrenched.

nn. The rise of the Pastoral Industry

• The first livestock came into the colony with the First Fleet. They were not meant for food production but for breeding and reproduction. Good grazing grass was not readily available around the Sydney Cove and the natives speared a number of the animals when the convict 'guards' fell asleep or strayed from their charges. The move to the cow-pastures area produced much better feed but still without any form of fencing the animals needed constant care. The Governor set up houses, pens and permanent yards to make the task of managing the animals a little easier. As Phillip began to make land grants to convicts completing their sentences and military officers, he also make suitable grants of animal pairs for breeding and further livestock production. The food shortage within the colony created great stress for settlers and convicts to see these growing herds and flocks grazing, ready for slaughter but out of touch for anyone. But with good control the herd grew and multiplied, as planned. The authorities considered that urban growth was limiting the available grazing lands for the growing flocks of sheep and herds of beef cattle. Marsden had been a recipient of a number of sheep and bred up sheep for meat as well as for wool, whilst the Macarthur family bred for wool alone. Marsden's sheep were well framed and hardy and were probably a more all-round success than Macarthur's sheep but Macarthur took wool samples to London and received large acreage in return for concentrating on improving both the quality and quantity of Australian wool production. Grants to free settlers (especially those with or access to capital) became the attraction for a growing colony, to the extent that by Macquarie's arrival the general assessment was that more grazing as well as farming land was needed. The exploration of new lands was encouraged and it took three free settlers – William Charles Wentworth (son of Darcy Wentworth) and William Lawson (military officer, pioneer official and farmer at Prospect) and Gregory Blaxland (a farmer at St. Marys and co-conspirator of John Macarthur in the deposition of William Bligh) – to find a passage over the Blue Mountains in 1813. Following this discovery, Macquarie sent Major Mitchell and John Oxley two surveyors and engineers over the mountains to further investigate the other side. They solved the great puzzle of the inland river system and formed a base at Bathurst establishing a starting point for the coming pastoral move into the inland open ranges. Macquarie was impressed by the Oxley reports of the potential of these grazing areas and planned a 'road' over the mountains to ensure the access was available to the many rather than just a few. The road was completed in six months at 'no cost' because the sixty handpicked convicts were given the added bonus of freedom if they completed the challenge for food and shelter only. This great movement of people and livestock opened the pastoral industry up to unprecedented growth and this industry became the leader of a national industry that was to lead Australia home on the sheep's back.

oo. The coming of the Railways

- The need for better and cheaper transport had been mounting since the early 1800s as the colony grew with free settlers. Initially, without horses available, the convicts provided the hauling and moving of goods, and this was followed by river transport. The Darling and Murray Rivers became large deliverers of water transport for both freighting of goods and the moving of people and produce.

- But the area needing most asdsistance was the transportation to decentralised country towns. It was at this time that the small rural areas were being to grow and neede support for transporting livestock and oproduce. Gold had recently been discovered and the country was going through a mini-boom of rural enterpridse, with increasing land prices, heavy demand for livestock and wool sales booming in London. The first rail link was between Sydney and Parramatta. Then came Liverpool, Goulburn, Newcastle and points west. Within 10 years most of New South Wales was linked to Sydney by rail, and rail business was booming.

The Commencement of Town Planning.

Phillip approved the earliest 'Public Buildings' with little benefit of forethought or planning. The earliest known layout of the colony is dated July 1788, showing Phillip's thoughts as to the layout of streets and the location of these public buildings. The references include"

- "A small house building for the Governor
- A farm of 9 acres in corn
- The lieutenant-Governor's house
- The principal streets marked out
- Ground intended for the Governor's new House, Main Guard House and Criminal Court
- Ground intended for building hereafter

- Ground intended for Church
- Grounds intended for Storehouses
- The Hospital
- The Observatory
- Temporary Buildings and huts—military and convict use."
  Phillip's plan showed that at the junction of the cove with today's bridge street, a road was marked. This road Phillip planned to be the town's principal street, 200 feet wide. The road was never made.
  This map was forwarded with Governor Phillip's despatch of 9th July 1788 to the Colonial Secretary, Lord Grenville, and is attached for reference purposes.
- Subsequent maps are dated 1800 (Grimes); 1807—drawn by ex-convict and official Surveyor James Meehan; 1808—Governor Bligh's plan of the Town of Sydney; undated Macquarie era plan (probably 1817-18) showing all town streets named and blocks marked and identifying main buildings and improvements; an 1822 map by Greenway, showing the prominent buildings and locations; and an 1827 'View of the Town of Sydney' showing the development in an elevation perspective, including items such as
- New goal
- Prisoners Barracks
- Government Domain
- General Hospital
- The various chapels and churches
- Botany Bay
- Road to Parramatta
- School of Industry
- Natives
- Orphan school
- Various official houses
- Fort Phillip
- Blue Mountains
- Law Courts

By 1800 the population of the town was 3,000. A further 3,000 residents were located in Parramatta, Toongabbie and Hawkesbury. Governor Hunter had opened up the fertile Hawkesbury River area for settlement in

1794, with Windsor being the first town centre of the region and replacing Parramatta as the principal rural district.

Earlier (in 1789), Phillip had given an acre of land at Rose Hill to James Rouse, an industrious ex-convict. Rouse became the colony's first independent farmer, and was followed by numerous other 'settlers, under Phillip's land grant scheme. Time-expired or pardoned convicts were 'granted' 30 acres with an additional 20 acres for a wife and 10 acres for every child. The obvious explanation is that Phillip wanted to encourage marriage in an otherwise immoral society and control the growing wave of orphan children roaming the streets. Phillip's hunt was for food production via an expanded agricultural base for the colony.

Phillips town planning was complicated by the need to separate and expand the colony into rural and town. Only the class responsible for town planning decisions understand the rationale behind their plan. The rationale was based on 'commonsense' for the colonial administration of the day, which policy was implicit in government for almost 100 years and is inherent in the building heritage of that period. Phillip built the town centre around the port, and the source of fresh water. The convict barracks were initially on the outskirts of the town boundaries, alongside the military barracks and main guard. The storehouses were centrally located to the wharf area and adjacent to the residential area whose inhabitants were the main customers of the public stores. The residential blocks were all sized 60 feet x 150 feet. There was commonsense symmetry in the street pattern—the main thoroughfares ran north/south from the wharves of today's circular quay towards Ultimo and Brickfield Hill and led the main thoroughfare all the way to Parramatta. The east/west streets traversed the main thoroughfares and linked the Domain to the smaller docks of Cockle Bay and today's Pyrmont. Macquarie completed and supplemented the first plan of Phillips, and although Bligh put his name to the 1808 map, his was a small contribution to the town plan.

By examining the public buildings and planned open public space we can understand a little better these 'commonsense' rules. The initial stage of military government was gradually transformed into the phase of civil type construction. Phillip and his two working associates, Hunter and King, had completed the basic structure and organisation of the town and it went to Macquarie to imprint the town with the embellishments that differentiate a town from a city. King & Hunter barely touched, let alone refined the Phillip plan mainly because they had had a hand in its formulation. Macquarie changed the pattern immediately because he found the town 'run down and decrepit looking, and wanted to make it a 'good place' to live, even though the majority of the residents were still convicts.

Buildings of new grandeur, buildings designed mostly by Greenway, an ex-convict, but also by Lafleur, made quite a contribution. The Macquarie era was the high point of the change, which affected the development of the primary and secondary towns as well as the styles of building. Macquarie developed Sydney's town centre on a plan 'for the ornament and regularity of the streets of Sydney, to secure the peace and tranquillity of the town'. The early timber structures had decayed rapidly, so Macquarie established the civic institutions in local sandstone: the schools, churches, public buildings of various kinds including even the asylums (for orphans and the aged), and the barracks. Through the architectural skills of Greenway, Macquarie placed the town centre further away from the shoreline. Macquarie also attempted to impose a town plan on an irregular topography and tidy up the rather haphazard streets and buildings clustered around the Tank Stream and Sydney Cove. This is in stark contrast to the geometric layout of Adelaide Streets on a level site beside the river Torrens set out by Colonel Light a generation later.

Macquarie encouraged the shift of the central civil authority away from the Rocks area, and allowed that part of the town (built literally on 'rock') to be the first area of urban decay. By re-locating the military barracks from Sydney Cove to Wynyard in George Street, Macquarie brought protection to the new middle class area around Hyde Park, Elizabeth Street and Macquarie Street. The gaol and police station remained in 'The Rocks' area and reminded the population that this was the original settlement of early convicts, as well as of trade and a source of great thievery and low-life haunts.

Macquarie was the colony's fifth official Governor and when he arrived in 1810 with his wife, Elizabeth, and his own regiment, he found the colony only just self-sufficient, with poor roads, crumbling building and a great deal of general maintenance work unfinished.

Macquarie had announced on 11th August 1811 a new town plan for Sydney, with road widths of 50 feet including footpaths and he set minimum building standards and construction regulations.

As well, the local agriculture and enterprise was at a low state. Public morale, after the removal of Bligh, was also at low ebb and the convicts after a tortuous period at the hands of the Rum Corps had lost all interest in other than just staying alive.

During the next eleven years of the Macquarie era, the colony would grow from 11,590 to 38,798 people and the amount of land under agriculture from 7,645 acres to 32,267 acres. Animal numbers grew in numbers enormously, particularly sheep; from a flock of 26,000 in 1810 to 290,000 in 1820; Cattle numbers increased 10 fold from 12,442 to 109,939. During these same years, the Bank of New South Wales was founded; a police force and police districts were created; currency was introduced, as was cart registration, horse racing and the first public markets. Sunday liquor sales was stopped and convicts were forced to attend church.

However, it was the public works program that brought Macquarie under special Colonial Office attention, and it was this program, along with his town planning skills, which have left the greatest legacy.

Macquarie had developed a proper plan for the town of Sydney as well as the settlement at Parramatta and the smaller towns in the Hawkesbury. Rather than allowing the city to develop in its own way, Macquarie named all the streets and, by regulation, required that all building plans be submitted for approval prior to construction.

He told Greenway that Government buildings should be of quality construction, and thus lead to a higher standard for all building work. In all he built 67 public buildings in Sydney itself (refer "Appendix A"), 20 in Parramatta, 15 at Windsor, 12 at Liverpool, as well as in Tasmania (Van Diemens Land) and Bathurst. Probably his greatest engineering achievement was the building of the Western Road over the Blue

Mountains; 60 convict workers and their overseers completed the 126 miles in just six months. The road had cost zero in labour. Macquarie had agreed that any convicts, who worked on the road at no pay other than food and shelter and completed the task quickly, would be given their freedom.

Macquarie chose to meet every convict transport ship arriving and 'select' qualified or suitable convicts for special government service. He justified new buildings, constructed in a belt-tightening era, in an unusual way. For example, he used a 'defence' need as justification for constructing the Government House Stables (now the Conservatorium of Music). The 'Rum' Hospital was a 'free' building—he exchanged the finished hospital for the free importation (free of duty) of 45,000 gallons of rum. However, Commissioner John Bigge brought the era to an end with the charge of extravagance against Macquarie, which led to his recall back to England.

If Macquarie were being examined today, in front of an enquiry panel into his actions, he would be applauded as choosing the most logical way of improving the economy. Increasing wealth within the colony and keeping costs (compared to benefits) to a manageable and justifiable level. However Bigge did not put it in this light. He reported excess expenditure (in his opinion) and reported scurrilous, damaging criticism to his superiors in London without ever placing Macquarie's explanations or justifications before the same authorities. Macquarie was damaged beyond redemption by the Bigge report, unjustly and unjustifiably, and as a result he personally and his health, suffered. He retired a shattered and broken man, without ever living to see the enormous contribution he had made to the fortunes of the colony.

"From the Records"

CHAPTER 27

BUILDING PROGRESS

From the Historical Records of New South Wales, we find from an attachment to an official Report to London, by Governor Hunter, a list of buildings completed between October 1796 and June 1797. This list includes:

1. Log prison in Parramatta 100 feet long x 24 feet wide
2. Log Prison in Sydney—80 feet long x 24 feet wide
3. Windmill in Sydney with a stone base
4. Granary in Sydney with a capacity of 10-12,000 bushels of wheat
5. Whitewashed & repaired all military barracks, storehouses, hospital,offices, houses, and all other brick buildings in Sydney
6. Widened and repaired the public roads
7. Built an additional storehouse in Sydney
8. Employed 24 men making bricks & tiles at Brickfield Hill and Rose Hill – producing over 25,000 bricks each week, but still not sufficient to meet the demand.
9. Built a windmill with stone base for Parramatta
10. 2 stockyards for Government livestock—Parramatta & Toongabbie
11. Rebuilt several Government boats
12. Prepared ground and sowed 300 acres of wheat
13. Divided the Town of Sydney into 4 sections, and placed a watchman in each
14. Built houses for the two assistant surgeons

15. New gaol—created from the 'Gaol Fund'—in Sydney.

In a Report by Phillip to Lord Sydney (Secretary for the Colonies) 9th July 1788, found in HRNSW—Vol 1 Part 2.

" . . . . 70-100 convicts are constantly employed on building the Military barracks."

Phillip enclosed the 'intended plan for the colony'. A house was being built for the Lt. Governor. The second Gov. House was to be built opposite the Lt Gov on a corner of Bridge Street adjacent to the Parade ground. Convict huts are located on both sides of the parade. An observatory was built at Dawes Point. The streets are 200 feet wide, and public buildings will be placed in situations that will allow for expansion. Only one house per allotment dimensioned 60 feet frontage and 150 feet depth.

I propose building barracks between the town area and the hospital. I shall next build a 'secure' storehouse and in future, all buildings shall be covered in shingles."

Further extracts from Phillip's reports demonstrate the progress as well as the difficulties of trying to create the new settlement:

Gov Phillip wrote to Lord Sydney on the 28th September 1788

"The officers now have separate houses. The former barracks are used as convict quarters. The barracks, officer's houses, hospital, storehouses for the military and for the public stores are going to last for many years. They are to be walled up with brick or stone, if limestone can be found in the country (it was found near Newcastle)" and again on 12th February 1790,

"All buildings are now of brick or stone. My house was only designed as three rooms but having as solid foundation, it was enlarged to 6 rooms and being well built should stand for many years."

Phillip wrote to Lord Grenville on the 4th March 1791

"The new stores in Sydney and Parramatta are of brick and tiled so there are no apprehensions of an accident from fire. A barracks is finished in Parramatta for 100 men; all the convicts are now in good huts."

We find that in 1800, King had determined to buy the house of retiring military officer Lt. Kent, and use the house for an Orphan lodging. He wrote to the Treasury in London looking for support on his having given Kent a Bill of Exchange in payment for the house. King justified the cost by 'valuing the replacement cost of the property.

The value of Lt Kent's house appeared to Gov. King as too expensive to acquire for an Orphan Home.

King wrote, "It is valued at 1,539 pound, made up of:

Bricklayers, plasterers, mason	568.02.3
Carpenters, Windows, shingles, nails, glue	818.00.0
Glaziers, glass putty	63.15.0
Locks, bolts, hinges, sashes, pulleys, etc	90.00.0
Total	£ 1539.17.3

Governor King

In 1800, King proposed to the Treasury Commissioners to build a new Orphan 'asylum' from revenue raised 'from the entry and clearance of ships, and a duty from landing articles for sale, together with revenue from fines, charitable donations. In the meantime, the Kent home would be bought for that purpose until sufficient revenue was accumulated to build a new building. This is the first recorded plan to raise local revenue other than Hunter's endeavours to replace the burnt down gaol with a new one funded by settler's subscriptions.

Public Buildings—Value at 13th August 1806

• Granary at Hawkesbury	600
• Church and school house at Hawkesbury	400
• Brewery at Parramatta	1,000
• Port Phillip works to-date	1,909

- Salt Works—Sydney   500
- Church—Sydney—Wk to-date   500
- Guard-house at Sydney   600
- Other works   1,000

(Gov. King assembled these figures from Commissary Accounts and other Public Documents

Governor Hunter

Governor Hunter (King's successor), writing in September 1800, stated that a great deal of repair work had been undertaken recently. He noted:

- that the large brick barracks in Parramatta (100 feet long) much decayed was now repaired, with an additional 60 feet to be added to serve as storage for wheat—there being no granary in the town.
- A strong windmill tower has been erected above Sydney town; the mill was finished and put to work
- A set of barracks, built of brick, built in Sydney between the hospitals and the surgeon's house
- A strong gaol of 80 feet in length, with separate cells for prisoners, built in Sydney
- Two log granaries—both 100 feet long for wheat and maize on Green Hills at Hawkesbury.
- Whitewashed two government houses, military barracks, store-houses, granaries, officers dwellings and all the public brick buildings—all for the purpose of preservation
- "Made good the public roads and repaired them at various times through the different parts of the settlement and threw bridges over the gullies"
- Converted the old Grose mill-house in Sydney into a good granary—72 feet by 21 feet wide, with two floors
- Built another stone windmill in Sydney 36 feet high
- Built a weatherboard store-house in Sydney with two wings, one wing being converted into a temporary church
- Built a blacksmith's workshop in Sydney with 6 forges

- Built a brick granary in Sydney of 100 feet by 22 feet wide with three floors. An addition was built of a further 70 feet for a kiln for drying grain
- Built an elegant church in Parramatta 100 feet by 44 feet with an extra room of 20 feet long for a council room
- Built a steeple tower in Sydney of brick for a town clock
- Built an apartment of brick in the yard of the old gaol for debtors containing three cells
- Built a stone house near the naval yard for the master boat-builder. On the same naval yard built a joiners and blacksmiths shop + sheds for repairing vessels, a storehouse, a steamer, a warders lodge and clerk's house.
- Built a stone gaol in Sydney
- Built a large and elegant Government House at Parramatta
- Built a new dispensary and hospital (with store attached)
- Prepared foundations for a new powder magazine in Sydney
- Fenced and paled in the military barracks and exercise ground in Sydney
- Paled in a cooperage beside the provision store at Sydney
- Paled in the public tanks and around the spring head at Sydney and cleaned them of filth.
- Built a Military Hospital and dispensary at Sydney
- Built an officers room at the Main Guard at Sydney
- Built sheds for Government boats
- Repaired a house for use as a School
- Erected nurses home in the hospital yard
- Built stockyards for the Government cattle

Buildings Required in the Colony

Gov. Hunter then submitted a list of Public Buildings he proposed to build, by utilising the convict labour readily available, but not overly willing:

a. **Water mill at Parramatta**
b. Church at Parramatta
c. Court-house at Parramatta
d. Church (made of stone) in Sydney

e. Gunpowder magazine—Windmill Hill, Sydney
f. 2 new stores + 1 guardhouse for Hawkesbury colony
g. Modify stone mill in Sydney to make it higher
h. Log Prison for Hawkesbury
i. Stockyard at Portland Place for Gov. cattle. Cut down 100 acres at Portland Place ready for buildings (near Parramatta)
j. Stockyard for Pendant Hills
k. Boat for coastal pursuit of deserters
l. Boat for carrying supply to and from Norfolk Island

Public Works in hand during 2nd Quarter 1803

a. Brick granary at Hawkesbury—101 feet x 25 feet wide; 23 feet high (3 floors)
b. Public School for boys
c. Public Brewery
d. 2 story Stone Barracks for convicts at Castle Hill—100 feet x 24 feet-
e. Stone Church at Sydney
f. Stone Gaol at Parramatta
g. Stone Bridge at Sydney Cove
h. Water-Mill at Sydney + associated dam
i. Enlarging the Wharfs, building vessels

Estimated values of completed work as of 1st July 1804 (Pound Sterling)
a. Colonial vessels and boats 2,250.00.0 b. Public Buildings 54,100.00.0

- Hospital   4,000
- Gov house   5,000
- Gaols   6,000
- Churches   7,000
- Granaries & Store-houses   12,000
- Barracks   8,000
- Mills   4,000
- Orphan houses   3,100
- Magazines   500
- Batteries   500
- Other   4,000

<u>Public Labour of Convicts as at 31st December 1805</u>

- Fort Phillip—Stonework—
- Building stone house over the salt pans + dwelling house + wharf
- House for Judge-Advocate
- Brick house for main guard + officers quarters
- Brick printing office
- Repairing store-houses, offices, soldiers barracks

Governor Lachlan Macquarie

At the time of Macquarie's arrival in the colony, at the head of his Regiment – the 73rd Dragoon Guards—Lt-Col Foveaux (as Acting Governor) wrote to Viscount Castlereagh on 9th November 1808 that a number of urgent repairs as well as new works were required in the colony.

"A substantial brick barracks (the Wynyard barracks) in Wynyard Square 180 feet in length and two stories high to accommodate the increased strength of the NSW Corps have been commenced, however, there is a present shortage of mechanics and labourers which does not allow me to carry on with new work or even the necessary repairs of existing buildings"

Foveaux wrote to Gov Macquarie, (shortly after Macquarie's arrival in the colony) on 27th February 1810 claiming to have completed the military barracks at Wynyard Square, together with officer's quarters and gaol, as well as the store granary at Parramatta and new brick convict barracks at Sydney; a new commissary store had been built and completed close to the waterside at Sydney Cove. Bridges were constructed which would afford land carriage and travelling in safety from Sydney town to other settlements."

In a communication from Macquarie to Castlereagh 8th March 1810, Macquarie wrote:

"I found the public stores almost empty of dry provisions—being occasioned by the flooding of the Hawkesbury River and the total ruination of all crops. There will be absolute necessity for building a new general hospital, the present one being in a ruinous state. Granaries and other public stores, as well as barracks for new male and female convicts are also very much wanted"

On the instruction of the British Treasury, in an attempt to make users of roads pay for their upkeep, Macquarie approved the installation of 'toll-bars' on roads between the Sydney markets and residential areas of Hawkesbury and Parramatta, for a period of seven years—the proceeds were to be used to improve and expand the public road system.

Macquarie appointed Samuel Marsden, Simeon Lord and Andrew Thompson to be trustees for a 'turnpike' between Sydney and Hawkesbury on the 31st March 1810. Marsden (because of an inability to work with the former convict—Lord-) declined to act and W.C. Wentworth was appointed in his place.

Macquarie declared, on that date—31st March 1810, "the cost of making the Sydney-Hawkesbury road would initially come from the Colonial Fund, which he had recently formed. Tolls would be used to repay the amount and to repair the road". (HRNSW) However Butlin writes in 'Forming a Colonial Economy' that the Colonial Fund was not formed until 1822.

Macquarie had announced on 11th August 1810 a new town plan for Sydney, with road widths of 50 feet including footpaths and set minimum building standards and construction regulations.

In the "Epitome of the Official History of NSW" (1883), it is recorded that "One of the most remarkable features of Governor Macquarie's time was the number of public buildings erected, the total reaching 250. Commissioner Bigge however, sets the accurate number at 73 (based on a submission from the Colonial Treasurer's office.

Macquarie returned to England in the middle of 1822. In defence of his policies, which had come under such severe, personalised attack from Bigge in his final report to the House of Commons, Macquarie wrote to Earl Bathurst, upon his arrival in London, as follows:

"I found the colony barely emerging from infantile imbecility, and suffering from various privations and disabilities; the country impenetrable beyond 40 miles from Sydney; agriculture in a yet languishing state; commerce in its early dawn; revenue unknown; threatened with famine; distracted by faction; the public buildings in a state of dilapidation and mouldering to decay; the population in general depressed poverty; no public credit nor private confidence; the morals of the great mass of the population in the lowest state of debasement and the religious worship almost totally neglected. Such was the state of New South Wales when I took charge of its administration in 1810. I left in February 1822, reaping incalculable advantages from my extensive and important discoveries in all directions, including my supposed insurmountable barrier called the Blue Mountains, to the westward of which are situated the fertile plains of Bathurst; and in all respects enjoying the state of private comfort and public prosperity.

John Thomas Bigge & the Bigge Report

From the Bigge Report Vol 3 P 101 (printed on 3rd July1823) we find that Bigge reported, "Such is the extent of demand for timber in the town of Sydney that timber is being used in an unseasoned state. The gangs of timber fellers working in Sydney and Pennant Hills were insufficient to meet the demand and 90,946 super feet of timber of all sorts was imported from Newcastle to Sydney valued at 1,136.16.6 pounds, in 1820. In addition New castle exported to Sydney 3,915 tons of coal and 42,800 bushels of lime. These were wholly expended upon the public works of Sydney . . .

I procured a list of buildings and works undertaken, in progress or completed since 1st February 1810. It appears (from this document) that 73 buildings of various kinds, including two vessels and several boats, have been commenced, and the greatest portion of them has been completed.

The most useful buildings on the list are:

- The Commissariat (King's) Store at Sydney
- St. Phillips Church at Sydney
- St. Matthews Church at Windsor
- Church at Liverpool

- Chapel at Castlereagh
- Improvement of Government Houses at Sydney and Parramatta
- Clearing of grounds contiguous to the Government Houses
- A Parsonage House at Sydney, Parramatta, Liverpool
- Military Barracks at Sydney
- Hospital at Parramatta
- Hospital at Windsor (formerly a brewery owned by Andrew Thompson)
- Hospital at Liverpool
- Military Hospital in Sydney
- Improvements to Lumber-Yard and Dockyard at Sydney
- Convict Barracks at Sydney and Parramatta
- Carters Barracks and gaol at Windsor
- Female Factory at Parramatta
- Light-house at Sydney South Head
- Houses for Judge-Advocate, Judge of Supreme Court
- Court-house, school-house and market house at Sydney,
- An asylum for the aged and infirm near Sydney
- Government stables at Sydney
- Fountain in Macquarie Place
- The Turnpike Gate
- Fort (Macquarie) at Bennelong Point
- Battery at Dawes Point
- 2 Windmills (built at Public Expense)—one at Garrison barracks, a second at the Domain.

At Newcastle the buildings erected were:

- Church
- Hospital
- Gaol
- Commandant House
- Surgeons Quarter
- Workhouse
- Blacksmiths Forge
- Pier
- Windmill
- Parsonage House "(Bigge Report)

Francis Greenway

M.H. Ellis in his biography of Francis Greenway records that a vitriolic and noisy opponent of Greenway was a Mr Henry Kitchen, who had become a 'voluntary and enthusiastic adviser to Bigge'. Kitchen, a 'sour rival of Greenway, was burning to revenge the ruin which Greenway had brought upon him' (Ellis)

Kitchen considered that the appropriateness of Greenway to be civil architect (Colonial Architect) could be judged from 'my opinion upon many of the principal works of his design and erection' (Ellis)

Kitchen pledged to examine the cost of the Government building program for Bigge, but decided that 'the obtaining of information as to what value any building or work has been to the Government is absolutely impossible'. (Ellis)

However "the assessment of the expense (apart from the Sydney hospital) is 922,857.13.11 pound." (Kitchen's estimate)

Kitchen's complaints were numerous and commenced with:

- The Government's energy was being devoted to the wrong sort of building eg only 2 months supply of grain can be stored instead of at least twelve months requirements.
- The sole attention of the Government is to employing the labours of a vast proportion of convicts (Here Kitchen was being mischievous, as this was the sole purpose of the colony and what the British Government was providing financial support to achieve.
- 'Enormous expense' and 'monopoly of useful labour' were the two main complaints of Kitchen, together with observations that the convicts were continually drunk, worked under a lax system and were lazy and unproductive
- Exorbitant and high expense can be demonstrated by the fact that one set of barracks for the convicts cost 36,000 pound. Thus, says Kitchen, the 'mere house rent of 700 convicts at the current rate

of interest (being 10%—the discount rate) is 3,600 pound per annum.'

- The workmanship was shoddy—the' barracks referred to above, had been completed for only two years but already needed re-shingling. The materials of the Macquarie lighthouse and Tower were extremely bad.

- The tollgate, says Kitchen, was an extravagantly expensive trifle. The commissariat stores in Parramatta were trembling to their fall. The female factory in Parramatta was defective in plan and building. The magazine at Fort Phillip was a 'trifling toy'. The church of St. James was too near adjacent buildings, and an obstruction to the thoroughfare.

Kitchen was not only criticising Greenway, but also the actions of Macquarie, who had chosen not to use Kitchen's drafting skills – probably for goods reason!

The following notes in relation to Greenway's architectural and Project Superintendence on behalf of Macquarie, in Sydney, are taken from the Greenway Papers A1451, as recorded in the M. H. Ellis biography of 'Francis Greenway' (Angus & Robertson—1949)

From an official copy of documents in the handwriting of Robert Crawford, Clerk to the Colonial Secretary between 1816 and 1820, it can be seen that Greenway credited himself with entitlement to a fee from the Colonial Treasury of 8% of the assessed value of all works done under his supervision by convict labour, including St. James' Church and other buildings which were only in the initial stages of erection when his estimate of what was owing to him was prepared.

Ellis records "It will be noted that his charges for travelling expenses for five buildings alone—Mr Marsden's parsonage, the Windsor Church. Liverpool Church. Parramatta Women's Factory and Parramatta Gaol—total 327 pound.

At the proper scale of 17 shillings each day, this works out at 387 days—a good indication of Greenway's unbusinesslike nature and the utter undependability of his mind when applied to practical matters. 387 days out of Sydney would have meant that two workdays each week between 1816 and 1820 were spent 'on the road' and away from his drawing table. 'Just not believable,' concludes Ellis.

Ellis further points out 'his figure does not square with his statement at the end of the document that 'it has cost me twenty pounds per annum travelling expenses more than I received from the Government'. Again, his estimate is in conflict with the fact that he was prepared, under Macquarie to accept 7 shillings per day travelling expenses before 1819, and that before the court in 1822 he affirmed under oath that he had spent more than 80 pounds more than the 32 pound he received before 1819.

However, the report by Greenway is of interest to us for reasons other than his poor business skills, and these relate to the listing he made for Commissioner Bigge of 'The measure and work done by Government men according to the plan and direction of F. H. Greenway, Acting Civil Architect, Assistant Engineer'

Construction Job Greenway's estimate of cost

Magazine Fort Phillip	1,240.
Macquarie Lighthouse	7,050
Hyde Park Barracks	30,600
Officer Quarters-Hyde Park	10,600
Fort Macquarie	21,000
Judge Field's House	4,800
Alts to Judge Advocate's Hse	600
Alts to Lumber Yd bldg	2,000
Alts to Dawes Battery	1,200
Windsor Church	5,600
Gov House Stables	9,000
Alts to Liverpool parsonage	520
Portico, Gov House, Parra	1,120
Alts to Orphan School, Syd	640
St. James Church, Hyde Pk	6,240
Court House	6,450
St.Andrews Church found'n	2,500
Market House Foundation	300

Alts to Gov House, Sydney	600
Dockyard & Offices	3,500
School Hse in Hyde Park	4,600

This list is most interesting not only because it outlines the range of new construction work undertaken by Macquarie, but also it gives us a basis of identifying direct costs, at that time, of materials and the skills available in the infant colony.

Greenway adds a personal observation to his list by stating " In carrying into effect these public buildings by government hands it has not cost Government one-half the sum it would have cost by the lower contract that would have been obtained, and the same buildings, five years ago, would have cost nearly double what is now calculated by contract."

In trying to explain his concept of changing building values, Greenway adds " The contracts carried into effect by me fore Government, but for the line of conduct pursued by me, would have cost Government double the money. The buildings carried into effect by my perseverance in getting better workmanship and materials, is of double value to Government, than they would otherwise would have been."

He then lists minor work completed by him such as:

- Plans for Mr Marsden's House at Parramatta
- Survey for the new General (Rum) Hospital
- Plans for the Windsor Church
- Plans for the Liverpool Church
- Plans for Judge Field's house
- Plans for Parramatta Female Factory
- Survey of Parramatta Bridge
- Survey of Sydney Gaol
- Measuring work by contractors at Sydney Gaol
- Plans for Windsor Court-house
- Plans for new toll-gate
- Plans for Obelisk in Macquarie Place
- Plans for fountain in Macquarie Place.

This latter list is the one Greenway presented to Commissioner Bigge in 1819 as part of a claim in which Greenway states he saved the Government (by not being paid for this work) over 11,000 pound.

However, Greenway helps us in another way—he sets down some cost figures for contract work at that time, and from these figures we can verify the Greenway estimate of how the Government stables should have cost only 2,500 pound, instead of the 9,000 pound Greenway quoted as the cost of contract labour and materials.

In the Appendix to the Bigge Report, we find an 'estimate ' by Greenway of the cost of replastering the interior of Chief Surgeon Sir John Jamison's house.

463 yards ceiling @2s 6d	= 57.17.6
1960 yards walls =	196.01.9
16 enriched blocks	16.0
1 centrepiece	10.0
Cornice 211.5 @2s 6d	26.08.9
30 @ 1s0d	4.10.0
TOTAL	286.03.3

The Greenway estimates for the Government Stables

16,686.5 days @ ave 1 shilling/day	834.06.6
(i.e. The No. of days worked by various 'mechanics')	
Bricks used—650,000 @10s/'000 (inc ctge)	325.00.0
Lime & loam required for brick laying	260.00.0
Scantling, nails, battens for 104 sq roofing	210.00.0
304 hundred lin.ft of joists & flrg brd	121.12.0
3 tons lead @46 pnd/ton	138.00.0
Cost to Finish Out (est.)	600.00.0
TOTAL	2,488.18.6

CHAPTER 28

THE PLAN FOR A SETTLEMENT

The development of the colony followed a relatively orderly and logical sequence, thwarted only temporarily by the continuing famine and understandable poor attitude of the convicts towards work. By the time Phillip returned to England, the basics had all been completed and everyone was housed, or at least had a roof over their head. Regular major storms over Sydney destroyed much of the early development, including the first gaol, giving residents and officials a good sign of just how flimsy the earliest method of construction was. The bowing and splitting of undried wood continued until a good stock of timber was available to the store and a 'Lumber Yard' was established at the top end of High Street (later George Street). The main role of the Lumber Yard was to organise the 'cutting crews' in the forests around the Town and haul the logs by hand to the Yard before sawing into useable lengths and placing on racks for proper drying. Until a stock of dried wood was built up, the Yard would release semi-green sawn timber, which after a time would split around the large nails as well as bow and bend. Eventually when the immediate need for lumber slowed the Yard built up its stocks and even made sawn timber available to private buyers.

It was only much later than the Lumber Yard found that Yellow, Blue and White Gum dried at the rate of about ½ inch per year, so the drying process is extremely slow. In addition, the whitewashing process acted as a sealer and kept as much moisture in the timber as it was meant to keep out. Being used to the cedar and birches found in England, the tools that came with the first fleet were both inadequate and inappropriate to meet the demands of local hardwoods and gum found around Sydney town.

Observations from Historians

F.L.W.Wood, a New Zealand Academic makes two statements of some extended interest, in his work "A Concise History of Australia"

It was the Greeks (2,350 years ago in 384-322BC) who first proved that the earth was round and who identified a 'terra Australis' – they were certain that it was vastly bigger than the lands and oceans that they knew. Their scientists knew that there was a temperate zone in the South, corresponding to that which they knew in the north. It followed, they thought, that there might well be a great southern continent where white men could live.

Wood surmised that when Cook and Banks returned to England their opinions were that—'if a colony was to be founded then it should be at New Zealand, Friendly Islands or the Sandwich Islands, but not at Botany Bay'. However, their journals were 'edited' and published by a Dr. Hawkesworth, who 'made considerable changes in what the two explorers had written, and in particular made Botany Bay seem a much better place for a colony than they had said it was.

In 1779, Banks recommended Botany Bay as a place to send convicts which is surprising when it is recalled that he wrote in his original journal that Botany Bay 'was the most barren place he had ever seen'. Possibly that is why he thought it may be a good place for convicts. He also thought that 'if the convicts worked hard, they could make the settlement self-supporting in a year'.

"If Phillip had great powers (he had been given despotic powers by the British Parliament) he also had great difficulties to overcome. Some of these were from the same Government that provided his powers – not enough tools had been sent out and many of these were bad. Then a party of marines had been sent to keep order. They refused to overseer the convicts and make them work. The greatest difficulty was that the great bulk of the people to be governed were convicts. It would be wrong to say that all of the convicts were lazy and wicked; however the bulk of the convicts were not suitable colonists and were unwilling to do more work than they could help. The barrenness of the land around Sydney Cove caused a problem of food production – there was no good grass for animals brought from South Africa. Crops were carefully sown but came to nothing. He scouted the harbour and inland areas and eventually discovered the fertile area of Rouse Hill where he started a second settlement. Then in June the next year (1789) he explored broken Bay and the Hawkesbury area – an untold value of fertile land.

The convicts were more use than the soldiers – freed convicts were given small parcels of land to cultivate for producing food, and it seemed that Australia was to become a country of small farmers.

Phillip opened up the Parramatta region in 1789 and determined to make it a rural urban location. It was clear that they could not make the colony self-sufficient in the two years foreseen, although the original food supply, brought with the first fleet was only intended to last two years.

The convicts came from a variety of backgrounds most having limited skills other than a nose for getting out of work. Poachers and Petty offenders headed the list but many future leaders were born of this initial misery. William Redfern became a leading doctor. Simon Lord a trader and magistrate; James Ruse an agriculturalist; Francis Greenway became the Colonial Architect. Wood believes that the convicts fared much better under the humane Macquarie than they did under a William Bligh or the stern Governor Arthur.

The happiness of a convict depended largely on the Governor's character with the policy of the Government towards rehabilitation being the task of the sentence and the conduct of the convict. Sometimes convicts flourished e.g. Greenway, Ruse, Lord, Redfern,

Phillip had carefully drawn up plans for the town of Sydney. All streets were to be 200 feet wide, straight and well laid out; public and private buildings were to be so placed and so built that Sydney would be a model town. But these plans were swept aside and the town grew up with narrow and criss-cross streets and badly planned buildings. By yielding to the interests of the military, Grose (the acting Governor after Phillip's departure,) made the officers wealthy, the colony self-supporting in food terms, an exporter of wool, furs etc and made the colony wealthy as well – a nation of traders and small farmers, at least until the rise of the pastoralists and their mighty sheep flocks, grazing the open western ranges.

The British Government could not allow the self-serving interests of the military officers to dominate the operations of the colony, but unfortunately put in place a weak, but honest and well-meaning Governor (John Hunter) who was not strong enough to deal with the selfish military. Wood states that practically every officer in the colony traded in rum. In September 1800 even the two chief medical officers had for sale about 4,500 gallons of spirits between them. Hunter failed and was recalled in disgrace. Both Hunter and his successor King were compatriots of Phillip and wanted to follow Phillip's initial plans for the colony.

The third Governor was Phillip King, who tried to strong-arm the military but who also failed to destroy the rum trade. The Irish revolt in 1804 was easily suppressed but the health of King failed him.

His successor was Captain Bligh, a career officer with a fierce reputation and a person much stronger than King. Again the military revolted when they determined that Bligh was going to have his way in policy matters and closing down the rum trade. He gave his enemies many chances to attack him until in 1807, Bligh quarrelled with McArthur, one of the richest and most enterprising residents in the colony. The officers chose rebellion and arrested Bligh in Government House, and the colony awaited his successor for almost two years – during which time the military resumed governing the colony.

Phillips ideas for town planning had been forgotten and the town moved into very bad condition. Phillips plans had been forgotten and the Sydney streets had grown up narrow and without plan. Macquarie set to work to make the streets straight and wide. By then most of the buildings were miserable – many being just wooden huts. Macquarie taught the colonists to build houses of brick and stone and set the good example by putting up fine public buildings. Many, including the British Government, thought he spent too much money on these buildings and this may have been so, however, when he arrived in the colony, many of the public buildings were falling to pieces for they had been built of green timber in the days of Phillip and the wood had warped. Macquarie's buildings were excellently planned, and gave accolades to Greenway as one of the best ever Australian architects. Under his guidance Sydney became more and more like a good-class English town, with well laid out streets and fine buildings. It was an orderly town for Macquarie successfully reorganized the police and made Sydney safer THAN London. Macquarie decided that the farmers would not flourish unless they could get their crops top market so he built roads from Sydney to all main settlements – Parramatta, Liverpool, Windsor and Bathurst. Altogether he built 276 miles of public roads.

In A History of the Colony from the Records, it is recorded that in 1794, acting-Governor Grose informed Chaplain Dundee that he had erected 'a church containing three hundred people, which contradicts what Revd Richard Johnson wrote to the Archbishop of Canterbury . . . 'there is no place for public worship except in a building put up at my own expense' . . . . and after six years of the colony this was the only sign of matters ecclesiastical' The Johnson chapel according to a Johnson letter to Dundee could accommodate 500 people and cost Johnson personally (subject to reimbursement) 67.12.11 ½ pound

Phillip reported to Lord Grenville on 4th March 1791, " Three stores, sufficient to contain two years provisions in Sydney and Rose Hill are built. They are brick and tile, so we no longer fear accidents from fire. A barrack is finished at Rose Hill for convicts and we are starting on barracks for officers and men in Sydney. Storehouses in Rose Hill –100 feet long x 24 feet wide, were begun and finished in November, a rainless month. In December the foundations for a storehouse in Sydney were laid. Although Phillip's dispatches show that a large proportion of the convict population was employed in erecting public buildings (there were only 450 men available for agriculture, including those given to officers and settlers, on 4th October, 1792) there is little reference in the dispatches to the building work undertaken. Collins diary records that a good deal was accomplished including two large storehouses at Parramatta together with a town hall and a hospital. The town hall included a market place, and the usual barracks for convicts and military men. Collins refers to brick huts for convicts and the construction at Sydney of a tank holding nearly 8,000 gallons of water. Collins records that the traditional barracks design was 100 feet by 24 feet, at each end were two apartments for officers, 75 feet x 18 feet, each apartment containing four rooms for their accommodation with a passage of 16 feet

In April 1794 shortly after Phillip departed the colony, Grose claimed that ' I have the satisfaction to say that military officers are all in good barracks. We have three large mills at work sand 2,962 acres of ground have been cleared.'

Contrary to thinking that development under Grose was haphazard, we learn that Grose's grand plan was 'to form a chain of farms between Sydney and Parramatta, the object being to bring the two centres of population into communication with each other. Most of the land grants issued in early 1793 after authority had been received to give land to all military officers were made in accordance with Grose' plan. HRA records that "the permission given to officers to hold lands had operated powerfully in favour of the colony. They were liberal in their employment of people to cultivate these lands; and such had been their exertions that it appeared many valuable acres had been cleared and cultivated and much food production had been completed" David Collins recorded in his diary of the same period that " the colony never wore so favourable an appearance as at this period; our public stores are filled with wholesome provisions; five ships are on the seas with additional supplies; and there is wheat enough in the ground to promise the realizing of many a golden dream; a rapidly increasing herd of livestock, new country gradually opening, and improving everywhere opening to us as it opens; with a spirit universally prevalent of cultivating it".

In 1788 the prefabricated canvas and timber house Phillip had brought on the first fleet and which he erected on the east side of Sydney cove had cost 125 pound and was the colony's first Government House.

During the 1790s stone footings and thresholds, whitewashed hessian ceilings and walls of grass reinforced mud and cow dung on timber frames were characteristics of early cottages. Measuring at least 7.3m x 3.6m, they were contained one room for sleeping and one room for eating.

In 1790 brick maker James Bloodworth completed the first dry store on the east side of Sydney Cove.

In 1793 Richard Johnson built the first chapel in the colony near the present day intersection of Hunter and Bligh Streets. It was 22.2m x 19.8m (built of wattle and daub) but burnt down in 1798 (arson)

In 1797, Governor Hunter began a building program of a new Government House, surgeon's quarters, a second St. Phillip's Church on Church Hill and a 45 m clock tower, which collapsed a few years later.

In 1798 the 2 storied Union Hotel was built of weatherboard exterior and plank lining on the inside

By 1800 tongue and grooved flooring, smooth lime-plastered internal walls and ceilings used cedar joinery and glazed windows were used on the typical house of free settlers.

In 1807 the Ebenezer Church was commenced, situated on the Hawkesbury River north of Windsor, it survives as the nation's oldest church.

On Dec 15, 1810 Macquarie set down the first building regulations. 'Dwellings were to be of brick or weatherboard with brick chimneys and shingle roofs

On 9th July 1788 Phillip submitted a town plan calling for 200 feet (60 m) streets, but the plan was not followed

In October 1788 the first bridge over the tank stream was construction (near the present corner of Pitt and Bridge Streets). David Collins recorded in his diary that a 'group of convicts were employed, rolling timber together to form a bridge'.

In 1794 Grose, acting Governor completed a bridge over the Parramatta River at Parramatta. It was washed away in the 1795 flood. He completed a road from Parramatta to Windsor.

In 1810 Macquarie introduced the turnpike or toll-road system for maintenance by contractors.

The 1881 stone arch bridge over the Tank Stream was crossed upon payment in spirits

In 1813, under Macquarie, the longest bridge in the colony was constructed being 200 feet long in 5 spans across South Creek at Windsor

In 1814 the Sydney—Liverpool road was opened and a cattle track was made down the Bulli Mountain north of Wollongong.

Before 1811 only three landing places existed around Sydney Cove: the Governor's Wharf on the east side of the cover; the Hospital Wharf adjacent to the market place and store house, and Robert Campbell's wharf further north on the western side. Neither the Hospital or Governor's wharves had any depth of water or any effective device for unloading equipment. In 1803 Campbell's wharf was described as being in good condition. Until Macquarie's arrival, all goods were unloaded at the rather dilapidated Hospital Wharf within easy reach of the market place, situated where the Cahill Expressway now passes over George Street. Its shallow water was only sufficient to accommodate the small craft coming down from Rose Hill with agricultural produce but Macquarie announced in 1811 a new wharf at Cockle Bay (now Darling Harbour). This new Market Street wharf was a factor in determining the geographic centre of the town and underpinned the new growth corridors of the settlement. In essence, the building of this important wharf created a new hub for the settlement and enabled Macquarie to establish a new system of streets extending back from Sydney Cove, with the new marketplace at the centre. The author of 'Seaport Sydney' observes that 'had this port facility been located elsewher5e on the peninsula, or even at Farm Cove, the future central city structure would have been established on very different lines.

a. The new wharf was to generate for Macquarie commercial development in the western sector of the town and became a determinant of urban development as well as heralding a period of significant and intensive growth in the Woolloomooloo area

b. Patrick White in Voss writes that 'the romance of the clipper sailing ship and the beautiful green-blue waters of the Sydney Cove at the heart of a delightful Georgian town ended with the impact of the great gold rushes on the economy.

M. H. Ellis wrote two detailed works by way of historical biographies of lives that for some significant period intertwined – the lives of Greenway & Macquarie ran together between 1814(when Greenway was transported to the Colony of New South Wales as a prisoner on a 14-year sentence. Macquarie had arrived in 1810 with the commission as Governor of the Colony replacing the disgraced Bligh. It was shortly after Greenway settled into his routine as convict that he showed signs of design experience and made observations on the ruinous condition of many Public Buildings. Macquarie, who was in the mindset of reform – keeping a growing number of convicts fully occupied in the colony, and himself wanting to leave a Macquarie 'stamp' on the development progress of the town – heard of Greenway's proposals, sent for him and requested some small designs to demonstrate his knowledge and art.

Coghlan (T.A. Coghlan –"Labour & industry in Australia") argues that the current wage rates in July 1800 were:

Felling, burning & breaking up 1 acre   = 5.03.0
Reaping wheat per acre   = 0.13.11
Sawing 100 feet of plank   =1.01.3
Day labour – no board   = 5.0

Macquarie, Governor from December 1809, continued the rates existing at that time, but there is no doubt that certain employers paid premiums for good labour. The premium payers were usually small settlers who had no assigned convicts. This practice was given in evidence before the Select Committee of the House of Commons in 1812. John Palmer who was Commissary-General for the colony until the arrival of Macquarie gave evidence that the lowest weekly wage was 24s, but skills brought a premium as well as scarcity of good labour – a shipwright could earn 10-s per day in 1808. Another witness stated that blacksmiths, carpenters, tailors and shoemakers could early 5 pound per day

Coghlan opines that Macquarie was a great builder. His roads, bridges, churches, public buildings required for their construction large numbers of labourers and he allowed assignment of convicts only on a small scale. Under Macquarie, an assigned servant/convicts whole time again became his masters as Phillip had contemplated, so the wage rates changed once more. The summary of official wages payments is:

Assigned servants not working after 3 pm:—no wages

Assigned servants working all day fully found	-7 pnd p.a.
Farm servants fully found	-10 pnd p.a.
Day labourers	-4s per day
Mechanics	-5s per day
Caulkers	-6s per day
Shoemakers	-5 s per day

From "An Economic History of Australia" by E.O Shann, we learn that:

"Macquarie's general order after a first tour of the settlements upbraided his subjects for their unsuitable houses, the absence of barns and their miserable clothing—a lack of standards bespeaking the despair of exiles. In spite of directions that 'no public buildings whatsoever, will be commenced unless indispensable to the public service'. The bills drawn by Macquarie for building materials soon mounted up:

25,000 pound	1818
16,738	1809
59,738	1810
71,085	1811
30869 (4 months)	1813
75,000	1815

Macquarie's defence was simple ' no-one else, in any of H.M colonies had been more rigidly vigilant and watchful of public expenditure of money, provisions and stores belonging to the crown'. Greenway won support by offering to 'erect more and better buildings in four years'. Greenway's best buildings included; Hyde Park Barracks; St. James Church, Sydney; St. Matthews, Windsor;

Burdekin House in Macquarie Street, and Subiaco in Rydalmere. He worked in a style 'simple and stately, although of humble execution'.

a. During the post-war period after 1813, a big surge of convicts arrived in the colony. The post Napoleonic era in Britain brought widespread industrial unrest and increased crime, thus the increase in the transportation program of prisoners to Botany Bay. From the high expenditure on public buildings, which had offended the cash-strapped Treasury, another form of public works commenced, enabling these convicts to be put to gainful work. Exploration over the Blue Mountains opened up large quantities of grazing land, which required access roads, clearing, sheep and cattle shepherding, and much assigned convict labour. Macquarie sanctioned a 'road ', a cart track according to Evans, over the Mountains to be made by convicts who, upon completion, would receive no remuneration but would receive their freedom. Macquarie decided that making bridges and permanent roads was ' one of the first steps in improving a country'. Any cost to an empty British treasury was a burden and Liverpool wrote to Macquarie that 'if the spirit duties were spent on roads, they could not be used to lessen the burden of sending and maintaining the convicts'. He (Liverpool) argued that 'if the free settlers could not pay for the roads, this proved the colony was not advanced enough to need them'. A new Secretary of State had sanctioned other turnpike (toll) roads on the ground that tolls would recoup the expense, but bridled at offering free roads whilst the Treasury is paying 100,000 pounds per annum for the support of the colony.

The Treasury thought Macquarie was out of control. With his excessive spending. However the circumstances required Macquarie's touch. The colony was growing; the colony had accepted 16,493 convicts between 1810 and 1820. 11,250 of who arrived between 1816 and 1820. Colonial revenues from import and port duties had increased from 10,000 in 1810 to 125,884 in 1820. But Macquarie spent them without much caution – 3,005 in 1811, 6,920 in 1815 and 16,486 in 1819 (all values are in pounds sterling). Floods along the Hawkesbury River had cost the colony much in lost production and thrown many assigned convicts back on

Government rations. The colony's bills drawn on Treasury for rations and stores had amounted to 227,000 in 1814 and 240,0000 in 1817

The Bigge Report

Bigge was initially complimentary in his report about the grants of land and the road-widening program commenced by Macquarie. He wrote " The regulations for building in the town of Sydney were promulgated by Governor Macquarie, by public order, on 18th August, 1810. Previous to that period very little attention had been paid to the regular progress or dimensions of town lots, or to the formation of streets. Much improvement was considered necessary and has been taken during this Governor's period in office. It was found necessary to purchase individual houses that obstructed improvement, or projected beyond the regular lines of the street. Payments had been made from the Police Fund."

Bigge observed that 'purchasing' of materials was done with great economy. (Goods were not usually purchased by contract, but from sellers who had large stocks on hand and who would negotiate a reasonable price). The Superintendent of Works was held responsible by Bigge, in the Report, for the alarming theft of tools from worksites. This was because, thought Bigge, that there were too many worksites operating at the same time with insufficient supervisors to attend them. It is more likely that the Superintendent was aware of both the problem and the solution but was being pushed by an impatient Macquarie.

Another continuing result of Macquarie's impatience, observed by Bigge, 'was the unseasoned state of the timber. Such was the demand for it in Sydney, and the rate of consumption, that the efforts of the numerous gangs of labourers at Newcastle and Pennant Hills were insufficient to meet it. In 1819 there appears to have been exported from Newcastle to Sydney 90,946 super feet of timber (of all sorts), valued at 1,1436.16.6 pound; in 1820 the export was 102,256 super feet valued at 1278.04.0 and 26,461 s.ft of plank valued at 641.08.6.

Newcastle at the same time exported to Sydney, 3,915 tons of coal and 42,800 bushels of lime. These were wholly expended upon public works in Sydney. It appears that, writes Bigge, 73 buildings of various kinds, including two vessels and several boats have been commenced since February 1, 1810 and that the greatest proportion have been completed I beg leave to state that the most useful buildings on this list are:

a. The King's Store (Commissariat) in Sydney
b. St. Phillips Church, Sydney
c. Windsor Church
d. Liverpool Church
e. Chapel at Castlereagh
f. Government House at Sydney
g. Government House at Parramatta
h. Clearing of grounds contiguous to these houses
i. A parsonage –house at Sydney, Liverpool, and Parramatta
j. Military Barracks at Sydney
k. Hospital at Parramatta
l. Military Hospital in Sydney
m. Dockyard in Sydney
n. Lumberyard in Sydney
o. Convict Barracks at Sydney
p. Convict Barracks at Parramatta
q. Carters Barrack & Gaol at Windsor
r. Female Factory at Parramatta
s. Lime-kiln at Bennelong's Point
t. Light-house on South Head
u. Enclosure around Burial Ground at Sydney
v. Residence for the Judge-advocate
w. Residence for Judge of Supreme Court
x. Court-house in Sydney
y. School-house in Hyde Park
z. New Market House
aa. Asylum for aged and infirm at Sydney

(This list comprises 27 of Bigge's 73. The full list is in the Bigge papers, but is not part of his report, even as an appendix. He listed items that were erected and constructed in Newcastle (11), Hobart (8) and George Town (7). But we are not advised if the Macquarie list of 73 includes items built in other sections of the colony. If this were to be so, then 53 of the 73 have been accounted for, but it is surprising that there are not more items for Windsor or the Hawkesbury (Castlereagh).

Bigge spoke highly of Greenway in his report 'I have spoken of the valuable services of Mr. Greenway, as far as they were employed in the public buildings I have mentioned, and the benefits derived from those services have been very conspicuous. Mr. Greenway's architectural skill has been the means of introducing into the buildings of the colony greater celerity and better taste than has previously prevailed.'

In relation to the General Hospital in Sydney – the 'Rum' Hospital – its foundations had failed and made it unoccupiable – Bigge claimed the pillars were made of very weak stone and the roof structure was poorly designed. He observes 'since there were no workmen in the colony who could construct a two story building of these dimensions it should not have been undertaken. However it should be remembered that the 'Rum' Hospital was a trade-off with Darcy Wentworth and two others for a permit to import 40,000 gallons of spirits without duty into the colony. The building was a gift in return. Macquarie oversaw the design of the building and was probably very demanding in what he wanted in exchange for such a bounty as duty free spirits.

Bigge then goes on to list the extravagances in the Macquarie building program (for so young a colony! states Bigge)

a. The Government Stables in Sydney
b. Fountain and Obelisk in Macquarie Place
c. The turn-pike gate
d. Fort Macquarie at Bennelong Point
e. Battery at Dawes Point

Bigge concludes 'although the general expense incurred in erecting public buildings in New South Wales is lessened by the employment of convicts in that labour, the materials might be used to other advantage and using local funds to the purchase of them, instead of defraying the cost of keeping, clothing and feeding the prisoners by Treasury Funds.

If a defence was to be made of the Macquarie policy, it could include these points.

The building program put many many convicts to gainful work who otherwise might have reengaged in more criminal activities

The contracting of material supplies created a trading environment, which was supporting early merchants (free men).

Since all non-locally produced materials were brought in from England then it created trade, shipping etc from England and employment 9in England. The colony was only marginally self-sufficient in food production and by putting work on the commissariat, the public works department, the engineers and architects; food production was the concentration of the agricultural sector, which had grown rapidly under Macquarie. The Macquarie program trained many convicts in skills which they could successfully and gainfully use after their release.

The Bigge bottom line was always the amount of Treasury expenditure in the colony. " The estimate of expenditure (he wrote) for the year ending 24th December, 1821 amounted to 189,008 pound, of which rations for the military, civil officers and convicts is 143,370 pound". As we have seen, the building material content of this sum was less than 20,000. Such a small cost with such great flow-on benefits to try to eliminate.

In 'A Land Half Won' by Geoffrey Blainey, we find he writes, that:

a. *"The east coast of Australia slipped into favour as a likely place of exile for the multiplying inhabitants of British gaols and hulks. As a penal colony in Australia would attract few free settlers in its first few years, a new system of transportation was necessary if Australia was chosen. The expense of transporting the prisoners, guarding and employing them required a compensating balance, naval or commercial. This came by way of any settlement at Botany Bay could off the advantage of expanding English commerce – English ships could call into Botany Bay on their voyage to China for tea, or on their way to trading fur seals in North America. Whaling was also a possibility. Another vital reward of a settlement on the east coast was a supply of two strategic materials; timber for ships' masts and flax for the making of ships' ropes and sails.*

- *Blainey had argued in his work 'The Tyranny of Distance' that ' the east coast was settled: to provide Britain with vital naval raw materials and to provide a useful place for exile of criminals. To these two main reasons could be added a third;*

- *Britain's need for a port of call on the new trade routes in the Pacific and Indian Oceans.*

- *Delusions of climate (because of Bank's misrepresentation of the local climate) must be regarded as a fourth vital cause of the settlement—in 1770 Banks had seen the country at its most flourishing; he found the soil rich and lush meadows. In 1788, the soil was found to be sandy and poor, the clearing of tree-stumps and roots was heavy work, and the tools and implements were meager. The soft-grained European wheat was not suited. The ideal season for planting had to be learned by trial and error. The challenges of starvation in 1789 and 1790 had not been planned for. Fish were expected to be a vital food. The settlement lacked suitable timbers to build fishing boats, and the English fishing techniques were not suitable. Aborigines and the colonists competed for fish in the same calm harbour. Meat could not be eaten until the breeding stock multiplied.*

CHAPTER 29

A COLONIAL EXPERIMENT
(Understanding the Colonial Economy)

The Rural Economy

    g.   Decentralization—growing towns and regions
    h.   Development of Agriculture

The Trade Economy

    i.   Trade & Exports
    j.   Transportation – river, road, rail
    k.   Communications

Remaining British

    l.   Method of control by the British Government
    m. Steps Leading to Self-government

a Colonial Experiment

(Understanding the Colonial Economy)

Introduction

Before an understanding can be commenced of the colonial economy we need to understand the background to this colonial experiment.

By the middle of the 1700s, Britain had progressed past the phase of reducing its prison numbers by hanging a substantial number of prisoners. Butlin, N.G. in 'Forming a Colonial Economy' makes the submission that during much of the 18th century, 'few criminals were apprehended and those that were caught and judged guilty were dealt with severely'. Apprehension came about firstly by the formation of a vigilante group by employers in an endeavour to restrict theft by employees, and secondly, by (in London) the Bow Street runners, and thirdly by implementation of The Criminal Law Act of 1826, which established a system of public payments of expenses of litigation and being a 'thief taker', leading to a conviction. Between apprehension and indictment, accused prisoners were held in privately operated lockups. There (according to Butlin) 'they faced squalor, disease and malnutrition' until facing summary punishment in absentia by magistrates or trial by open jury before a judge. As the reluctance to execute grew during the 1700s, a range of crimes was punished through transportation. Hanging was now limited to capital crimes whilst lesser crimes were punished by transportation for 7 to 14 years, if not life. That is not to say that the prisoners, having satisfied their punishment, were welcomed to return to England. Many forms of dissuasion were used to stop their return. This legal system contributed to a substantial number of prisoners facing transportation, and to a lesser extent, fostered the concept of emigration to the colonies. Shaw, A.G.L. in his 1966 study of 'Convicts and the Colonies' estimates that in the first half of the 18th century, over 2,000 prisoners were executed by hanging each year. By the second half, he estimates that less than 200 were hanged each year, whilst transportations to the American plantations had grown to substantial numbers of over 5,000 per annum. Butlin concludes that of those persons indicted, on average approx. 70% were convicted and of those convicted an average of 20% were transported.

Transportation to the American colonies had worked well even if it was cut short by the American War of Independence. Prisoners, having been physically transported to the new colony, were made available for sale to plantation owners—they would pay from 8 to 25 pound per worker, according to his or her usefulness. In this way, the British Government, received a small monetary reimbursement for their costs of handling the prisoners to-date and in addition were relieved of the responsibility of maintaining them into the future.

When this move towards independence from the British caught on and gained momentum, this transportation program ceased and the British gaols began, once again, to overflow. The British vainly sought alternatives and considered their existing African colonies but the prevalence of disease, and the insufferable heat turned the official minds to other considerations. They turned their minds, with the gentle and persuasive assistance of Sir Joseph Banks, to the great southland –Terra Australis.

A New Zealand academic, F.L.W. Wood, writing (1935) a 'Concise History of Australia' concludes that the

'Origins of man's beliefs in Terra Australis lay in the teachings of Greek scientists who lived more than 2,000 years ago. Men like Aristotle (382-322BC) had proved that the earth was round . . . and it seemed reasonable to think that the unknown regions of the world would be partly land and partly sea. Scientists of that time were aware that there was a temperate zone in the south, corresponding to that which they knew in the north. It followed that there might well be a great Southern continent where white men could live'.

Wood's also writes that the Dutch had come across the west coast of Cape York Peninsula in March 1606 whilst, exploring New Guinea for ' a great store of gold'. The discovery of another part of the western Australian coast was by accident. Woods explains that 'when the Dutch first came to the East Indies (1595) they followed the same track as the Portuguese. They sailed up the coast to Madagascar and thence to India or Java. But the winds were not always reliable and the route was studded with over 12,700 islands. In 1611, Henrik Brouwer tried a different route. He sailed 4,000 miles due east after leaving the Cape of Good Hope and then turned north to the East Indies. It was easy for a captain to sail too far east before making his turn north and this is what happened to Dirck Hartog in 1616.

So some little information was known to the seafarers of 1760, such as Cook, on his first venture of discovery into the southern seas. Leaving New Zealand at the end of March 1770, Cook decided to return home by the East Indies and on 20th April, 1770, sighted land at what is now Point Hicks on the east coast of Australia. Cook stayed in Botany Bay for 8 days, endeavoring to find wood and water. Banks was especially interested to find many plants previously unknown to science. According to Banks it was a botanists' paradise, and it was Cook's decision to change the name of their safe harbour from Stingray May to Botany Bay, in honour of Banks' discoveries. Leaving this Bay in May 1770, Cook sailed past Port Jackson and Broken Bay, not bothering to investigate.

In July 1771 Cook brought news of his discovery of New South Wales. The journals of Cook and Banks were edited and published by Dr. Hawkesworth, and according to Woods 'he made considerable changes in what Banks and Cook had written, and in particular he made Botany

Bay sound a much better place for a colony than their verbal reports said it was. Cook's recommendations would have been, if asked, New Zealand o the Friendly Islands – not Botany Bay'.

The concept of transportation was simple. After the death penalty, it was considered to be the severest penalty inflicted. At the same time, transportation could help a new country to grow up; and after his time was expired, the emancipee would become a citizen of that new country and have a chance to start life again. Over a thousand prisoners had been transported to the American colony each year until 1775, but the numbers in English gaols since the American War was increasing so greatly (at well over 1,000 per year) that the official expectations for any new transportation program would be significantly higher. These prisoners were kept in prison and in hulks tethered in mid-stream on the Thames River. Both holdings soon became over-full, and the government looked for a new place to send them. In 1779, Banks suggested Botany Bay—even though Banks had reported initially that 'it was the most barren place he had ever seen'. It must have been just right for a penal settlement, especially since 'the natives were few and cowardly. Banks concluded that 'if they did work hard, they could make the settlement self-supporting in a year'. It was Matra that determined the related cost of transporting to the southern lands rather than the Americas. Matra reported to the House of Commons Committee into revising transportation matters, in 1785, that the additional cost of food and clothing for the new colony would be 30,000 pound extra. A visit to Africa found that there was no suitable site for a colony and so the committee determined to accept Bank's advice to adopt Botany Bay in New South Wales as the site for a new penal settlement. Captain Arthur Phillip R.N. was chosen to take the First Fleet, of convicts, stores and military personnel, and the few selected civil personnel, such as the surgeon, judge, surveyor etc.

So the new colony of Botany Bay in New South Wales was to be established by early 1788, as a penal settlement for transportees, whose crimes to our present day observation would be considered minimal, since capital punishment had already taken the lives of the murderers and the most violent former members of society.

Our present goal is to examine and understand the formation of the new colony, mainly from an economic standpoint. There were a number of key economic events that fostered development and diversity within the settlement and these will be considered firstly. The second tier of events can then be considered under the broad headings of finance, trade, education, agriculture and building, construction and transport.

Obviously the history of early Australia is bound integrally with economic factors.

- Transportation brought over 160,000 men and women into the colony between 1788 and 1840.
- Free immigrants followed for reasons of married partners to many of the convicts; sponsored and paid immigrants; investment in the colony
- British Investment in the colony was substantial, and London-based merchant banks saw opportunities to obtain a quick return on their money
- The Discovery of Gold reflected a new and better side of the local economy and attracted development, investment and population
- Exploration meant the opening of new pastoral lands, the commencement of new settlements but also a new role for the Legislative Council to make new roads, survey new lands, establish laws for crown land leasing and later sale and the continuing demand for much greater revenue, to meet the growing needs of the settlers.
- Railways brought decentralization, cheaper goods to both country and city and the opportunity of farm produce reaching the cities in good condition.
- Export trade was encouraged and soon exports grew and almost matched the continuous need for imports. Current account was most usually in deficit but exports grew into a major economic stimulus.
- The sale of crown land meant that the British Government achieved the goal of self-sufficiency for the colony especially in slowing the annual support payments.
- Education became an important economic event. During the first 30 years of the colony, illiteracy ran about 70% with few

convicts being able to read or write After even the most basic stage of an education program being introduced by the Rev'd Richard Johnson, the illiteracy rate dropped to about 25%. The implications are clear that in an emerging colony and one under great development, literacy amongst the working class makes a special contribution.

- Self-government in 1852 meant an end to the British payment of people on the civil list but also the foregoing of revenue from the sale of crown lands. The British Government under self-government for the colonies in Australia abdicated all payments to the colony and claims on revenue.
- Although it was challenged in its day by Commissioner J.T. Bigge, the most important development in the first25 years of the economy was the impetus shown by the Macquarie construction program. The 76 new buildings constructed between 1810 and 1821 set firm foundations for future growth. Not only did Macquarie spend over 900,000 pound on building materials, he gainfully employed the growing number of convicts brought to the colony; quickly took many off the Commissary support list, created jobs, encouraged exports of wool, furs, grain, coal and timber. He supported local ventures into building materials; a timber harvesting and sawing industry, local manufacture of nails, hinges, bricks, tiles and only a little later stone and blocks. Macquarie's contribution has been underestimated as has been the 'opportunity' cost benefits to the British Government and its people. Although it is claimed that British 'invested' many millions of pounds into the colony, they saved, on account of using the colony as a penal settlement over 140 million pounds in building prisons, feeding, guarding and putting prisoners to work in their own country.

So, it is important in an understanding of our colonial history to place all these economic events into perspective, and to start we'll consider the establishing of the colonial economy.

Before we discuss these main events further let us review the progress Phillip made in the earliest days of the settlement.

Establishing the Early Economy

Phillip's change of location

Governor Phillip's first major decision was to change the projected located of the settlement from Botany Bay to Port Jackson. Upon his arrival with his Fleet, Phillip found the barren land first described by Banks, but even worse, a lacking of fresh water. He took his small ship around through the entrance to Port Jackson and was immediately stunned by the magnificent harbour appearing before him. Using row boats for closer inspection he decided that Manley Cove (aptly named because of the proud bearing of the native men his crew had seen on the shore.

Setting up at Sydney Cove

Before the all the anchored ships could be moved from Botany Bay to Port Jackson, Phillip had again changed his mind, and decided on settling on Sydney Cove. A gentle slope to the waters edge; good sized trees in the immediate area, large rocks on the western side of the cove suitable for a fortress in case of attack by the French navy; fresh water from a stream coming into the Cove, and a large rock overhand on the eastern side to afford some shelter from storms.

Phillip was not to learn until a few days later that there was no depth to the soil and nothing would be grown at the cove. On the good side, it was a safe mooring for his fleet and stores and passengers could be disembarked safely by rowboats, and unloaded onto the beach, without damaging the boats or their cargo.

David Collins in his diary 'Account of the English Colony in New South Wales' records the first days of the settlement.

"The disembarkation of the troops and convicts took place from the day after (27th January) the governor and officers raised the flag and drank the health of his Majesty, and success to the new colony (26th January), until the whole were landed. The confusion that ensued will not be wondered at; when it is considered that every man stepped from the boat literally into a wood. Parties of people were everywhere heard and seen variously employed; some clearing ground for the different encampments; others in pitching tents, or bringing up such stores as were more immediately wanted, and the original spot recently the abode of silence and tranquility was now changed to that of noise, clamour and confusion; but after a time order gradually prevailed every where."

The cove had been named Sydney as a compliment to the principal secretary of state for the home department. The east side of the cove (now Bennelong Point) contained the portable canvas house brought for the governor, and the tents of a small quantity of convicts. The marines were camped at the head of the cove near the stream, and on the West side, were placed the main body of convicts, plus tents for the sick. When the women were finally disembarked on the 6th February, there were a total of 1030 persons in the settlement. A small farming area had been cleared behind the governor's canvas house, and there as Collins records " we soon had the satisfaction of seeing the grape, the fig, the orange, the pear, and the apple taking root and establishing themselves in the New World. The livestock, consisting of 'one bull, one bull-calf, one stallion, three mares and three colts', having depastured their first small area on the east point of the cove, were moved to the head of the adjoining cove and allowed to graze.

Phillip's difficulties

Although Phillip had extensive powers, he also had great obstacles to overcome, if he were to succeed in his mission. For example he had insufficient tools and of those that had been provided many were bad. Phillip wrote that 'they were as bad as those sold to the Negroes of Africa'. His next problem was the attitude of the party of marines sent with Phillip. Most refused to give him any help, for they said it was not part of their duty as soldiers to supervise convicts and make them work. Although it would be incorrect to claim that all the transported convicts were lazy and wicked, men of all types had been transported and as Roberts discovered, the bulk of them were not suitable colonists and were unwilling to do more work than they could avoid.

Phillip's powers

Once the camps had been erected in Sydney Cove, Phillip summoned the whole population before him and read aloud the official documents establishing the colony. Phillip was appointed governor of the whole east coast and the nearby islands of the Pacific. England was not yet claiming the western part of Australia, which had been found by the Dutch. Phillip's rule was to be not unlike that of a despot. He had the powers of Commander-in-chief, Prime Minister and Parliament. He could pardon criminals, make land grants, make laws, and even be the judge himself. No one had the right to disobey his orders

The first farming

Phillip's difficulties were greatly increased by the barrenness of the land around Sydney Cove. A good choice for unloading ships, and access to fresh water, but the land was incapable of growing the necessary vegetables. Even good grass was hard to find to feed the livestock brought from South Africa, and most of them died. Crops were carefully sown, but came to nothing. Phillip, who had been a farmer, quickly decided that much better land had to be found. He led little parties through thick bush or in rowboats around the harbour and even broken Bay and in April, 1788 he found the good land he was seeking at the head of the harbour in an area he named Rose Hill (Parramatta). In June, whilst rowing around Broken Bay he found the mouth of the Hawkesbury and determined that fertile land of untold value was available in the future.

Phillip had found at least two of the patches of good soil that Joseph Banks had predicted would be available to the settlers.

Phillip by his actions laid a firm foundation for the colony to grow and even prosper. Phillip was aware of the bright future for the colony and made his thoughts known to the British Colonial Secretaries, but his immediate problem was a coming shortage of food. The second fleet with its supply ships had not arrived as planned, and almost in desperation, Phillip sent Hunter off to open up Norfolk Island with a little more than half the convicts. The land was supposed to be fertile on the Island, Hunter was a good organizer and leader, and in the right circumstances this group should not only survive and become self-sufficient long before the Sydney group would be, but if the exercise went well, it was possible that the Island could provide a surplus of food for shipment back to Sydney.

Let us return temporarily to the special events that grew the colony and made it attractive for investment and migration.

CHAPTER 30

THE GRIM ARMADA OF THE SECOND FLEET

Michael Flynn in his work 'The Second Fleet' records the bad conditions imposed on over the 1,000 convicts that made up the 2nd Fleet from Britain to Australia.

Here are three extracts:

"The Surprize was to reach Sydney Cove on 26th June, 1790, 59 days after leaving the Cape, with the other two ships, the Neptune and Scarborough, arriving two days later. The voyage was a nightmare for the convicts on board, especially those of the Neptune. Heavy gales and high seas lashed the ships, interrupting the cooking of food, preventing exercise on the deck, and sending water cascading through the compartments of sickening convicts. They were, at time, up to their middle in water for extended times. The southern winter brought very cold temperatures. In addition to the scurvy, which continued to spread, a violent epidemical fever broke out in the Neptune. It was almost certainly the fever, which John Macarthur contracted at the Cape everyone being affected to a more or less degree, wrote Captain Trail. "

"By the time the ships reached Sydney 267 of the approx 1006 convicts on the three ships were dead; a staggering rate of 26.5%. The Neptune had lost 158 out of 502 or 31%, with a further 269 hospitalised upon arrival. The Scarborough lost 73 out of 259 or 28%, and the Surprize lost 37 out of 256 or 14% with 126 hospitalised. These figures suggest that less than 250 out of the original 1006 arrived in any degree of health."

"The Reverend Johnson witnessed the terrible scene at the Port of Sydney upon arrival. He wrote" The landing of these people was truly affecting and shocking:—great numbers were not able to walk, nor to move hand or foot; and, such were slung over the ship's side in the same manner as a cask or box. Upon being brought into the fresh air, some fainted, some died in the deck, and others died in the boat before they reached shore. When they came on shore many were unable to walk or stand or stir themselves in the least, hence some were led by others. Some creeped upon their hands and knees and some were carried upon the backs of others."

CHAPTER 31

THE CONSEQUENCES OF TRANSPORTATION TO THE COLONY OF NEW SOUTH WALES

a. Economic-Consequences:

During the time that the convicts were the principal source of labour for government purposes and private enterprise, the consequences of transportation appeared to be measurable. One of the indirect consequences was the 'opportunity' cost to both Britain and the Colony of the transportation program. The Molesworth Committee in 1838 stated that it was their definitive opinion that 'on the value of transported labor, the British Government could only justify its continuation as an obstacle to economic growth. An advocate* of transportation, some twelve years later produced figures to show that just the opposite was true. (*Archibald Atchison—Crime and Transportation—London 1850). He concluded that there were many benefits and gains to come from continuing the transportation program.

b. Social Consequences:

The transfer of so many male convicts led, by 1841, to 'a dearth of females', a situation named as alarming by Ralph Mansfield 'Analytical view of the census of 1841 in New South Wales'—published in 1841. Other social consequences included the spread of illiterate persons and children for number of years. Illiteracy led to poverty; poverty led to crime and abandonment of children and one parent homes. The Orphan home in Sydney tried to cater for many of the nearly 1,000 orphaned or abandoned children in Sydney before 1810.

c. Political Consequences:

The nature of the penal settlement required a 'peculiar form of government'. The British laws adopted wholesale by Governor Phillip and successive Governors and Justices needed modification if it was to be suitable for the climate of the colonies.

The Molesworth Committee Report—Some Conclusions

(British Parliamentary Reports 1838)

"Some persons contend that the pecuniary interests of the penal Colony require the continuation of transportation; that as the extraordinary commercial prosperity of these colonies was occasioned by the constant supply of convict labor, if that supply be cut off the colonies would be ruined, from great wealth they would be reduced to great poverty; and that this change in the fortune of inhabitants, especially if it were sudden, would necessarily produce the worst moral effects upon their character, and still further demoralize the already demoralized.

"The extraordinary wealth of these colonies was occasioned by the regular and increasing supply of convict laborers. The convicts were assigned to settlers as slaves, they were forced to work in combination, and raised more produce than they could consume; for this surplus produce Government provided a market, by maintaining military and convict establishments, which have cost this country above 7,000,000 pound of the public money.

"Labor is in short supply whilst capital has amazingly increased. The flocks of sheep are double the size they ought to be; a vast number perish for want of care; labor must be furnished from sources, other than convicts, if the colonies are to continue to flourish"

Analysing the Benefits to the United Kingdom

Although the consequences of transportation of British convicts to the Colony of New South Wales may have been both economic and social, the consequences of transportation of British convicts out of the United Kingdom are numerous and quantifiable.

The essential question becomes—Would the United Kingdom have pursued a Colonial expansion policy if there had not been a need to transfer convicts from the Americas elsewhere?

The answer is of course, a simple—'yes'. The trade, defense, and colonization policies, in place, and under discussion, made territorial acquisition essential. The British Navy needed supplies of masts and spars to maintain its fleet in sailing condition. The British Trade tsars wanted to see further expansion, after a successful entrance into the Caribbean area, and the eyes of the East India Company wanted to spread further across the Asian region. Terra Australis—the great south land—was an obvious and desirable conquest.

So, it is fair to say that the gains to Britain were enormous in economic terms, especially in terms of opportunity cost in dealing with the housing, feeding and guarding of the great surge of prisoners between 1750 and 1850.

Some of the advantages to Britain include:

a. The build-up of trade by the East-India Company
b. The advantage of a secure, in-house, supply of raw wool, to keep the spinning mills occupied
c. the opportunity cost of housing, feeding and guarding prisoners
d. The use of convict labour in the new Colony, for such as

- land clearing, farming, food production
  - for road construction building projects such as:
  - public wharves
  - barracks
  - Public Buildings

- production of Materials supply eg brick & tile production.
- as unpaid day labour for the pastoral & agricultural industry.

e. We can assume that Land grants , in the Colony, to men on the military and civil list was a form of 'fringe benefits' and should be quantified as an alternative to paid remuneration for these people. Even land grants to emancipists were used as an incentive to increase food production.

f. We can quantify items C, D and E into a 'value of direct gain to the British economy of nearly 140,000,000 pound(refer details in 'Statistics'), compared with the publicly recorded expenditure on transportation, supplies, and military personnel of 5,600,000 pound, between 1788 and 1822.

The purposes of trying to quantify these benefits is to challenge to traditional concept that 'the British invested millions of pounds in the Colony of New South Wales'.

It is obviously only the case when the outlay is shown and not the on-going benefits for over fifty years, and indeed two hundred years. It is still arguable that the Continent of Australia is, in Captain Arthur Phillip's words ' the best investment Britain will ever make'.

CHAPTER 32

THE ECONOMICS OF GOLD

Introduction

The discovery of gold on the mainland, in all states, had so powerful an effect that a special analysis of its benefits, must be made. We observe that the main bonuses to the Colonies was population and wealth. By-products became an increase in exports, offset by an increase in consumption goods, all designed to improve the quality of life, the dramatic growth of the railways system which brought with it extensive overseas borrowing, additional employment and new skills.

This section will review each of these benefits and explore the race problems that arose in the Colonies and the Commonwealth (originating with the gold rush), and see if this was limited to politician's minds or if it pervaded the lives of the peoples. Edward Pulsford claimed, as a rabid open-immigration supporter that the people of Australia supported the right of the Chinese and the Japanese to migrate to this country, the same as the majority of them had, not too many years previously.

Another by-product became the exploration for other minerals such as silver, copper and silver-lead, which became important export items from 1884.

Background

An extract from an address to the New South Wales Legislative Council by Governor Fitzroy on 11th May, 1853 gives an interesting insight into one aspect of the discovery of gold in the Colony and the improvement in the prosperity of its settlers.

"I desire first to acknowledge, with gratitude to Divine Providence, the general prosperity presently enjoyed by all classes of the community. At no former period of the existence of the colony has the material condition of its inhabitants been in a more satisfactory or progressive state. Although the prices of the necessities of life have been very considerably advanced, I am happy to say that they still continue abundant; whilst the increased means at the disposal of the people generally have enabled them without difficulty or inconvenience to meet the additional expenditure to which they are subjected. I must except from this satisfactory state of things, the paid servants of the crown, whose incomes, fixed with reference to former prices, now prove inadequate to their proper position and reasonable support. It will be my duty to invite your concurrence in such an advance in their present remuneration as the altered circumstances of the Colony may appear to render just and expedient.

Whilst in the enjoyment of so large a measure of material prosperity, we must not forget the duty which devolves on this Legislature to make some corresponding provision for promoting the intellectual and moral advancement of the community. Measures are being prepared for augmenting the amount allotted for education, with a view to extension of primary schools, as well as the encouragement of institutions destined to promote the higher branches of literature and science"

The British Colonial Secretary commissioned a report on the subject of the effects of gold discovery in 1852, and the report noted:

"assuming there are 30,000 men engaged at the gold mines in Victoria alone, then 15,000 of that number have been diverted from their previous occupations in that province, along with a further 5,000 from South Australia. To supply the places of these 20,000 , there would be required, under the regulations of the commissioners, 100,000 persons and these would only restore the labouring population to the state it was before the discovery of gold. Thus the immediate need is for a regular and uninterrupted supply of labouring immigrants, because every careful servant soon becomes an employer".'

In real terms, most of the gold was 'sold' overseas, rather than treated in the Colony..

In what well may be the first legislative statement of fiscal and monetary management in the Colonies, the South Australian Bullion Assay Act of 1852 heralded significant changes in the currency management of the Colonies. The Act enabled rates of exchange to be fixed, which prevented further speculation of gold in Adelaide, it stopped the drain on the Banks of coinage, encouraged former South Australian Colonists to return 'home' from the Victorian gold-fields, with their gains, and enabled the three banks of the day to survive the panic, namely The South Australian Bank, Bank of Australasia and the Union Bank of Australia. These banks were formed following the success of the Bank of New South Wales (founded in 1817 for the purpose of keeping the public account).

The discovery of Gold was kept secret whilst convict transfers were still being undertaken, lest the 'dream' of great wealth became stronger than the requirement to work out a penal service.

The discovery of large tracts of good grazing land and its associated export development of wool, and the discovery of large gold deposits rapidly boosted the fortunes of the Colony.

a. Gold Production & Value

The Wealth and Progress of New South Wales, published by the Colonial Statistician (Mr T. A. Coghlan) in 1900 records the value of gold produced in the Colony between the years 1851 and 1901, as being close to 50 million pounds. For the Australia wide production, this figure becomes close to 450 million pound, with the largest value being attributed to the State of Victoria at 210 million pound or close to half the total Australasian value of production.

Another side effect of the discovery of gold in the eastern states was the emigration of population from South Australia to the eastern states. In January 1852, the South Australian Parliament passed 'The South Australian Bullion Act' with the major background speech by the Premier observing "Throughout 1851 and 1852, South Australia has rapidly lost population to the adjacent Victorian goldfields. Worried bankers ,merchants and shopkeepers wonder what they ought to do about the situation, as it looked as if they might all be heading towards bankruptcy. The Burra Burra copper miners had been amongst the first to leave for the El Dorado, and soon most of the towns in the country districts were nearly cleared of their menfolk. There has been a general depreciation of land and property values. Every emigrant took whatever money he had in gold, thereby reducing specie to the banks, but diggers who returned with gold could not find buyers for it. The Chamber of Commerce and the Bank Managers conferred, and in January 1852, George Tinline, the Manager of the Bank of South Australia, had the idea of assaying gold into stamped ingots and then allowing it to pass as legal tender.

A hurried meeting of the S. A. Legislative Council was called and a special act was passed on January 28, 1852 to 'provide for the assaying of uncoined gold and to make banknotes, under certain conditions, a legal tender for the next twelve months'.

Owners of the ingots were authorised to convert the gold for bank notes at the rate of 3 pounds 11 shillings per ounce. The Bullion Act should not have been assented to by the SA Governor as it interfered with currency but the Act restored confidence in trade, and helped save the Colony of South Australia from insolvency, and it led to the importation of 1,500 million pound of gold from Victoria.

b. Population Growth

The statistician's figures of population on the goldfields are probably not very reliable because of the difficulty in collecting such information but the estimates for December 1861 shows there were over 17,000 miner's rights and business licenses on issue and an estimated working population of over 28,000. This compares to an estimated working population in the Victorian goldfields in April 1854 of 67,000 (there were 40,000 licenses on issue in 1852), including approx 2,000 Chinese. The Ballarat District had 17,000 workers, The Bendigo/Sandhurst District had 16,000 workers, and the Castlemaine district had over 23,000 workers. There was estimated to be, in total, nearly 7,000 itinerant travellers at any one time in the 5 gold mining districts in Victoria.

c. Government Revenue from Mining

MAIN SOURCE OF GOVERNMENT MINING REVENUE—(1885)

Year 1885	'000
Mineral Leases	20,750
Mineral Licenses	2,311
Miners Rights	4,143
Leases of Mining Lands	4,510
TOTAL REVENUES—MINING	31,714

This compares with Revenue from General Fines and forfeitures of £20,171 pounds for 1885.

Dr. G. L. Buxton (The Riverina 1861-1891) submitted that ,

"influx of population during the gold-rush years would, as a result of natural increase, have generated substantial pressure on existing resources, including land, and that this may have inevitably led to a struggle for redistribution of wealth."

But that is when he then goes on to say

"recently N. G. Butlin has suggested in 'Investment in Australian Economic Development" that the selector-squatter struggle has been over-emphasised by historians, but an adequate knowledge of this struggle is necessary for any real understanding of the course of pastoral investment in New South Wales and the development of Australian rural society and its politics."

That the British over-lorded the Colony for the first 112 years and imposed their own ways, standards and conditions, might well be considered another significant step in our economic history, and then the growth of the rural economy and the definite boost thereto from the coming of the railway system should be another.

Customs revenues peaked in 1842 at 182 thousand pound, at a time when, for the first time, the Colony's total revenue leapt to 700 million pound. These spikes were on account of the gold discovery and the importation of goods and the inflow of people to the gold fields.

The discovery of gold and the burgeoning wealth of the Colony prompted the Legislative Council in 1852 to seek the British Government's acceptance of an offset arrangement whereby the Colony of New South Wales would accept responsibility for all civil (ie official) salaries, provided the British Government surrendered all Colonial revenues to the discretion (under a proposed new constitution) of the Legislature.

The verification that the British authorities accepted Colonial funds, raised from the earliest sale and lease of Crown Land, and to be used for the funding of 'free immigration' to the Colony.

The concurrent Napoleonic wars being undertaken by the British, as well as the ongoing American War of Independence placed a substantial burden on the public purse, and the British Treasury was seeking every opportunity to limit, defray or offset expenses relating to the Colony in the Great South Land.

N. G. Butlin in the introduction to Chapter 7 of Historical Australian Records—Statistics—'The Economy before 1850', suggests there is a great deal of statistical data available on the new settlement before the discovery of gold. 'It represents some indication of the nature of the workforce of the settlements, the arrivals of convicts and free settlers, the economic activities they developed to support themselves and the heavy expenditure by the British Government to make the settlement a success. The Colony was supposed to support itself, increasingly so as pressures for public economy grew in post-Napoleonic Britain. The tables on Colonial Fund and Land Fund Revenues show this increasing shift to local self-support'. Butlin, by implication, is suggesting the financial pressures on Britain by the Colony would have caused the use of Crown Land sales to become a relief in the homeland Budgets.

The gold 'rush' brought great wealth not only to many individuals but also to each of the Colonies of Victoria, New South Wales, Queensland and Western Australia. A great leveling followed also immediately when the depression of 1890-3 came about.

The use of all this gold extracted in such a relatively short-period is interesting, and the Colonial Statistician records that ' Gold is coined only at the Sydney mint, and the weight of gold sent for coining in the period 1885 to 1886 was 15,005,884 ounces, and valued at 56 million 880 thousand pound(56,880,142); but of this amount New South Wales produced only 6,994,135 ounces or 26,716,196 pound. Queensland was the second largest contributor followed by New Zealand and then Victoria. The greater part of the gold extracted in New South Wales, Queensland and New Zealand came to Sydney for coinage, but by far the largest portion of the balance of gold extracted goes to Melbourne. Of the total gold extracted, some 317,312,707 pounds value, nearly 18 percent passed through the mint of the Colony, being sovereigns and half-sovereigns.'

Gold produced in the Colony of New South Wales peaked in 1862 at 620 thousand ounces but fell away consistently until in 1886 less than 100 thousand ounces was produced. This decrease is explained by the Colonial Statistician's office as being:

"the fact that the rich alluvial deposits discovered in the early days had been exhausted, and other resources of a more permanent nature are being developed. These ventures offer more regular employment to the labouring classes, perhaps without the chance of accumulating rapid fortunes but with more security against loss. The key New South Wales gold production areas were Bathurst, Mudgee districts, Tumut and Adelong, Temora, New England District. In the early days many mines were abandoned by reason of the want of proper appliances for the saving of gold. Now these mines have been re-opened and a revival of mining in these various districts is being seen. However the dry weather over the last few years has had an important influence on alluvial gold-mining, and large areas of payable ground are now deserted, owing to the want of water for sluicing purposes.

The economy was strengthened because it added gold to the powerful list of woollen exports. Wool temporarily lost its number one export title to gold from 1856 to 1870 but then returned to the top of the list.

The discovery of gold strengthened the Australian demands for the introduction of responsible government. By the end of 1852 the British Government had accepted these arguments, and invited the members of the legislatures of New South Wales, Victoria, Tasmania and South Australia to draft new constitutions. This request drew two events to the fore. Firstly a split occurred in Australian politics between the conservative constitutionalists and the liberal constitutionalists. Secondly, responsible government became the architect of chronic instability of governments that followed. The Australian delegation to London had accepted uncritically that responsible government—governing for one's own people—was the one way of ensuring control over domestic questions. But it was soon learnt that responsible government assumes two main parties, and to have two main political parties you need groups with clearly defined principles and interests. 'Between 1856 and 1878 it was found that there were differences of 'interest' but no serious differences of principle' (Clark—Select Documents in Australian History Vol 2 P.321)

The rest of the world watched change take place over centuries whilst Australia abbreviated all those same changes into less than 100 years. During that time Australia grew in monetary, population and self reliant terms. The changes in Australia were compressed into a shorter period but driven by the need to catch the rest of the world and make a mark.

At the time of the first gold rush in 1851, only 4 out 10 children attended school. By 1861, education was free, compulsory, secular and schools were well attended.

At the time gold was discovered, license fees and duties on exports of gold and duties on the domestic conversion of gold were applied and this revenue helped fill the Treasury coffers.

A short time before had come the first Appropriation Bills and 'Ways and Means' through the Legislative Assembly in 1832 under Governor Bourke. This was a major step forward in Government economic planning, as was the limited deficit budgeting that commenced at this time. The improvement in Government economic planning simplified the analysis of and planning for the dramatic increase in revenues and thus availability of funds for improving social infrastructure such as railways, roads, new inland settlements, schools, law courts, mechanics institutes and libraries, cottage hospitals. Government played a different role in those early days, when development of government and community assets was a much higher priority than maintenance of those assets, as is the case today. The Treasurers of the 1850s were in demand to understand and carefully formulate priorities that served their colony, rather than the select few.

Effects of Gold Discovery

a. A number of immediate results came from the discovery of gold: it assisted in terminating transportation it assisted in bringing responsible government forward land and political reforms came about as a result of the digger's demands for such reforms a general consequence was a rise in prices, wages, rents and charges
b. A shortage of general labour supply.

Self-Government

It is pointed out above that the discovery of gold was hidden and suppressed for many years. It was recorded in 1896 by the Colonial Statistician that the existence of gold had been known to the authorities during the early days, when the Colony was a convict settlement, but for obvious reasons of State, the matter remained secret. The first authenticated discovery of gold is contained in the field notes of Assistant Surveyor McBrian bearing the date of 16th February, 1823, with the reference being to a location on the Fish River just out of Bathurst, where Edward Hargraves made his big and public find twenty-eight years later. In 1839, Count Strezlecki , the namer of Mount Kosciusko, found gold in the Goulburn area, and was asked by Governor Gipps to keep the matter secret. The Rev. Clarke found gold in 1841 in the Macquarie Valley and expressed his belief publicly that 'the precious metal would be found abundantly dispersed throughout the Colony'. Edward Hargrave's discovery in 1851 was the first officially recognised find and led to the 'Gold Rush'.

Finding a Place for Gold

Gold occupies a foremost place in the country, both on account of the quantity found and the influence which the discovery had on the settlement of the country.

Coghlan, T. A. (Wealth & Progress of NSW-1900-1901) expresses a concern over the actual discovery date.

"The date of the discovery of gold in New South Wales was, for a long time, the theme of much controversy, and the question as to the original discoverer was long disputed. It is now agreed, that the existence of gold was known to the authorities during the early days when the state was a convict settlement, but for obvious official reasons the matter remained secret. As set out previously, the first authentic record of its discovery is contained in an extract from Assistant-Surveyor McBrian's Field-book, bearing date 126th February, 1823, in which the following note appears.—'At 8 chains 50 links to river, and marked gum-tree—at this place I found numerous particles of gold in the sand and in the hills convenient to the river.' The river referred to is the Fish River, at about 15 miles from Bathurst, not far from the spot to which the first gold rush was made twenty-eight years afterwards. "

In 1839, Count Strzelwcki found gold in Clwydd and communicated the discovery to Governor Gipps, but was requested to keep the matter secret, lest the existence of gold should 'imperil the safety and discipline of the Colony' (Coghlan P371). The Rev'd W.B. Clarke found gold in 1841 in the Macquarie Valley, but it was not until 1851 (the last convict had been shipped to the Colony some years previously in 1840, and by 1850 most had been released) that payable deposits were proved, by Edward Hargraves, a British immigrant and a recent traveller from California, in the area of Bathurst, on the banks of the Macquarie River. Only a few weeks later, deposits were found in Ballarat and Sandhurst (Bendigo) and Mount Alexander, all in the Colony of Victoria. For his find and public announcement in the SMH of 15th May, 1851, Hargraves was awarded 10,000 pound and appointed a Commissioner for Crown Lands.

The finds were all located in easily worked alluvial deposits, and therefore without costly diggings or appliances. Coghlan suggests "Rich they may be (and thus attracting the greater number of miners), alluvial deposits are very soon worked out, their area generally being of limited extent."

In July 1851 a 'mass' of gold was found in the Maitland area gold-fields which weighed 106 lb or 1,272 oz. Coghlan clarifies the description and says although called a 'nugget, it was really a piece of reef gold.' Another nugget in 1858 was found near Orange, which was melted at the Sydney mint and weighed 1,182 oz with a value of 4,389 pound 8 shillings and 10 pence. Numerous other large nuggets were found around the Colony, including Temora, Maitland, Mudgee, Hargraves and Delegate (via Cooma).

From 1851 to 1901, a quantity of 13,475,633 ounces was produced in New South Wales with a value of 49,661,815 Pound. Values increased during this period and although 1862 produced the most quantity (640,622 oz worth 2467,780), 1899 exceeded the value of any other year (496,196 oz worth 11,751,815).

The quantity of gold produced in 1901 fell from 345,650 to 267,061 whilst the number of miners employed dropped 5,894 for that period.

The Gold Dredging Act validated all leases and applications until 1899, and authorised a system of sluicing and dredging which has 'awaked considerable activity in certain districts where gold is being saved from the beds of rivers and creeks, as well as from wetlands which the ordinary miner experienced considerable difficulty in working.' (V & P NSW LA 1899)

Coghlan comments on the irregularity of gold-mining (P376)—"It is a well known fact that in years of prosperity, when employment of all kinds is easily obtainable, people are attracted from gold-mining to other pursuits, which, while offering smaller chances of rapidly acquiring wealth, nevertheless gives steady employment, and when working in steady occupations is scarce, these persons again give their attention to gold-mining. The depression in trade experienced during the last few years had the effect, therefore, of largely increasing the seekers after gold, many of the unemployed being supplied with Miner's Rights and with railway passes to take them to likely spots where a living could be made by fossicking, on the condition that the cost could afterwards be refunded, when the men were in a position to repay the money." Another benefit to the Colony of this process was that, in addition to the miner's right, the government hoped many men, and their families would take up residency in the area, on the gold-fields. The benevolence of the state was masterful in its manipulation for the betterment of all!

When the names of the districts where alluvial ,quartz and gold were found in the late 1800s is listed, one finds the areas where new population growth was taking place at increased rates.

Armidale, Bathurst, Orange, Parkes, Wyalong, Cobar, Peak Hill, Gundagai, Wellington, Forbes, Nowra, Gulgong, Temora and the Lachlan District. Discoveries covered much of the State, and even as late as 1894, the discovery of riches in the Lachlan District attracted more than 10,000 men of whom 4,600 were still there in 1901. However much gold was discovered, the average gold won per miner was 17.24 ounces, valued at 62.1.10 pound.

There were growing factors, other than just the population. There were 318 steam engines used in mining in 1899, 1762 crushing machines and 1,986 stamp heads. All this equipment was made in the Colony and valued at 975,000 pound. It also required skilled workers to maintain and operate the equipment.

Coghlan records (P381) that "from the date of the first discovery of payable gold, in 1851, to the end of the year 1900, the quantity of gold produced in the Commonwealth and New Zealand represents a total of 443,550,310 pound, extracted in the short space of 49 years. The share of each state is as follows:"

Gold Production by State 1851-1900		
State	Value	%
NSW	48,740,533	11.0
Victoria	257,386,448	58.0
Queensland	40,209,783	11.3
South Australia	2,294,973	0.5
West Australia	22,914,059	5.2
Tasmania	4,598,412	1.0
Com'wealth	386,144,210	87.0
New Zealand	57,406,100	13.0
Australasia	443,550,310	100.0

Compared to the world's production of gold, the Commonwealth of Australia only produced, in 1900 about 26% with NSW only being 2.3% and Victoria being 12%.

Population of Gold Towns in 1900

Armidale	4,249	Bathurst	,9,223
Orange,	6,331	Parkes	3,181
Wyalong,	1,510	Cobar,	3,374
Peak Hill,	1,107	Gundagai	1,487
Wellington,	2,984	Forbes	4,294
Nowra,	1,904	Gulgong	1,579
Temora	1,603		
The Lachlan District	10,000		

The Chinese Problem

Timothy Coghlan, a close friend and admirer of our Federationist Senator Edward Pulsford, made a controversial observation on the Chinese question.

He wrote, in 'Labour & Industry in Australia' " The unanimity with which the Australian states have passed laws restricting the immigration of Chinese may be taken as some evidence of the un-desirability of the race as colonists. At the census of 1861 there were, in New South Wales, 12,988

Chinese. In November 1861, a duty of 10 pound per head was imposed upon Chinese male immigrants. This continued until November 1967, and led to a decline in the number of Chinese in the State to 7,220. By 1881 the number had risen to 10,205 and to 15,445 at the end of 1888. Numerous departures followed and only 12,156 were found in 1891 and less than 11,000 in 1901. For many years New South Wales offered little inducement to the Chinese as a place of settlement, the superior attractiveness of Victoria and other States as gold producers claimed their attention. During the riots at Lambing Flat in 1860, large numbers of Chinese came across the border from NSW and established themselves in Victoria, their strength being constantly supported by new arrivals, but they did not remain in NSW as is shown above. The violent anti-Chinese attack on the Burrangong goldfield near Young NSW ('Lambing Flat') on 30th June, 1860, by 3,000 diggers led to many Chinese being beaten and their camps destroyed. Tensions were reduced by the departure of many of the Chinese and the passing of the Chinese immigration restriction bill in November 1861.

From 1878 to 1888 over 27,000 Chinese arrived in New South Wales whilst 16,000 departed."

This second rush in 1878 caused the introduction of the 'Influx of Chinese Restriction Act' in 1881, re-imposing the poll tax of 10 pound. The next measure by the Parliament followed a meeting of all state representatives where it was agreed that they were witnessing a 'growing danger'. The new Act came into force on 11th July 1888 and prohibited any vessels from carrying into the State more than 1 Chinese passenger to every 300 ton of cargo, and each Chinese landed are required to pay a poll-tax of 100 pound; they were not to engage in mining except with the permission of the Minister for Mining, nor were they permitted to take advantage of the Naturalisation Act. Any Chinese that come as British subjects (from Hong Kong) had to pass the educational test prescribed by the Immigration Restriction Act of 1898.

The penalty for breach of the Chinese Restriction Act was 500 pound. The Act had greatly reduced Chinese immigration, but it was believed that a large number of Chinese found their way into NSW through the other States.

The 'History of the Australian Gold Rushes' edited by Nancy Keesing records an extract of an unpublished manuscript by the Manager of the Robe branch of the Bank of South Australia (Thomas Drury Smeaton) written in 1865.

"in 1858 there were 33,000 Chinese on the Victorian gold-fields, whilst in 1853 there were fewer than 2,000. The Chinese coolies were highly unpopular among the miners often for reasons based on ignorance and prejudice. In 1855, Victoria passed an Act imposing a poll tax of ten pound on each Chinese immigrant and forbidding ships to carry more than one Chinese passenger for every ten tons of the vessel's tonnage. The shipping masters promptly evaded the tax by landing coolies at South Australian ports, from which they travelled overland to the goldfields. The town of Robe on Guichen Bay in South Australia was a favoured port. In all about 16,500 Chinese passed through Robe on their way to the diggings. Of this large number all were males"

Conclusion

Our goal was to determine the quantity and value of gold extracts in the Colony of New South Wales and the country as a whole. Another purpose was to determine which areas of the State were most influenced and how the proceeds were utilised. What labour was involved and what by-products were advantaged?

In summary then we learnt that New South Wales produced 12,862,922 ounces of gold valued at 48,740,533 pound, whilst the Commonwealth produced 63,464,717 ounces valued at 443,550,310 pound. Of this amount 96,676,500 pound was put into circulation as coinage and over 2 million ounces were exported, valued at about 16 million pound.

Over One million pounds worth of equipment was employed, including the steam engines valued at 970,000 pound.

New businesses flourished on the gold-fields—sale of stores and provisions, prostitution, tent-makers, log houses, basic furniture, firewood cutting and sale, tool making, Cobb & Co. coaches—and gold escort services, sly grog production (officially alcohol was not allowed onto the gold fields), policing, licensing and clothing makers.

The biggest benefit of the gold discoveries was the move by the British Government to provide responsible government to each of the Colonies.

Edward Pulsford in 'Trade and Commerce in New South Wales' (1892) writes

"The most important event which occurred in the decade 1850-1860 was the discovery of gold, which will for ever stamp 1851 as the most remarkable year in the commercial history of New South Wales, from the foundation of the Colony to the present. Volumes could be written to record the successes and failures of gold mining, the way in which new towns are settled, and development both retarded and promoted.

On 22nd May 1851 the Governor of New South Wales had proclaimed the Government's right solely to sell all gold removed from the Colony's diggings. And then provided that a license fee of 30 shillings per month was to be paid to dig on Crown lands. From the first find, the Government had been determined to have a two-way control over the gold successes, so that the Government received its share.

Frank Crowley in Colonial History—Volume 2, 1841-1874 records (P206) a detailed report, dated 10th October, 1851 by Lieutenant-Governor Latrobe to the Colonial Secretary (Earl Grey) in London:—

"The immediate effect of the gold discoveries were a sudden increase in the size of the population in Eastern Australia and the export of large quantities of gold bullion to Britain. At first, wool growing and cattle raising suffered from loss of workmen, but squatters quickly adapted to the new situation. There was a large meat-market on every goldfield, and mass production of cheap galvanised fencing wire enabled a small number of boundary riders to replace the army of shepherds. Freight costs were greatly reduced by the keen competition between shipowners, at a time when wool prices were steadily rising. Farming was at first disturbed and then stimulated by the rising population and the increased demand for food. Many small industries in and around Sydney were adversely affected by the shortage of labour, rising wages and competition from the flood of cheap imported goods from Britain. Every ship that brought immigrants and gold-finders had its holds jammed tight with pots and pans, picks, shovels, shop clothing, lanterns and cheap furniture. The commercial boom in Sydney and Melbourne lasted until 1855 and the sudden increase in capital available for investment and speculation resulted in a building bonanza, especially in Melbourne City and the towns centred around the goldfields such as Bendigo and Ballarat. "

The associated boom in trade and commerce also brought fortunes to Melbourne merchants as well as to the farmers and squatters who were close to the diggings. Storekeepers on the fields made a great deal of profit from their buying and selling. Flour resold at 3 d per pound, mutton at 3.5 d per lb., sugar was 2s 6 d per lb.; tea was 4 shillings/lb, boots 2 pound; blankets 2 pound.

The Sydney Morning Herald of 4th August 1852 announced 'Steam Communication with England at last' and reported that steam powered ships were now running between Britain and Australia on a frequent basis.

In the middle of 1852 the diggings at Bendigo held about the same number of workers as did the Ballarat diggings—30—40,000 people at each. It was reported that about 2,000 carts and drays were on the road from Melbourne at any time of the day.

An ex-convict writing in the Melbourne Argus questioned the acceptance of the ill-effects of the gold fever—the increase in crime, the high price of labour, the stopping of the public works, in particular the unfinished sewerage system in Melbourne and other burdens of the 'root of all evil'

Another less obvious problem with the gold-fever came from the society ladies of Sydney, who claimed that' the town had gone downhill rapidly during the last two years, mainly because of the extortionate prices being charged and the scarcity of domestic servants'. (SMH 10.7.1853)

Because of the local shortage of coins in Sydney, and fluctuations in the price of raw gold and in the exchange rate between Australia and Britain, the Royal Mint was invited to and accepted, the opportunity of opening a mint in Sydney on 14th May, 1855.

The goldfields, concludes Crowley (Colonial Australia Vol 2, P404) in a very short time contributed a major economic boost to the Australian Colonies that had only received sixty years of Imperial Expenditure from the convict system.

The Albury Border Post of 22nd February, 1860 waxed poetic in its article on the value of the goldfields.

"The traffic from Sydney to Melbourne will bring a population to the fine port and district of Twofold Bay. In this manner are the gold discoveries utilising themselves, and we imagine that each unoccupied portion of this vast continent will in its turn be visited by the wave of population, the flowing and ebbing of which will leave there a deposit, turning the wilderness into a fertile valley, and bidding the desert to bloom as the rose."

So we conclude with the recognition of some of the essential gains from the discovery of gold and can say that the country was much better off having discovered the riches under the ground, and transferred some of them to the top of the ground.

CHAPTER 33

RAILWAYS AND ECONOMIC GROWTH IN THE AUSTRALIAN COLONIES

Introduction

It would be considered natural that one of the key factors contributing to economic growth in a new country would be the creation of a railway network to service the rural and regional areas of that country. That an investment of 34 million pound and the creation of up to an estimated 50,000 jobs would assist as well, is unquestionable. But what other benefits could follow? A settlement system of towns developed because of the railways, and the infrastructure for those towns developed quickly and the railways rapidly attracted additional population.

Most assuredly the railways provided alternative transport to the bullock teams and horse drawn drays that were in common use and were so slow. The fact that steam engines relied on coal and that the tracks were laid on wooden sleepers cut from the forests contributed to the growth of these primary industries?

The wool industry had reached the stage when sheep numbers were growing rapidly, the yield of wool per sheep grew and the mills of England were still starved for wool. Here again the railway movement of both wool and livestock was an important task.

But what else might have resulted from an investment of 34 million pound starting just as the gold fields were at full operation? Did the overseas borrowing help or hurt the colony? Would the rail system, passengers and freight be able to service the debt? Or would the interest become a burden on the Colonial finances?

a. Railway growth in New South Wales

Boundary changes in the Colony of New South Wales were completed with the transfer of the Queensland region in 1859. The Colony of Victoria had been formally transferred in 1855. Self-government in New South Wales was achieved in 1856 and from that time the Colony became more a master of its own destiny than at any time previously.

The topography of New South Wales is not naturally conducive to a network of rail links throughout the Colony, since much of the coastal area is bordered by a mountain range and traversed with sizeable rivers which would need to be to be bridged. The State can, in fact, be divided into three distinct zones each differing widely in character and physical aspect with The Great Dividing Range providing a clear demarcation between the coastal zone and the Great Plains. So there were and are natural limitations when planning a railway system.

The first part of a 'network' was one of meeting the principal aims of constructing a railway—a network must link towns to the city, and to the ports. Rail communication—the revolution of steam that had already transformed so much of England and Europe , had also brought great wealth and growth to the United States, and it was expected the same benefits would accrue in Australia.

In 1846, the Government agreed to carry out a survey, and if found to be feasible, it was decided to construct a line between Sydney and the city of Goulburn. Two years later, the Sydney Railroad and Tramway Company was formed, with a capital of 100,000 pound, and an object of construction of rail-lines from Sydney to Parramatta and Liverpool, with extensions to Bathurst and Goulburn. On July 3rd, 1850 the daughter of Governor Sir Charles Fitzroy (Mrs.Keith Stewart) turned the sod of the first railway in Australia. The private company did not succeed and the

Government took over the works. A second private company, formed to complete a rail-link between Newcastle and Maitland suffered the same fate and so the Government quickly owned two potential rail services. The Government saw a solid future in completing the rail service and went to work on construction with such vigour that the Parramatta line was declared open on 26th September 1855 and the Goulburn line was opened on 27th May, 1869. If we were planning the same exercise today, the variety of considerations would still include the following facts:-

- Parramatta was still an out-of-Sydney location with 12,500 people (in 1855)
- Wollongong was a growing area with 3,500 people but access from Bulli and Nowra was extremely difficult because of the terrain and steep mountain passes.
- Newcastle was already a significant area with 13,000 people but traversing the Hawkesbury would be both difficult and expensive.
- Dubbo and Orange were attractive areas but the Blue Mountains were again the impasse with a high cost and a major engineering challenge—crossing the Mountains and handling the extreme gradients.
- That left Goulburn (10,600) and Wagga (5,100) as the two areas with a growing population that were penetrable by rail.

For ease of access and the lowest cost of laying the line and serving a good population with potential passenger and freight traffic, a line to Parramatta and a main southern line to Goulburn, which could be linked to a interstate line and branches to Wagga, Hay etc was the most practical decision.

However, further progress over the next twenty years was very slow and in 1875 the length of the line had only reached 435 miles. However from 1875 to 1889 much progress was made and by 1889 a further 1,748 miles was completed. This work was being carried out at the average rate of 125 miles per year. In 1899 the Berrigan to Finley line was opened (14 miles). In the next two years, the Tamworth to Manilla and the Moree to Inverell lines were both opened and in the following year the Broken Hill to Tarrawingee line became the property of the Government. The privately built Broken Hill—Silverton Rail line was to remain in private hands but was open to all freight and passenger movement for 5 years before reverting to Government ownership. It was to be become (because of the quantity of ore being shipped) the potentially most profitable line in the Commonwealth. The amount of rail line under construction by the end of 1901 was a further 540 mile.

Table A

RAILWAY CONSTRUCTION 1855-1901

Year	Miles Opened	Total Opened
1855	16	16
1856	9	25
1857	17	42
1879	45	733
1880	115	848
1881	148	996
1900	105	2811
1901	34	2845

Because exact figures are not available, we can only speculate on the number of men employed on construction, and of the total people including women and children who made a contribution to life on the construction projects.

We still can hear stories today of grandparents living in tents beside the tracks, where the men worked on the line and the women were paid cooks and providers. Permanent railway settlements at crossings, signal boxes and railway terminals started many small rural towns, created employment and were soon to be serviced by schools, stores and churches

Table B

POPULATION PER MILE

Year	Popln/Mile	Train miles run	Train miles/hd popln
1860	4979	174249	0.5

1870	1467	901139	1.8
1880	882	3,239462	4.4
1890	502	8,008826	7.4
1891	521	8,410421	7.5
1892	538	7,505310	6.3
1898	492	8,340338	6.4
1899	497	8,806647	6.7
1900	464	8,894352	6.6

Table C

COLONIAL RAILWAY LINES CONSTRUCTED AS OF 1901

State	Gov Line Op'nd	Private Lines	Total
NSW	2845	85	2930
Vic	3238	0	3238
Qld	2801	55	2856
SA	1882	19	1901
WA	1355	623	1978
Tas	446	148	594
C'wlth	12567	930	13497
NZ	2212	88	2300

These tables are sourced from 'The Wealth and Progress of New South Wales 1990-1901' by T.A. Coghlan (P472-3-4)

Coghlan makes one final comparison between the railway systems of the old world and the new world and for brief illustration we will review the length of lines, the population per mile of line, and the area per mile of line in selected countries. The latter measurement is just for comparison purposes and like many of the Coghlan statistics was used to show the superiority in many areas (but mainly New South Wales) over Victoria.

Table D

INTERNATIONAL COMPARISON OF INSTALLED
RAIL SERVICE LINKS—1875

Country	Length of Railway	Popln per mile of Line
NSW	2930	466
Victoria	3238	370
Argentine	10595	432
Austria-Hungary	22147	2,030
Britain	21,700	1,885
USA	190,833	396
Sweden	6649	767
Japan	3481	12571

Edward Pulsford (the leader of the Free Trade movement within Australia) and a Federationist, wrote in his 1892 tract—'Trade & Commerce in New South Wales' (P45):-

"In 1871 the number of miles of railway open was 358 by 1881 this had been increased to about 1,000 and by 1887 to 2,000. Since then the pace has moderated, and the aggregate is now about 2,200 miles. A small number in comparison with the United States aggregate, yet in proportion to the population it is not a bad exhibit. The railways consist almost wholly of main lines. A line from the Queensland border, in the north, to the Victorian border, in the south, passing through Sydney on the way, is the principal one—the total length being 869 miles. The second in importance runs from Sydney in a north-westerly direction to Bourke, on the River Darling, its length being 503 miles. Railway development has also proceeded rapidly in the other colonies, and it is now possible to journey by train from Adelaide, the capital of South Australia, to Melbourne, the capital of Victoria, 509 miles; on from Melbourne to Sydney, the capital of New South Wales, a further 576 miles, then on from Sydney to Brisbane, the capital of Queensland, 723 miles more. Making in all 1,808 miles of what is practically one railway line. The total mileage throughout Australasia is about 12,000 (in 1892)."

Our task is to examine the associated development that came with the railway system, to try to ascertain the number of direct and indirect employees working on the railway system, show the benefits of population growth coming with the gains of decentralisation and the general improvement in the rural quality of life.

The three distinct rail systems provide the basis for the potential growth and development that would follow the opening of the railway lines

a. The southern system, including the principal line in the State, (through Goulburn to Cootamundra), branches at Junee and placed the important district of Riverina, as far as Hay in one direction and Finley in another, in direct communication with Sydney from which they are distant 454 and 448 miles respectively (756 & 746 Km). Several other branches link onto this south-western line, connecting other important districts with Sydney. Culcairn connects with Corowa, on the Murray; and Culcairn to Wagga via The Rock; from Cootamundra to Gundagai; and Cootamundra to Temora. A line between Murrumburrah to Blayney connects the Western and Southern systems. The connection allows the direct shipment of western livestock to the markets in Victoria. A branch from Cooma to Goulburn connects the rich Monaro grazing district to the Sydney markets.

b. The North-South Main line passed through, by 1901, the most thickly populated districts in NSW and places Brisbane, Newcastle, Sydney, Melbourne and Adelaide in direct communication. The first sleeping cars were used in 1901 in New South Wales at Albury and provided for the comfort of passengers. European and British mails are landed in Adelaide (in 1900) by ship and transported 1,085 miles overland to all parts of Victoria, New South Wales and Queensland. A branch line connected the Illawarra on the South Coast to Sydney and Nowra.

c. The western system extends from Sydney towards the Blue Mountains and onto Mudgee through the Bathurst Plains and connects the rich agricultural lands of Bathurst, Orange, Wellington, Dubbo and Bourke (on the Darling River) to the all-important Sydney markets. A branch line from Orange connects to Parkes, Condobolin, Warren and Nyngan. Another branch connects the mining town of Cobar to the Sydney port (for mineral exports) and agricultural market (for rural products). This line is extended to Broken Hill and connects onto the South Australian system.

d.   The Northern System, commences in Newcastle, with connections to Sydney through Strathfield, making Sydney the Hub of all rail services in New South Wales by July 1901. This northern line accesses the great coal centres and on through the rich Hunter Valley into the New England areas and towns such as Maitland, Tamworth, Armidale, Glenn Innes and Tenterfield. The wide Hawkesbury River was finally bridged in 1889 by the Union Bridge Company of America. Its construction was hazardous and spectacular. It was the largest structure of its kind in the southern hemisphere. Its total length was almost 3,000 feet. Five piers had to be sunk to a depth of up to 160 feet below high-water level in swift-running currents, a record achievement at that time.

The Hawkesbury River was crossed by this iron bridge at a cost of 327,000 pound, thus completed the connection from Adelaide, Melbourne, Sydney and Brisbane a total end-to-end distance of 1,808 miles, but between Oodnadatta in South Australia and Cunnamulla in Queensland there is a continuous line of 3,100 miles opening up and inter-linking these four key states. The earliest development of the Colonies had depended on the port systems, creating inter-Colonial trade by sea, but the rail system had developed a two-fold benefit, the opening of the inland areas to markets, new towns with people migration to the rural areas, as well as creating an inter-state rail system.

A number of engineering feats accompanied the construction of the overall system. There were difficult gradients in all three systems with over 2,807 miles involved with a gradient, especially through the Illawarra, Blue Mountains and Hawkesbury areas. From the beginning, Australia's railways were modelled on British lines and then modified to suit local conditions. English-type rails were used at first, later to be replaced by lighter ones. All rails were imported until 1906 because the New South Wales Government had wanted to wait until the new Commonwealth Government imposed import duties in 1901, to confirm that protection would be offered to a local industry making iron rails, without the State having to guarantee either a minimum quantity to buy or accept an inflated price. In any case the State lost an important industry because by the time the tariff was announced most rail lines in the country had been installed.

As in the USA, rails were spiked to the sleepers rather than chaired as they were in Britain, and wood fuel was used as an alternative fuel when coal was not available. It fell to NSW to inaugurate the first government-owned railway in the country and in fact, in the British Empire. It was this methodology of spiking that essentially restricts the use of existing rail lines for the planned VFT (very fast train) in NSW in the year 2000.

b. Expenditure, population served and revenues

The first major benefit to the Colony of New South Wales was the investment in the Rail system at a total cost 38,932,781 pound or 13,682 pound per mile. This cost included 4,677,001 pound for rolling-stock; 340,657 pound on machinery; 638,698 on workshops and 10,036 pound on furniture for a total, of 5,666,392 pound for ancillary equipment, plus the rail laying cost 33,266,389 pound. The benefits of constructing rail rolling stock in NSW created great employment opportunities for newly emerging engineering industries, including Mort's Dock (employing over 1,000 men) and the Government-owned rolling stock workshops (employing over 4,000 men) .

Of the 38,932,781 pound 903,565 was provided from Consolidated Revenue of the State, with the balance being raised by the issue of debentures and other stock. These long-term low interest bonds yielded their investors about 4.5% on average and were almost self-servicing from year one in 1856 because of the passenger and produce traffic they handled.

The net revenue for the year ended June, 1901, after paying for working expenses, was 1,530,578 pound or a return of 3.94 % on the total outlay or 4.24% on the borrowed funds. Based on the early years of full operations, only a good rate of growth could be expected in the future years of operation. The Parliament had also allocated 1,000,000 pound for extending and improving the metropolitan lines and by 1901 75%

of this amount had been repaid from revenue. In spite of the extensive gradients and obstacles the cost per mile of line compared favourably with international costs but topped the costs within Australasia.

From humble beginnings in 1855, when the first lines attracted only 350,000 passengers for the year, by June 1901, the number of passengers numbered 29,261,324. An even more dramatic growth can be seen from the tonnage of goods carried. From 2,469 tons in 1855, this grew to 6,398,227 tons in 1901, a growth of 2,591 times the original tonnage. It was not until the line crossed the Blue Mountains and serviced the far interior that goods traffic became a major source of revenue for the railways.

It was recognised that there were numerous unprofitable lines and the Government of the day (in 1901) agreed to review all lines and branches for local benefit rather than on strict terms of profit before making any closures. This consideration was based on the cyclical nature of freight and passenger movements and the imposition of the then current drought effecting the movements. The June 1901 results showed that there was 1,368 miles of line, originally costing 14,545,000 pound that was losing an average of 320,000 pound per annum. The Railways Commissioners suggested in 1901 that surplus crown land on either side of the line be sold with proceeds going to the Railway Capital Fund.

So, at this point, we can start to see the full impact of the railway investment of nearly 40,000,000 pound in the Colony of New South Wales.

Employment was created in laying the line; building the rolling stock; maintaining the lines and rolling stock; servicing and operation staff such as drivers, signalmen and station staff; and many rural towns built family living accommodation for rail-staff in remote areas and this population growth assisted schools, townships, local building jobs; and, in addition, there was the furthering of coal extraction to power the steam locomotives.

Other benefits included the provision of skilled workmen who now had the capabilities of completing other major projects of a similar dimension, including ship construction at Mort's Dock & Shipbuilding in Sydney.

For the less populous states, Labour came from inter-state as well as overseas to work with the railways.

"Many of the navvies who built Queensland's first railways were Irish migrants and were known as 'Jordan's Lambs' after Henry Jordan, Queensland's immigration agent in London. These 'lambs ' were early agitators for the 8-hour working day. They were to suffer when economic depression forced the Queensland Government to suspend public works. A great many skilled railwaymen were thus lost to Queensland, when they moved south in search of work." (Illustrated History of Australia—Hamlyn P574) .

A big labour problem came about due to the low population of the western states (mainly Western Australia) which were vast in size and grossly-underpopulated and was being slowed down by a shortage of workmen in its construction program.

It is interesting to analyse the expenditures on operating costs:

From 1891 through 1901, working or operating expenses as a percentage to gross earnings averaged 59 percent.

In 1901 operating expenses per passenger broke down as follows:

Line and easement maintenance	10.81 d
Locomotive powering	16.98 d
Repairs & renewals	3.89 d
Traffic expenses	11.98 d
Compensation	0.25 d
General expenses	1.65 d

These expenses totaled 45.56 pence against an average per passenger ticket price of 50 pence. For a while the railway system in the colony was healthy and paying its own way. TOTAL 45.56 d healthy and paying its own way.

Again in 1901, the statistics on intra-state travel in NSW also shows an interesting picture:-

Total passenger journeys	25,489,985 passengers
Number of miles travelled	150,956,272 miles
ave. miles per passenger	5.93 miles
gross receipts from passengers	315,723 pound
Ave. receipts per mile, per passenger	0.50 d
Ave. operating cost per mile	0.4556d
Ave. receipts per head pa	20s 3.8 d

The goods traffic has risen to 4.7 tons per head of population in 1901 which compared favourably to Victoria at 2.8, Queensland at 3.1, South Australia at 4.5 and Western Australia at 9.5. These figures reflect the importance of the rail system to the economy in each State.

From 1855, when tonnage and goods freight revenue in New South Wales stood at 140 (tons) for 156 (pound), these figures had grown to 6,398,227 (tons) and 2,203,249 (pound revenue), in 1901.

The largest commodity categories in the goods freight being carried in 1901 were:-

Coal, coke and shale	3,956,033 ton
Firewood	218,058
Grain, flour	504,880
Hay, straw and chaff	154,403
Wool	99,164
*	
Livestock	200,339
'A' & 'B' class goods	398,402
All other goods	867,000
TOTAL TONS	6,398,227 Tons

Before we move along to review population growth in the larger towns, we can summarize some of the direct and tangible benefits from the railways. The direct employment numbers used in construction and operating of the railroads is not provided by Coghlan's Wealth and Progress of New South Wales but by interpolation of the average pay rates in 1901, we can conclude that approx 50 man years was used to complete an average mile of preparing and laying track. Other employment numbers can be derived in the same manner.

Direct Employment (using ave. pay rate assumptions)

Per mile construction	50 man years
For total track laid	140,000 man years
(+/-3,800 men per year employed)	
Construction of rolling stock	8,000 man-years
(+/-1,000 men employed per year)	
Maintenance and Operations	10,000 men
Repairs on rolling stock	4,000 men

These figures show that a substantial amount of available labour was used on the construction and operating duties of the railways. Part verification comes from Manning Clark who states in 'Select Documents in Australian History' that

"by 1890, the NSW Railway workshop alone employed over 4,000 men, which was about one-third of the total number of workers employed on the railways in that Colony. Furthermore, the need for carriages, goods wagons and locomotives provided an expanding market for the products of Australian foundries and general engineering shops. "

Each Colonial Government established big repair and maintenance workshops in their colony, and these expanded rapidly with the railway boom of the 1880s.

The volume of goods being transported by rail is indicative of the importance of the rail system to the rural sector and the ability to move goods to market and to port for export quickly and economically.

The main goods to benefit from the rail system are:

Minerals
Wood
Wool
Coal

Grains
Livestock.

An intangible benefit was the engineering skills developed during construction of iron bridges (Hawkesbury), tunneling (Blue Mountains), gradient engineering and management and manufacture and design of rolling stock (Sydney Workshops). The hardwood sleepers for the tracks were easily obtained from the eucalypt forests of the coastal region, and wood fuel was used to fire the boilers when coal was not available.

The slow bullock wagons were the only means of transporting wool to the ocean and sometimes, as in the Victorian gold-rush, even these wagons disappeared, leaving stations not only without an outlet for their wool but also without vital supplies. So the rail system was a major boost for the pastoralist as well as the agriculturalists, who wanted to ship fresh produce to the markets.

For many years, Echuca (serviced by a line by the Victorian Railways through Bendigo from Melbourne) boomed with anything up to 5000 bales of wool a day being transferred from steamers and barges on the Murray to freight trains. The wool came from as far away as Bourke in NSW and had been humped by camels across the wide-open plains to the Darling River. To shippers in Melbourne and Sydney that wool was most valuable. Transportation within Australia was being diversified. Paddle steamers, coaches, bullock trains, steam trains and ocean vessels all played an important part.

Another service provided by the railway was its special 'starving livestock' program whereby livestock was moved from drought conditions in one area to fresh feed in other areas. Likewise the program encouraged the moving of hay and packaged feed from grower to the livestock and this benefited many pastoralists who were able to maintain stock in good condition. Both programs were heavily subsidised (a 30% discount) by the State Government.

It was more than coincidence that following the gold rush with its enormous claim to workers rushing to the fields to find their fortune, and once the easy 'surface' gold was depleted, the workers wanted earned income for stability. These workers were largely put to work on the railway system in rural areas and so the potential huge unemployment problem was tempered by the attraction of hard but regular work, building a railway system throughout the State.

The gold rush had , in other ways, provided a powerful impetus for the building of the railways that had contributed so much to conquer the inland of the vast continent. The discovery of gold created both general prosperity and a scarcity of labour, and so the available workers became more independent and employers were forced to make valuable concessions.

Workers returning from the goldfields also brought with them a strong attitude of militancy. In May 1856, the eight-hour day had been achieved in the building industry in NSW—and without any reduction in daily wages. The movement then spread to workers in the 'indoor' trades in Melbourne such as cabinet-makers, coachbuilders and iron trade craftsmen.

But, the eight-hour day was a misnomer. They were really fighting for a 48-hour week, and as work ended early on Saturdays, the standard hours on other working days were about 8.75 (8 ¾) c. Confusion caused by the Railway Gauge Conflict

An extract from The Illustrated History of Australia shows the way confusion came about over the rail gauges in the mainland states.

The NSW Board of Railway Commissioners recommended to Earl Grey (the Colonial Secretary) in 1848 that the English standard 4' 8 ½" be adopted throughout Australia. Since Victoria was not separated at that time, that area, as well as Queensland was covered under this proposal.

"Two years later, an Irish Engineer, F.W. Shields, joined the Railway in NSW, and even though the Irish railways gauge was a broad one (5 ft 3 inches), and thus more expensive to lay and maintain, he persuaded the Legislative Council of NSW to use that gauge instead of the planned English gauge. The authorities in Britain did not see anything wrong with the idea, or perhaps they just did not care. Shields resigned soon after during a pay dispute and his successor changed back to the 4 ft 8 ½ inch. Victoria and South Australia, both of whom had ordered rolling stock from overseas continued to use the broad gauge and could not change, whilst Queensland and Western Australia, for reasons of economy adopted the narrow 3 foot 6 inch gauge. The Trans-continental railway opened by Commonwealth Railways in 1917 used the 4 foot 8 ½ inch gauge and brought Western Australian isolation to an end. The west became joined to the east for the first time. d. Population Growth in Selected Areas

It is not a surprising result to find that the great cities of Australia, like their counter-parts in all other parts of the world, accumulated the majority of the population and achieved the highest growth rates. One of the results of the industrial revolution that improved farm productivity, was that rural population commenced to decrease. Farm workers were attracted to the cities by electricity, schools for their families, stable employment and for a while, a better quality of life. That trend is still taking place but may be at a turning point for the very same reasons that the population once used as justification for moving away from rural areas.

In 1861 the native-born population amounted to only 46% of the total Colonial population and the native-born population of the Sydney metropolitan population was only 42%. The British born residents generally preferred the city living whilst the non-British residents generally preferred the rural districts. The growing Chinese population also preferred the city life.

The metropolitan trend grew as follows, along with the Sydney residents:-

1861	23.78	
1871	26.73	136,483
1881	30.34	237,300
1891	34.47	308,270
1901	35.90	400,650

This trend is explained in a thoughtful work, following the 1899 census of the Colony.

"The growth of the Australian cities is due mainly to the physical configuration of the continent, which makes no other mode of development possible—for there are no great rivers with leagues of navigable waterway stretching into the heart of the country far remote from seaports. To some extent the growth of cities has also been favoured by the commercial development of the states. For many years wool-growing has been the staple industry of the country; and while the actual tending of flocks needs few hands, and those widely scattered, the handling of bales of wool at a convenient place of shipment demands all the resources of a great commercial centre. Also, gold-digging, to which the state owe so much, is not an industry likely to promote permanent settlement in the interior. The miner of the past was in every respect a nomad: if successful in his quest after the precious metal, he became an emigrant to the Old World or a sojourner in an Australian capital."

The growing population in the city and the country can be seen from the following:-

Year	City	Country	% country
1870	134,578	364,081	73
1880	223,886	524,064	70
1890	380,048	741,820	66
1900	590,630	873,960	59
1901(census)	487,900	871,233	64

The railways provided the much needed access to markets for rural and agricultural output. The railways boomed and caused the Railway Department to place more orders for rolling stock and engines and commenced building more branch lines. The Government started again to borrow from overseas to pay for the capital improvements and with the import of capital came immigrants and labour. In the period just prior to World War One, there was a large inflow of migrants and they helped to expand the market and the work force. Agricultural expansion stimulated manufacturing, especially of agricultural implements and machinery Manufacturing made a rapid growth and diversified, and shared a growing proportion of the national product rising to about 14% in 1913. This growth was also due to the growing average income for each working family, the protectionist policy under Deakin and the Labour Party, and the population increases. Family income was supported by a rise of women in the workplace. The number of men employed in NSW manufacturing increased by 78 % between 1900 and 1914 but the number of women employed rose by 158%. Sydney was included in the building boom of the 1907-1912 period, and in 1911 the NSW Statistician wrote ' The city of Sydney is undergoing a process of rebuilding, and inferior buildings are giving way to superior factories and premises'.

Three selected inland towns make an interesting study for population and economic growth.

Town	Population 1901	Population 2000.
Goulburnn	10,612	22,500
Dubbo	3,409	30,000
Orange	3,990	30,000
Tamworth	5,799	32,500
Wagga	5,108	58,200
Broken Hill	27.500	25,000

The development of Goulburn is typical of most of these inland towns.

The stockade (in Goulburn) became the principal penal establishment in the southern district and was noted for its harsh discipline. There were usually 250 convicts hutted there. They slept on bare boards with a blanket apiece. 10 men to a box or cell.

The first school and church opened in 1839 and the 'Goulburn Herald' was established in 1848. It was later incorporated into the 'Post' which is still published today.

a. The settlement began to expand after 1850 due to a number of factors. the pastoral industry had expanded gold was discovered in Braidwood in the early 1850s (a local labour shortage was the immediate result) settlers began to arrive from the 1860s the railway arrived in 1869, facilitating access to the Sydney markets. The town remained the southern railhead until 1875.

As a result, Goulburn became the first inland city in 1863 after being gazetted as a municipality in 1859.

The railway was especially crucial as a catalyst for the town's boom period in the 1870s and 1880s when industries such as coach building, iron foundries and saddlery making began to develop. A dairy factory was set up in 1901 and woollen mills in 1922. The town has been a major wool sales centre since 1930.

Another contributor to economic growth was the closer settlement program that broke up huge pastoral holdings into smaller family holdings, which saw the early addition of fruitgrowing and dairying to the local agricultural production.

Electricity did not arrive until 1922. Bushrangers added adventure to the local area and kept the civilian prisons busy.

The story of Wagga, Dubbo, Orange and Tamworth follow much the same pattern. A slow start, discovery of gold, a growing settlement, building of schools and churches, the coming of the railway, and each major town having a huge edifice of a rail station to recognise the importance of the rail service to the town and closer settlement, small engineering shops, retailing of farm machinery, manufacturing and servicing standard farm machines, diversification of agriculture, growing wealth, electricity, retail stores, surfaced roads, wagons, Cobb & Co coaches, quicker rail access to the City, war service and with it a rural male population in decline. The Railway Commissioners assisted, perhaps unwittingly, in directing growth by selecting certain rural towns as transfer hubs, where trains would be 'parked' overnight, and goods re-assigned to another train, and the location for rail families to take up permanent residence.

An economic profile of Goulburn today can be compiled, for analysis, from the ABS Regional Statistics for 1999.

When Goulburn was proclaimed a municipality in 1859, its area of potential township as laid out by the Surveyor-General's office was approx 30 square miles. Those geographic and statistical boundaries remain today.

The population has remained relatively stable during the 1990s at 21,000, whilst its age distribution , like much of rural NSW has aged overall with post-school leavers moving away from the City. Today's population age grouping is :

20-54 years
55-64 years
65 years and over 2,77

It is noteworthy that in 1996-97 there was positive gain in population numbers with births (304) exceeding deaths (198)

Driving through the main street of Goulburn today, one does not appear to see many (if any) vacant shops but the building rate in 1997-98 was a record $7,092,000 made up of shops ($635m), factories ($180m) offices ($205m) and other ($6,072,000—accounted for by a new shopping centre). Housing generated $7,183,000 in new dwellings (73) thus averaging a little less than $100,000 each in estimated construction costs.

Obviously little farming is carried on in such a small geographic area and this is confirmed by there being only 27 farm units totalling 5633 hectares with an output of $1,2386,000. This was essentially sheep with lamb production numbering 15,563 and only 1,531 head of cattle.

The main activity within the city boundaries was manufacturing production, estimated to be $161 million from 40 manufacturing units, employing 1,083 people.

The 12 motels and hotels could accommodate 984 bed nights and employ 144 people. The city sponsors a number of annual events including The Lilac Festival, the Music Jamboree, a Blues Music Festival and the Goulburn Rodeo. The Goulburn Show and Rose Festival in March is also a major drawcard for tourists. The motor racing on most weekends, reverses the norm of high occupancy rates during the week and empty rooms of a weekend. In Goulburn, it is very difficult to find a room on a weekend but there are some vacancy's during week nights.

Being the centre of renewed interest in rural activities Goulburn is naturally poised to enjoy major growth as a tourist town. Like many inland cities, it has still not found its real competitive edge but is actively seeking any industry that may be looking to relocate. The concept of cluster industry development has not been adopted as it is considered too restrictive, narrow and limiting rather than bringing any and all industries to town and let them shake out to see who and what holds together. Goulburn has become the regional hub, where for many decades a wealthy pastoral setting known in the region for the strong wool merino in Gunning and the ideal lambing conditions around the Marulan area. Goulburn, for over 150 years, was the mainstay for the wool and pastoral industry and remains so today. The original railway brought much progress to the town and the idea of a VFT passing through and possibly stopping in Goulburn has made the City campaign to be the location for the second Sydney airport, the focus of a community project. The next 'railway' phenomenon has been witnessed on the horizon.

Dr. G. L. Buxton , as Lecturer in Economic History at Adelaide University published his doctoral work 'The Riverina 1861-1891' in 1967, and makes references to the effect of the railways coming to the region in the late 1800s.

"From the time that New South Wales had ignored the instruction that the Murrumbidgee was to be the inter-colonial boundary and had fixed it at the Murray—and on the south bank at that—Victorian Governments had cast covetous eyes at the Riverina. The whole of the area as far northeast as Wagga lies nearer Melbourne than Sydney. Its economic ties were with Melbourne, and Victorian Governments said that they would continue tapping the area and if possible annex it. In 1863 a Victorian Select Committee on the Riverina District had been appointed specifically 'to take evidence and report on the best method of securing to the Victorian Railways the Trade of the River in the districts of Murray, Murrumbidgee and Darling Rivers. Partly on the basis of the report the Victorian railway had been extended in 1864 to Echuca, 120 miles from Melbourne and only forty-five from Deniliquin. Two years later petitioners were urging the New South Wales Government that the railway should be extended to Deniliquin. By 1870 the Deniliquin and Moama Railway Company had been formed and in 1876 the Victorian-gauge line was thus extended by private enterprise to Deniliquin."

(P209)"The Railway Commissioners were to be informed of the hardship under which farmers laboured, under existing railway tariffs and the rates were to be revised; millers were to return bags to the producers of cereal, or reimburse them with two-thirds of the original cost; the government was to be urged so as to have the statistics of farm produce collected as to form reliable records of the cereal products of the colony, and finally, the union advocated the advisability of farmers cooperating with the object of building grain sheds for the purpose of storing their grain. By 1891, closer settlement, under the Robertson's Act, had given the selectors their land; railway extensions and differential rates were giving them access to metropolitan markets, and cooperation was breaking the political and commercial monopolies of the labour unions. But it was in fact the very land sales revenue which selectors had helped to boost which had saved New South Wales governments from having to resort to an extensive protective tariff system like Victoria. It is true that the southern Riverina declined earlier as a result of the general movement of population in a north-westerly direction. Selectors selling out to squatters or their fellows and accompanying rationalisation of holdings caused depopulation of the southern towns; as did the progressive outward movement of casual workers and contractors, including Chinese, engaged in fencing, dam sinking and ringbarking; while teamsters and those employed in coaching and the river-steamer traffic continually retreated before the advancing railways."

If the several hundred temporary residents engaged in building railways and associated works at Albury are excluded, and some allowance made for Wagga having become a Municipality with consequent boundary extensions between 1861 and 1871, the growth rates of Albury and Wagga are parallel. Both grew rapidly in the seventies but were required to share with other towns which developed as rural service centres the prosperity resulting from closer settlement. Deniliquin grew rapidly with the fat stock market of the late fifties, declining as that traffic did in the sixties. Growth recovered during the seventies, with rising prosperity from family selection and a further boost from the private railway link with Melbourne. The extension of the New South Wales government railways to the area in the early eighties, partly in answer to Victorian economic aggression, effectively reduced Deniliquin's economic hinterland, while movement of selectors out of the district further decreased the need for services. A combined flour mill and brewery, a wool scour, soap factory and the railway marked the limits of local industrial enterprise. The seasonal wool traffic to the railhead provided Deniliquin's major annual economic activity, with livestock movements of less importance as the Victorian protective tariff increased. Brick-works and saw mills, as in other towns, operated according to the demands of the building trade. In southern Riverina, building activity generally declined during the period, Between 1881 and 1891 the number of houses in Narrandera increased from 248 to 370 and in Wagga from 594 to 921. By contrast the number of houses in Albury rose only from 1,051 to 1,097 and in Deniliquin from 545 to 549."

"The railways to Hay and Jerilderie ended the domination of Deniliquin in the western Riverina, both of these towns growing at Deniliquin's expense. Within a year of the railway reaching Jerilderie a flour-mill had been built. During the seventies Hay had grown in importance as a transport centre for teamsters, Cobb & Co. coaches, and river steamers loaded with wool or station supplies, including fencing wire. Thousands of tons of copper ore brought by teams from Mount Hope, 160 miles north, and the Araunah mine in Nymagee, 220 miles north, were loaded on to steamers at Hay for smelting in Adelaide, and machinery passed back along the same route. Until the railway reached Hay in 1882 the bridge was opened for as many as six steamers a day, but in the whole of the following year only six passed through. Some squatters, accustomed to dealing with Melbourne, continued to send wool by steamer to Echuca when the river was high, but the differential rates netted an increasing amount of this traffic for Sydney, while the existence of the railhead enabled Hay's prosperity as the centre of the outback transport system to be maintained."

Narrandera and Corowa both grew as a result of selection activity, the need for services increasing as the district was more closely settled. Corowa's agricultural and pastoral hinterland gave rise to flour-mills and a wool scour; saw-mills cut red gum and pine; and in 1892 the completion of the Culcairn—Corowa railway link to Sydney assured further growth. By 1891, Narrandera, on a population basis, was the most highly industrialised town in the Riverina. Besides being a railway junction for the Hay and Jerilderie lines, and before that a steamer port, Narrandera was the centre of an extensive timber trade which drew on the surrounding natural pine forests. Timber from its several sawmills was sent all over the Riverina and as far as the upper Darling. A coach factory, a brewery and cordial factory, flour-mill(1884), wool scour(1886), and meat freezing works (1890)—in which rabbits increasingly replaced sheep—all contributed to the towns stability; while earlier gold had been mined. Narrandera's most rapid growth had been from 1871 to 1881, from a population of 142 to 1,142 . The 1871 census return included only twenty-two householders—the rest were recorded as 'persons sleeping on premises'.

Amongst the more general changes were the westward and northward movement of the 'selection frontier' and the 'ringbarking and fencing frontier'. The first followed available land, the second the spread of improvement techniques to an ever increasing area. Both led to a movement of land seekers and casual labour to areas progressively 'further out'. Similarly as the railway fan opened out, a further outward migration followed; that of the teamsters and those engaged in coaching and river traffic. All too often the program of railway development in eastern Australia was directed by inter-colonial rivalry, as the use of different (rail) gauges and differential rates indicates. The line to Hay effectively cut off Deniliquin's northern hinterland; that to Jerilderie severed it from the east.. This was the New South Wales Government's eventual answer to the Victorian policy off tapping the Riverina at a series of points along the Murray. Thereafter Deniliquin' linked with Melbourne rather than Sydney, though on a more limited scale than previously because of its reduced hinterland. Socially it made less difference. Even in the eighties it was said of the residents of Hay that they wore Melbourne clothes, read the Melbourne newspapers and drank Melbourne beer; and in the four southern Riverina counties, half the population were Victorian born. At the same time the extension of railways contributed to the growth of a number of small service centres, particularly in the wheat belt nearer Wagga and Albury. These railway towns, scattered at regular intervals, along the line formed focal points for the activities of farming communities. Often the extension of the railway was the result of successful closer settlement in the more favoured areas of the Riverina. However even today the largest towns remain those on the major permanent rivers."

Considerable changes had also taken place in the carriage of wool. Stations with a frontage to navigable rivers preferred to load wool direct on to steamers or barges by which it travelled to Echuca and thence by rail to Melbourne. From other stations it was carted by dray to the nearest railway. With the advent of the rail to Echuca , Wodonga, and Deniliquin, Wagga, Albury, Narrandera, Hay and Jerilderie, and the introduction of differential rates, river traffic declined. Inevitably wool-growers sold to the highest bidder—in this case, the colony offering the cheapest access to the sea-ports. Except for 1890, when the shearer's strike held up 10,000 Melbourne-bound bales of wool at Wodonga, there had been no difficulties in transporting wool, the quality of which had been continually improving, as had the yield per sheep.

The movement of livestock was another matter. Victorian protection, ministering to the commercial interests of Melbourne, had avoided a tariff on wool. But protection for meat-producers led to ever-increasing duties on livestock imports. In the late 1870s, despite the 1s. per head tax on sheep, as many as 12,000 per week were railed to Melbourne via Moama(on the NSW side of the Murray River at Echuca). Until 1891 it was reckoned that 75% of the cattle marketed in Melbourne came from Queensland and New South Wales, but in 1892, with protection an election issue, tariffs became prohibitive—rising from 5s to One pound per head on cattle—and smuggling was rife. Some of the problems of moving livestock cheaply and efficiently were avoided by the introduction of meat freezing and chilling works at Narrandera. By 1891 meetings had been held in other towns to encourage the building of freezing works there.

A typical pattern of development in the regions saw a rapid increase in town population in the seventies, relative decline with waning opportunities in the eighties as the selector frontier moved further north-west, and some recovery in the nineties. The migrations of the seventies resulted, in spite of the general slow down of growth and economic activity in the sixties, and with natural increase, the Riverina had seen a six-fold growth of population in thirty years, much of the increase being in the numbers of women and children. This growth in the respectable urban and farming communities and the vastly increased number of schools and churches took much of the roughness from the pastoral society typical of the fifties.

Conclusion

The overall answer to the question as to what benefits came with the railways investment can now be suggested.

What resulted was a blend of masterful engineering and construction works, employing many men returning from the gold fields and looking for permanent steady work, railway towns, transfer hubs, and workshops were all developed as part of the growth of the railway system, and these operational and maintenance facilities also put many thousands of men, and women to permanent long-term employment. Railway owns were established and commenced small settlements, all to be serviced with stores, schools, churches, roads and buildings.

The engineering work provided skills in bridging, tunnelling, gradient management, and these skills were then used all over Australia and New Zealand.

The associated construction involved major railway stations throughout the Sydney area and in every country town. Many large construction jobs were undertaken in the bigger towns such as Orange, Goulburn, Albury and Wagga, where huge station terminals and complexes were built.

Many railway towns sprung up with the Railway Commissioners funding the cost of houses for railway families.

Transfer hubs were built at junctions where undercover workshops for cleaning and maintenance and storage buildings were constructed, and many employees engaged. Train crews were generally housed and maintained in these hubs.

Workshops were built in the Sydney area to meet manufacturing, maintenance and cleaning obligations.

At the peak in 1885 over 12,000 men were employed by the Railway system in New South Wales alone. This was replicated in each Colony but, with the exception of Victoria, on a smaller scale.

Immediate associated development took place in the coal industry in New South Wales where production increased steadily to meet the needs of steam generation for the railway systems in New South Wales and Victoria. Victoria accepted shipment of over 160,000 tons of coal to keep its trains operating.

Other development occurred in the hubs by new industries starting such as, coach building, woollen mills, iron foundries, fencing contractors, Cobb & Co coaches, meat works with refrigeration and freezers (all of which needed installing and servicing). Electricity was being distributed through rural towns by the late 1910s, and larger mining operations were opening up because of the ability to transport the ore to refineries and ports.

The investment of under 40,000,000 pound in the Colony of New South Wales achieved great results. It created huge employment opportunities, opened up the inland areas for new towns and served the rural economies by providing fast and cheaper access to the markets and ports than previously available. But most importantly the capital came from overseas which meant that many new arrivals followed the importation of capital, and that the capital was serviced from operational revenues was unique. The Government of New South Wales, as opposed to the Governments of the other colonies did not have to burden itself with meeting debt or interest payment from current revenues.

This gain meant that other services in the Colony could grow as planned without the colony losing revenue. The economic growth continued with the on-going development of electricity to both town and country people and the growth of the telegraph system that would eventually link all the colonies to each other and overseas.

The gap created by the tyranny of distance was swiftly closing.

CHAPTER 34

LAND REFORM IN AUSTRALIA

The Problem

By 1860, the need for new land legislation in the eastern colonies became urgent because the leases of the squatters issued under the authority of the Order in Council of 1847, expired in 1861.

The attempt to pass new land legislation was one of the immediate causes of conflict between the Legislative Assemblies and the Legislative Councils of the colony of New South Wales.

The two New South Wales Acts did provide for other forms of land tenure, other than 'conditional purchase' and 'leasehold' eg there was purchase by auction, purchase of timber reserves, stock reserves, etc However these acts dealt exclusively with the disposal of crown lands, and did not affect private sales of land.

The author of the Alienation and Occupations Bill (leading to the above mentioned Acts) in NSW, John Robertson, insisted that the interests of the squatters and selectors be safeguarded. The Bill made ample provision for the obtainment of lands by those who really desired to settle upon the land and improve it, whatever might be attempted to be done for the advancement of the masses of the people, the squatter's interests were by no means overlooked.

An editorial in the SMH of 8th October 1860 sets out the record of the crown lands

"the origin and basis for our colonial prosperity has been pastoral occupation of the waste (Crown) lands. For a time it was the only thing possible, and it answered excellently its purpose of creating a valuable export, and spreading civilisation over the interior. But the growth of society requires modification to the system. Experience seems to point out that the advantages it has offered are too much confined to a particular class—that the scope offered to the agriculturalist and the small squatter is too limited, and a demand has arisen that greater freedom and opportunity should be given to those who are willing to invest their industry and their savings in rural pursuits. It is natural that those who feel, and who have perhaps felt for some time, the pressure of restrictions, should be prompted to advocate rather violent rearrangements—to sweep away, not only without compunction, but with a certain grim satisfaction, all the vested interests that have grown up, without sufficient considering the evils that would result even to themselves and their friends from such an iconoclastic policy. "

The SMH of 10th October, 1860 had reported some of the speeches in the Legislative Assembly:

"The moral argument for the squatters was presented by, Mr. O'Shanassy (himself a squatter): ' Within a few days of the end of the year, would it be thought fair to say ' Here, you pastoral tenants, whose rights have been recognised under law for the past twenty years,—you who opened up the wilderness, risked all your invested capital—and after all your pains and trouble, you are within fourteen days of losing your tenure. Go about your business!. No man in the community would deal in this way with slaves, let alone men of character and respectability.'

Some further background

A Member of the NSW Legislative Assembly—Mr Jenkins—spoke during the debate:

' It has been said that the produce of the pastoral districts did not stand so high on the list of exports as those of the gold districts. Now I do not wish to deprecate that interest, but I can show that a mistake was make in those statements, for the pastoral exports are far greater over a period than those of gold (the amount of gold dust exported annually is between 2 & 3 million pound; whilst the pastoral exports are between 3 & 4 million pound. But which industry employs the most labour. The amount of grain imported into the Colony has practically declined to zero, whilst the local production was fast overtaking demand.'

Alternatives

Following the earlier acts, an inquiry into 'Public Lands' was completed by Messrs. Morris and Rankin, who roundly condemned the entire system and concluded that the 'most noteworthy matter that has come to light, and the most ominous for the future well-being of the Colony (of NSW), is the class contest for the possession of its lands which has covered five-sixths of the surface. The huge area of 86 million acres has provided a field on which every form of abuse has been carried out in defiance of the public interest. It needs little argument to prove the vice of a policy which of its very essence divides the rural population into two hostile camps; and it would be superfluous to state that the personal virtues of veracity and honourable dealing have been tarnished by the daily habit of intrigue, and the practice of evading the law and by declaration in defiance of fact universally made. '

The most radical solution to the Land Reform Movement was adopted in New South Wales, where it was called ' Free selection before survey'. The essential feature of this system of selling Crown land, was not the sale price of the land, but its immediate release to homesteaders; they paid one-quarter of the price as a deposit, and received their title deeds after three years and completion of the payment. John Robertson successfully piloted two Bills through both Chambers incorporating these principles., after a political crisis involving strong opposition from squatters with seats in the Upper House. The Two Acts gave adequate protection to squatters by granting them long leases of Crown Land in pastoral areas, but allowed selectors to take up Crown land in agricultural or mixed farming and grazing areas with the minimum of delays and with only a low deposit. They could then begin cultivation immediately, and wait for the government surveyor to arrive later. However, they could get their freehold only if they made improvements.

'The new system worked!

A Brief History of Crown Land Disposal

The practice of recording money derived from the sale of crown land as a separate entry to which only the British Treasury was entitled (refer 'The Land Fund") was common to all colonies and formed one of the largest items of their annual income. Auction sales raised significant income before being suspended in 1883, when 'it became evident that this indiscriminate sale of the public estate and its alienation was threatening to endanger the true interests of the country" (Wealth & Progress of NSW 1886-87—P385). This alienation was due to rivalry between the two principal classes of settlers—the pastoral tenants and the free selectors, and the fact that the sales were concluded without conditions relating to use, improvement or settlement. Sales were temporarily suspended by auction and it was decided to sell only limited area during any one year.

Under the Crown Lands Act of 1861, the Governor was empowered to sell crown leasehold lands (upon which improvements had been made) to the owners of the improvements, without competitive bids, at a price determined by valuation, the minimum price being fixed at One pound sterling per acre. The area of land able to be purchased in this way was increased from 320 acres to 640 acres. This privilege of purchasing, without competition, Crown Lands held under lease did not extend merely to the pastoral tenant of the crown but to leaseholders in general including goldfield leases. Broad acre Pastoral leases could also be freeholded in lumps of 25 square miles. All conversions of crown land generated revenues of two hundred and ten thousand in 1871 and two hundred and sixty thousand pounds in 1886. The Government entered into 'conditional' or terms sales which in 1862 amounted to twenty-five million acres and generated a total of eleven million five hundred thousand pounds. Interest accrued on such terms transactions and in 1886 amounted to two million 605 thousand pounds.

Full details of annual sales and lease of crown land and revenue therefrom can be found in the Statistics section of this volume.

Pastoral leases generated generous revenues but a significant element of default occurred. In 1886 revenue obtained from these leases amounted to only 374 thousand pounds, but lease payments in default amounted to over 500 thousand pounds.

Revenue from Government services was the largest sector of overall Government revenue.

In 1886, the percentage breakdown was as follows:

Services	40.7
Taxation	4.4
Land sales	21.6
miscellaneous	3.3

CHAPTER 35

TRAVELS WITH JOHN OXLEY— AN INTIMATE ACCOUNT

John Oxley solved the challenge put before him by Governor Lachlan Macquarie to solve the puzzle of the rivers. The challenge was to find their source and where they emptied and to establish whether or not there was a large inland body of water with greatly fertile lands surrounding it which contributed to the river system of the Colony of New South Wales.

Oxley had arrived in the Colony in 1803 and in 1814 was appointed Surveyor-General of the Colony.

In 1816, Macquarie requested Oxley to head up an expedition to follow the trail of the recently returned Blaxland, Lawson and Wentworth over the Blue Mountains. Macquarie had a number of reasons for this request Firstly he had been doubtful of the full truth of the Wentworth expedition and wanted independent verification; secondly, Oxley was a reticent 'explorer' and Macquarie wanted to see him gain both confidence and experience in discovering the new challenge of surveying in the unknown; and thirdly, Macquarie needed to open up new areas for the pastoral industry which, with over 1 million sheep and a hundred thousand cattle, desperately needed new open grazing lands.

Oxley left , accompanied by Lieutenant Evans, a sound , reliable engineer and architect in early 1817, and upon his return on the 30th August, 1817 wrote to Macquarie reporting the highlights of his journey. The Oxley

Journal is hundreds of pages but his letter highlights the essential aspects of the journey and is recorded in full in W.C. Wentworth's volume (1814) 'A Statistical Account of the Colony of New South Wales'. Oxley wrote his account from Bathurst, which, after the Wentworth journey over the mountains, became the base camp for future expeditions and the start of a township and watering point for squatters and pastoralists taking up new land in the west.

"I proceeded down the Lachlan in company with the boats until the 12th May, 1817, the country rapidly descending until the waters of the river rose to a level with it, and then dividing into numerous branches, inundated the country to the west and north-west, and prevented any further progress by boat, the river being lost in marshes.

We then proceeded with the horses, in a course towards the coast to determine if there were any intersecting streams that might come into the Lachlan.

I continued this course until the 9th of June , when having lost two horses through fatigue and want, and the others in a deplorable condition, I changed our course to north, along a range of lofty hills, running in that direction, as they afforded the only means of procuring water until we should fall in with some running stream. On this course I continued until the 23rd June, when we again fell in with a stream, which we had at first some difficulty to recognise as the Lachlan, it being little larger than one of the marshes of it, where it was quitted on the 17th of May.

I was unwilling to have the slightest doubt that any navigable waters falling westward into the sea, between the limits pointed out in my instructions. I continued along the banks of the stream until the 8th of July, it having taken during this period a westerly direction, and passing through a perfectly level country, barren in the extreme, and being evidently at periods entirely under water. We were a full five hundred miles west of Sydney, and nearly in its latitude; and it had taken us ten weeks of unremitted exertion to proceed so far. We had demonstrated beyond the shadow of a doubt, that no river whatever could fall into the sea, between Cape Otway and Spencer's Gulf.

It now became my duty to make our remaining resources as extensively useful to the colony as our circumstances would allow: these were much diminished: an accident to one of the boats, at the outset of the expedition, had deprived us of one-third of our dry provisions, of which we had originally but eighteen weeks; and we had been in consequence for some time on a reduced ration of two quarts of flour per man, per week. To return to the depot by the route we had come, would have been as useless as impossible.

It was my intention to take a northeast course, to intersect the country, and if possible ascertain what had become of the Macquarie River, which it was clear had never joined the Lachlan. On the 7th of August we were now quitting the area of the Lachlan and had passed to the north-east of the high range of hills, which on this parallel bounds the low country to the north of that river. This renewed our hopes of soon falling in with the Macquarie, and we continued upon the same course, occasionally inclining to the eastward, until the 19th passing through a fine luxuriant country, well watered, crossing in that space of time nine streams, having a northerly course through rich valleys; the country in every direction being moderately high and open, and as generally as fine as can be imagined.

An accident let us down this stream about a mile, when we were surprised by its junction with a river coming from the south, of such width and magnitude, as to dispel all doubts as to this last being the river we had so long anxiously looked for. Short as our resources were, we could not resist the temptation this beautiful country offered us, to remain two days on that junction of the river, for the purpose of examining the vicinity to as great an extent as possible . . . . as far as the eye could see in every direction, a rich and picturesque country extended, abounding in limestone, slate, good timber, and every other requisite that could render an uncultivated country desirable. The soil cannot be excelled, whilst a noble river of the first magnitude affords the means of conveying its productions from one part to the other.

It appeared to me that the Macquarie had taken a northwest course from Bathurst, and that it must have received immense accessions of water in its course from that place. We viewed it at a period best calculated to form an accurate judgement of its importance, when it was neither swelled by floods beyond its natural and usual height, nor contracted within its limits by summer droughts; from the boldness and height of the country, I presume, must be at least as many, some idea may be formed, when at this point it exceeded in breadth and apparent depth, the Hawkesbury at Windsor. Many of the branches were of grander and more extended proportion than the admired one on the Nepean River from the Warragambia to Emu Plains. On the 22nd we proceeded up the river and between the point quitted and Bathurst, crossed the sources of numberless streams, all running into the Macquarie; two of them were nearly as large as that river itself at Bathurst. The country from whence all these streams derive their source, was mountainous and irregular, and appeared equally so on the east side of the Macquarie. This description of country extended to the immediate vicinity of Bathurst; but to the west of those lofty ranges, the country was broken into low grassy hills, and fine valleys watered by rivulets rising on the west side of the mountains, which on their eastern side pour their waters directly into the Macquarie.

I shall hasten to lay before your Excellency the journals, charts and drawings, explanatory of the various occurrences of our diversified route; infinitely gratified if our exertions should appear to your Excellency commensurate with your expectations, and the ample means which your care and liberality placed at my disposal.

I express my appreciation and thanks to Mr. Evans, the deputy Surveyor, Mr. Alan Cunningham, the King's botanist, Mr. Fraser and Mr. Parr."

CHAPTER 36

RECONSTRUCTING THE MACQUARIE ERA CONSTRUCTION PROGRAM

The Bigge's Report provides a partial list of building work completed by Macquarie. The items, which to Bigge are the most useful buildings on the list, include:

(The numbers refer to references in Greenway's –1822 Map of Sydney)

Sydney Items

- The Commissariat (King's) Store at Sydney (8)
- St. Phillips Church at Sydney (12)
- Improvement of Government House at Sydney (1)
- Sydney Gaol (30)
- Clearing of grounds contiguous to the Government Houses (1)
- A Parsonage House at Sydney (30)
- Military Barracks at Sydney—Wynyard Square (13)
- Hospital in Sydney –"Rum" Hospital –Macquarie Street (21)
- Hyde Park Convict Barracks (20)
- Military Hospital in Sydney – Wynyard Square (27)
- Improvements to Lumber-Yard at Sydney (28)
- Improvements to Dockyard at Sydney (29)
- St. James Church (19)

- Colonial Secretary's House & Office (4)
- Sydney Cove-Governor's Wharf (26)
- Water Bailiff—House and landing (31)
- Houses for Judge-Advocate (Judge of Supreme Court) – (4)
- Court-house at Sydney (18)
- School-house at Hyde Park (16)
- Market house at George Street, Sydney (15)
- Government stables at Sydney (2)
- Fountain in Macquarie Place (6)
- Obelisk in Macquarie Place (7)
- The Turnpike Gate—Lower George Street (22)
- Fort (Macquarie) at Bennelong Point (3)
- Battery at Dawes Point (10)
- Greenway's House and office (9)
- Windmill—(built at Public Expense)—at Garrison barracks (23)
- Windmill—(built at Public Expense)—at the Domain. (24)
- Magazine at Fort Phillip (11)
- St.Andrew's Church foundation (15)
- Orphan House in Sydney (25)

Parramatta, Windsor, Liverpool & Outer Sydney Area Items

- Carters Barracks and gaol at Windsor
- Female Factory at Parramatta
- St. Matthews Church at Windsor
- Church at Liverpool
- Chapel at Castlereagh
- A Parsonage House at Parramatta
- A Parsonage House at Liverpool
- Hospital at Parramatta
- Hospital at Windsor (a converted brewery formerly owned by Andrew Thompson)
- Hospital at Liverpool
- Convict Barracks at Parramatta
- Improvement of Government House at Parramatta
- An asylum for the aged and infirm near Sydney
- Bridge at Rushcutter's Bay—South Head Road
- Macquarie Light-house at Sydney South Head

(This list accounts for 46 items on Bigge's 63 reference)

Newcastle Items

- Hospital
- Gaol
- Commandant House
- Surgeons Quarter
- Workhouse
- Blacksmiths Forge
- Pier
- Windmill
- Parsonage House "(Bigge Report)

(We now account for 55 out of the 63)

Greenway Items (drawn but under construction)

- Officer Quarters-Hyde Park
- Alterations to Judge Advocate's House
- Alterations to Lumber Yard building
- Alterations to Dawes Battery
- Alterations to Liverpool parsonage
- Portico, Gov House, Parramatta
- Alterations to Orphan School, Sydney
- Alterations to Government House, Sydney
- Judge Field's House –Sydney
- Plans for Mr. Marsden's House at Parramatta
- Survey for the new General (Rum) Hospital
- Plans for the Windsor Church
- Plans for the Liverpool Church
- Plans for Judge Field's house
- Plans for Parramatta Female Factory
- Survey of Parramatta Bridge
- Survey of Sydney Gaol
- Measuring work by contractors at Sydney Gaols
- Plans for Windsor Court-house
- Plans for new toll-gate

- Plans for Obelisk in Macquarie Place
- Plans for fountain in Macquarie Place.

(If we count 'alterations' to buildings, we can account for the whole 63 items stated by Commissioner Bigge to have been undertaken in the Macquarie Era)

APPENDIX B – CALCULATED COST OF CONSTRUCTION

CONSTRUCTION ITEM Greenway Estimate Author Estimate

CONSTRUCTION ITEM	Greenway Estimate	Author Estimate
The Commissariat (King's) Store at Sydney (8)		`17500
St. Phillips Church at Sydney (12)		6250
Improvement of Government House at Sydney (1)	600	
Sydney Gaol (30)	6000	
Clearing of grounds contiguous to the Government Houses (1)		200
A Parsonage House at Sydney (30)		850
Military Barracks at Sydney—Wynyard Square (13)		21000
Hospital in Sydney –"Rum" Hospital –Macquarie Street (21)		0
Military Hospital in Sydney – Wynyard Square (27)		16750
Improvements to Lumber-Yard at Sydney (28)		2000
Improvements to Dockyard at Sydney (29)		1000
St. James Church (19)	6240	
Colonial Secretary's House & Office (4)		875
Sydney Cove-Governor's Wharf (26)		5500
Water Bailiff—House and landing (31)		1250
Houses for Judge-Advocate (Judge of Supreme Court (4)		4800
Court-house at Sydney (18)	6450	
School-house at Hyde Park (16)		8500
Market house at George Street, Sydney (15)	300	
Government stables at Sydney (2)	9000	
Fountain in Macquarie Place (6)		500
Obelisk in Macquarie Place (7)		375

The Turnpike Gate—Lower George Street (22)		2750
Fort (Macquarie) at Bennelong Point (3		21000
Battery at Dawes Point (10)		14675
Greenway's House and office (9)		1695
Windmill—(built at Public Expense)—at Garrison barracks (23)		6250
Windmill—(built at Public Expense)—at the Domain. (24)		6230
Magazine at Fort Phillip (11)	1240	
St.Andrew's Church foundation (15)	2500	
Orphan House in Sydney (25)	2180	
Parramatta, Windsor, Liverpool & Outer Sydney Area		
Carters Barracks and gaol at Windsor		19750
Female Factory at Parramatta		37500
St. Matthews Church at Windsor		5600
Church at Liverpool		5250
Chapel at Castlereagh		4750
A Parsonage House at Parramatta		1250
A Parsonage House at Liverpool	520	
Hospital at Parramatta		16500
Hospital at Windsor (a converted brewery formerly owned by Andrew Thompson)		3365
Hospital at Liverpool		15850
Convict Barracks at Parramatta		31500
Improvement of Government House at Parramatta	1120	
An asylum for the aged and infirm near Sydney		8625
Bridge at Rushcutter's Bay—South Head Road		2275
Macquarie Light-house at Sydney South Head	7050	
(This list accounts for 46 items on Bigge's 63 reference)		
Newcastle Items		
Hospital		16693
Gaol		18824
Commandant House		1356
Surgeons Quarter		1569
Workhouse		5228
Blacksmiths Forge		2135

Pier		3556
Windmill		2150
Parsonage House "(Bigge Report)		1189
(We now account for 55 out of the 63)		
Greenway Items (drawn but under construction)		
Officer Quarters-Hyde Park	10600	
Alterations to Judge Advocate's House	600	
Alterations to Lumber Yard building	2000	
Alterations to Dawes Battery	1200	
Alterations to Liverpool parsonage	520	
TOTALS	55600	344865

Kitchen Estimates (furnished to Bigge) is 922,857.13.11

Since the actual total for the estimated 60 buildings construction work completed in the Macquarie era is only $400,000, and it is most unlikely that the total could have reached $922,000, then it is safe to assume that Henry Kitchen, in producing this misleading estimate to Commissioner Bigge was intent only in providing with the goal of further blackening the names of both Greenway and Macquarie – both of whom disliked and were disliked by Kitchen. It was a deliberately malicious and deceptive piece of disinformation by Kitchen.

There is another possible explanation that stretches credulity somewhat but could be justified as a possibility. It is always assumed that convict labour was essentially 'free', and should therefore not count or contribute to the total cost of the finished construction.

If we make a number of assumptions concerning equivalent day rates of pay, and about the productivity level of the convicts in a major construction job, keeping in mind they were supervised by other convicts, then we may be able to say that the 400,000 pound of cost assembled in the Table above is for materials only and that the equivalent value of the convict labour makes the difference of the 522,000 to bring the total estimate up to Kitchen's estimate of 922,000 pound.

a.   The relevant assumptions are (based on Greenways cost estimates above) the number of days of mechanics labour to complete the Government House Stables was 16,686.5 the average cost per man day was 1 shilling labour reflected a 33% content of the total finished cost.

So applying these assumptions to the construction work in the rest of the table, we find that all the projects would have taken 2,683,108 days of mechanics labour or approx 8,450 man years. The convict population increased between 1812 and 1820 by 10,800 men and totaled 19,000 men by 1820, and to suppose that 44% of the male convicts were employed in construction work is not unreasonable. At the minimum rate of 1s per day, our labour cost total becomes 134155 pound; thus, at an average of 3 shillings (compared with Coghlan's cost for 'free' mechanics at 5s per day, we would achieve the difference of 480,000 pound. Coghlan estimates that a convict would only produce about 60% of a 'free' labourer.

Our conclusion, if we stretch the point, is that Kitchen's estimate of a construction cost for the period of 900,000 is valid if our materials are valued at 402,000 and our labour accounts (at the average rate of 3 shillings per day) to a further 470,000-pound.

Phillip's Town Planning

In a work commissioned for the sesqui-centenary of the City of Sydney, Paul Ashton writes in 'Planning Sydney-The Accidental City', " within months of the initial European colonization, New South Wales' first governor, Arthur Phillip, had marked out the 'principal street of the intended town', defined 'the limits of future building' and ordered the preparation of a plan for the town of Sydney. Most likely executed by Lt William Dawes and Augustus Alt, Phillip's plan envisaged the 'principal streets . . . . placed so as to admit a free circulation of air'; they were also to be 200 feet wide. Other provisions were made to 'preserve uniformity in the buildings, prevent narrow streets, and the many inconveniences which the increase of inhabitants would otherwise occasion hereafter'.

Phillips early administrative decision to segregate convict, military and a number of civil establishments from bureaucratic and legal functions was to influence Sydney's development. Building was to concentrate in the western part of the fledgling town, while the eastern area, naturally separated by the Tank Stream, was to be characterized by open spaces and later provide the location of the Sydney's first 'genteel' suburbs. But the Governors somewhat ambitious plan did not materialize. His last order, that the crown within the town of Sydney retain land was likewise ineffective. After Phillip's departure from the colony in 1792, some of his successors leased into private hands and, from 1808, granted title to land within Sydney town. The alienation of town sites compounded Sydney's disorderly growth, so much so that by 1807 its most irascible governor, William Bligh, was to complain to his superiors in England 'how much government (was) . . . . confined in any arrangement it may think proper to make for its own use or ornament of the town'.

When Macquarie arrived in Sydney in late 1809, the conditions were not conducive to planned growth, nor to his goal of 'having all Edifices within the town built on a regular plan, so as to combine convenience with ornament, and preserve the regularity of the streets and houses'. Macquarie had clocks installed in the major buildings (those commissioned by Macquarie himself) in order to 'instill discipline into the colonial workforce, and he had also had a host of regulations decreed to bring order to the town. Thoroughfares were regularized and named; narrow streets were widened; building rules were promulgated. But he further alienated land from the crown and helped create property relations. All those 'able and willing to erect substantial and handsome buildings within the town' were also encouraged to do so by promises of land grants instead of leases.

WILLIAM CHARLES WENTWORTH WROTE IN HIS 'HISTORICAL AND STATISTICAL ACCOUNT OF THE COLONY OF NEW SOUTH WALES':

"Until the administration of Governor Macquarie, little or no attention had been paid to the paving of streets, and each proprietor was left to build on his lease, where and how his caprice inclined him . . . The town upon the whole may be pronounced to be tolerably regular; and, as in all future additions that may be made to it, the proprietors of leases will not be allowed to deviate from the lines marked out by the surveyor-general, the new part will of course be free from the faults and inconveniences of the old".

Timothy Coghlan in "Labour & Industry in Australia records that

"Phillip was expressly enjoined to pay attention to the laying out of townships, reserving land in each for military purposes, and for naval purposes also where such seemed desirable. The interests of religion as represented by the Establish Church were not forgotten, and he was instructed to set apart a site for a church in each township, close to which 400 acres were to be reserved for the support of a clergyman; a site for a school was also to be reserved, together with 200 acres for the schoolmaster.

In 1832 Surveyor General Mitchell recorded in his report ' Reports on the limits of Sydney' that " most of the peripheral town land has been alienated and that roads and boundary lines were oblique and irregular" Mitchell's decision to straighten roads and property boundaries resulted in many claims for compensation from land-holders and led to the appointment of a select commission on compensation. The commission decided not to pay compensation but did decide that " owners would not be compelled to follow the street alignments" and this in effect gave them carte blanche to build where ever they chose, and houses were even built across the very roads that formed the basis of Mitchell's grand plan for the extension of the town".

In 'Significant Sites' edited by Lenore Coltheart, we can find the confirmation that in the Police Act of 1833 a signal of the changeover to civil society from penal society was demonstrated. The Act allowed for the regulation of shop awnings and house guttering directed that carriage and footways 'be marked by posts at the corners and intersections of streets; and ordered that the Surveyor General 'set out and name with sufficient marks the limits of the town' and its immediate port. The Act also made provision for the erection of boarding and scaffolding. A Street Alignment Act was then passed in 1834, which aimed to straighten and widen thoroughfares. The Sydney Building Act of 1837 was in effect only concerned with structural considerations and the 'security of property' within the town boundaries against the ravages of fire.

The Police and Orphan Funds

Between 1802 and 1822, the Treasury reporting function was, in fact, privatised and outsourced—the only time in Australia's history and indeed a rare occurrence any where in the civilized world. Treasury recording and reporting has always been a task for official Government.

However it was Governor King, who having been driven into action by the hasty recall and dismissal of Hunter from the position, decided that a number of matters could be handled less expensively by combining duties. The Reverend Samuel Marsden was already the Deputy Chaplain in the Colony and was 'interfering' in Colonial Politics (such as they were), so an answer to two problems came to King's mind and in reality he solved all three problems with one sweep of the pen.

A senior officer and good citizen of the early settlement – a Lieutenant Kent, was leaving the service and returning to England. Kent had built a large (some said a 'magnificent' house (which Kent couldn't sell when he was about to leave the colony. He lobbied King for the Government to buy it for official purposes, at its valuation, but King did not have authority for those types of extravagances. But he did see its use in connection with the second problem.

The penal colony had grown such as a penal colony would – a low morale, little respect for social niceties, especially marriage or responsibility towards each other; spirits were consumed to excess, whilst spirits were the 'currency' of the streets. Men and women drank to cope and debauchery reigned. This lifestyle, although officially frowned upon, led to a state of children, of all ages, running the streets, most from one parent homes and unmarried mothers. There was estimated to be 500 children of both sexes living on the streets as the nineteenth century came into being. King came to the idea that female orphans could be house, educated and 'found', as wards of the state – largely the influence of Wilberforce back in England, who Marsden had been corresponding with and informing of the conditions and inactions in the colony. Marsden had forcibly lobbied both Hunter and King. Since Hunter was no longer around, Marsden directed the full force of his ideas at King, not expecting the repercussions that came swiftly.

Marsden was becoming a thorn in King's side. His plea for more churches – Parramatta, Windsor and Liverpool, could not be justified in terms of buildings or more preachers to service them.

So Kings three-pronged action solved all three problems at one time.

King bought Kent's house for use as the Female Orphanage and set up a committee (including Marsden) to organize it. 80-100 female orphans were planned o be housed, fed, clothed and educated. Marsden's task was to, not only chair the committee but be its Treasurer. Shortly, King having arranged a source of regular revenue for the Orphan treasury, extended the role of the treasurer's function and kept Marsden extremely well occupied and away from the Government residence.

That was how the Orphan Fund commenced and was still going strong in 1821, when Macquarie was told by the British Treasury to abandon his simplistic accounting systems and adopt the 'Blue Book' methods.

The second prong of the 'privatized' treasury recording system was the Gaol Fund, with the Police Fund being simply the successor (by name change) to the Gaol Fund.

When the original Sydney Gaol burnt down by suspected arson, King decided to rally the citizens of Sydney and build a larger, stronger and more attractive replacement. He was encouraged in his plan by the directions of the Treasury in London to keep costs down, so King decided to make it a building by subscription. He rallied the free settlers and 'encouraged' them to donate money to a building fund. Subscriptions were slow but initially sufficient to get the building started. But progress was then slow and after two years of construction, the building was still not complete and donated funds had run out. So King decided to finish the Gaol with Government money. Thus the Gaol Building Fund was converted into the 'Police Fund', given an expanded role and placed into the hands of a second treasurer – Darcy Wentworth. Wentworth who was also the assistant surgeon in the colony was to be the father of William Charles Wentworth after marrying an ex-convict. Both Marsden and Wentworth filled their roles from 1802 through 1821.

It was Macquarie who decided to make the accounts and the reporting more transparent. In 1810 Macquarie subjected the payments from the two funds to scrutiny and set up a committee led by the Lieutenant Governor to review each months payments, after which Macquarie put his name on them and had the published in the Sydney Gazette for all the citizens to read and enjoy.

The reading was probably not the exciting news from 'home' that the residents wanted to hear but since the Sydney Gazette had become the official government organ for disseminating information to the populace, it was as good as the next story.

The source of revenues for both funds was the mainly import duties, imposed first by King in 1802, without official authorization but readily welcomed by the British Treasury. Import duties were applied to all imported goods at an initial flat rate of 5%, but naturally this rate grew until by Macquarie's time it had grown well into double figures (see accompanying table). Other revenues raised were fees from tavern licenses, auction licenses, tolls (from June 1811) and Market duties, for stalls in the open-air market, near Sydney Cove.

Revenue varied significantly from quarter to quarter, such was the small size and irregular visit of traders to the Harbour.

The usage of funds was broad and never ending. It ranged from paying for repair work on the existing roads and bridges of Sydney to building new roads and bridges and even government buildings. In the early days, revenue was small and expenditures limited by the need to remain in credit and build to some type of surplus. Between July 1810 and November 1818 total revenue raised for the police fund was 125,598 pound, and this was all spent other than the final balance on hand (16,859) on

- ➢ Salaries   52927
- ➢ Repair work   9409
- ➢ New Wharf   2000
- ➢ New roads   6280
- ➢ Other contracts 15779
- ➢ Govt buildings   9920

> ➢ Sundry payments   4000
> ➢ Hospital supplies   2624

Macquarie's Loan Bank

Timothy Coghlan writing in his 'Labour & Industry in Australia – Volume 1' states that

"At an early period in his governorship, Macquarie prepared a plan for the establishment of a loan bank, on the model of that founded by the Dutch at the Cape. His idea was that the Bank should issue loans to landowners at the rate of 6%, taking a mortgage of their property as security; thereby he hoped to stimulate agriculture and establish credit for those who deserved it while doing away with the need for promissory notes. The Committee for Trade and Plantations in England was unwilling to sanction the experiment, and nothing more was heard of the matter. But then in November 1816 an official notice was issued to the effect that certain subscribers had obtained permission to establish a bank. This was the Bank of New South Wales which was to have a capital of 20,000 pound divided into 200 shares of 100 pound each, and was authorized to do all the usual business of banking, including the issue of notes. Very soon the evils of an unstable paper currency disappeared as the notes of the bank were everywhere received and the promissory notes of private persons were speedily withdrawn from circulation".

For an explanation of early revenues we can turn to James Thomson's 'The financial Statements of New South Wales' where we find in the Appendix an explanation and An account of the Rise, Progress and present condition of the Revenue of the Colony.

Thomson records that "early in the year 1800, import duties on other articles of luxury were resorted to, which, with slight modifications, were continued to be collected under Proclamations of successive governors till the year 1840.

When Major-General Macquarie assumed the Government in 1810 the population was 11,590 and the port duties about 8,000 pound per annum.

On his retirement from office, in 1821, the population had increased to 29,783 and the annual port duties to nearly 30,000 pounds.

Some explanation is necessary to show where local revenues were used to supplement the civil list, since all military, government officials, legal and medical, surveying and superintendence, were meant to be allayed from the civil salaries provided by the British Treasury. Upon Macquarie's establishment of the permanency of the Police & Orphan Funds, salary payments began to appear with frequency. The first quarter of 1810 showed only 49 pound but this grew quarterly until second quarter 1812 it was 325 pound and by the fourth quarter of 1815 it had reached 4,012 pound. By the third quarter of 1818 it was consistently 2,500 pound, giving in total for Macquarie's period over 50,000 pound of payments in the form of salaries not met by the civil; list from the British Treasury.

The expenditure on roads and bridges is likewise interesting to analyse. Darcy Wentworth was, as well as an assistant surgeon, appointed as a Police Magistrate. As treasurer of the Police Fund, he had an interesting conflict of interest and he used his position in an unusual way. Most of the road repairs were carried out under the direction of a police representative or military officer. In the early 1800s the military was in its prime as controllers of the trading scene in Sydney and especially the flow of spirits. But not all military officers were proficient or successful as traders, and this is where Wentworth was able to supplement those incomes by offering them supervisory work over road repair gangs. Over the period, 1810 – 1818, supplementary payments amounted to nearly 10,000 pound. Another source of supplementary income for the military officers not otherwise engaged in trade was to 'bring back' absconding convicts. This work generally carried a 25 pound per head fee, and was not difficult work for military men with some experience of tracking.

The most important question now that we have considered the rise of local revenues and the use of those funds is how to explain the 'gap' between the use of local building funds about 25,000 pounds between 1810 and 1818, but the known expenditure on new buildings by Macquarie of over $900,000.

The Henry Kitchen submission to Commissioner Bigge of 922,000 pound is obviously an attempt to blacken the reputations of both Macquarie and Greenway. We also know that it includes an 'allowance' of 3 shillings per day for convict labour which we have to ignore because the convict maintenance fund was separated kept by the British Treasury. Thus the generally agreed upon cost of materials for the period (accepting the Bigge papers identification of 63 buildings completed during this time) is approx 412,000 pound. The payment of 25,000 pound from local revenues (assuming it all contributed towards public buildings) leaves this gap of about 375,000 pound and we need to identify its source.

N.G.Butlin wrote 'Forming a Colonial Economy' but is silent on public funds prior to the commencement of official statistics in 1822, sourced from The Blue Books. He fails to discuss these early Funds, which became the 'unofficial' treasury of the colony between 1802 and 1821.

Macquarie commenced his rule in 1810 with a meager surplus in the funds of less than 4,000 pounds – his predecessor. King, having spent rather lavishly on boat building and raising little revenue. Macquarie operated in surplus for most years in his era except for 1812 when he had a deficit of 523 pound; 1814, a deficit of 4,000 pound; and 1815 a further deficit of 4,000 pound. Prior year surplus covered these shortages, as did the accruals of government revenue for debts uncollected by the government on duties and other taxes imposed.

The answer to our question lies in the remarkable increase in the annual value of bills drawn and paid from the commencement of the Macquarie era, in 1810. Governors had the authority to arrange for bills to be drawn on the British Treasury in payment for goods and services purchased on behalf of the colony. From the last days of King when the total of bills drawn was less than 12,000 pound, Macquarie's first year was 78,000 and it rose from there.

Bills Drawn on British Treasury 1810-1819

Year	Amount of bills	Cumulative
1810	78805	78805
1811	92128	170933

1812	91019	261952
1813	57948	319900
1814	74174	394074
1815	86021	480095
1816	109118	589213
1817	101163	690376
1818	145520	835896
1919	163465	999361

(These figures sourced from the Bigge Report to the House of Commons and Australian Historical Statistics)

Although the British Government reacted to this high level of 'bill' expenditure and appointed John Thomas Bigge as Commissioner to investigate the operations of the colony, Macquarie's successor, Major General, Sir Thomas Brisbane was not able or unwilling to reduce the amount of annual expenditure in any category. One area of explanation for Macquarie's high expenditure over say, King's was that the costs for convict transportation also rose dramatically, a confirmation that a huge increase in convict numbers had occurred. To Macquarie's credit the cost of stores fluctuated downwards which indicated the movement towards self-sufficiency within the colony, and an explanation for the high cost of salary payments from local revenue is that Macquarie kept the civil list, for his whole ten years at less that the last year of King and in fact reduced it from 13,309 pound in 1811 to 12,423in 1816.The cost of victualling the colony continued to rise which indicates that in despite of the system of 'assignment' the demand for daily rations did not decrease but rather increased over the 10 year period.. Macquarie had kept the majority of the arriving convicts out of the assignment program in order to use them in his construction program. The total of bills paid under Macquarie at close to One million pound was obviously not all allocated to the construction work but would have covered most of operating costs for the colony by way of injection of funds for public finance, and community works in particular. Macquarie provided new sources of public water, and commenced a basic sewerage works program – both a considerable expenditure of colonial funds.

CHAPTER 37

THE DEVELOPMENT OF COLONIAL LABOUR & INDUSTRY

Coghlan in 'Labour and Industry in Australia' evaluates industry in the early colony as being concerned with

- Farming and stock raising
- Timber
- Whale fisheries and sealing
- Coal-mining

He points out that the second phase of industrial development included

- Wool exports & by-products (tallow, skins, oil)
- Wool scouring & weaving tanneries
- Exploration and decentralization
- Grain sales & value adding
- Cattle-breeding–export& domestic consumption – salt beef
- Dairy products–export & domestic consumption
- Other agriculture –viniculture, tobacco
- Mining industry development—copper, lead, silver
- Manufacturers in 1838 numbered 77

    o   Grain mills;
    o   Distilleries 2;
    o   Breweries 7;

o Soap-works 5;
o Tanneries 12;
o Brass and iron foundries 5;
o Woollen factories 7;
o Salt 1;
o Hat 1;
o Tobacco works 1
o Sugar refining 1
o Salting/preserving meat 2
o Coal mining 1
o Lime manufacturing 1
o Ship building 1
o Agricultural implement manufacturing 1
o Smelting works 1

These industries were all located in New South Wales

By 1848, the industrial establishments of Australia numbered 479

- Distilleries 2
- Rectifying/compounding works 2
- Breweries 51
- Sugar refineries 2
- Soap and candle works 30
- Tobacco and snuff factories 5
- Woollen mills 8
- Hat manufacturers 4
- Rope works 7 tanneries 62
- Salt works 5
- Starch manufacturers 2
- Blacking makers 2
- Meat preserving and salting 5
- Potteries 9
- Glass works 1
- Copper-smelting 1
- Iron & brass foundries 27
- Gas works 1
- Ship & boat building 12

- Flour mills 223
- Oatmeal and groat mills 1

These industries were located:

- 272 in New South Wales
- 41 in Port Phillip
- 99 in VDL
- 67 in South Australia

The third phase was encouraged by broad economic events

- Gold discovery
- Free immigration
- Railways
- Crown Land sales
- Invention of agricultural machines
- Introduction of tariffs & protection for Victorian industry
- Growing British Investment in Australia

Hourly Rates for Workers

- Hunter's Regulation rates <u>pound</u>
- Felling, burning off & breaking ground—1 acre 5.03.0
- Reaping Wheat—1 acre 0.13.11
- Sawing plank – 100 feet 1.01.3
- Day labourers (no board) 0.05.0

Convict rates

- Full day –assigned 7.00.0 pa

Macquarie Rates-1817

- Farm workers 10.00.0
- Mechanics, carpenters, bricklayers etc 05.0pd
- Caulkers 6.0pd
- Day labourers—no board 4.0pd

- Shoemakers 5.0pd

Commentary

➢ As early as 1826 the application for male convicts exceeded the supply, and the governor was in a position to withdraw convicts from the employment of persons who were considered unfit to have assigned convicts.
➢ In NSW in 1835 over 20,000 convicts were assigned out of a total of 27,000
➢ For the purpose of regulation, one mechanic was estimated to be equivalent to two or three labourers. Convicts with skills in certain trades, bakers, candle-makers, slaters, and printers might be distributed to employers in these callings.

<u>Women Domestics</u>

General servants	11.10.0 pa
Nursery maids	11.0.0 pa
Housemaids	13.15.0 pa
Laundresses	13.00.0 pa
Cooks	13.10.0 pa

<u>General Commodity Prices</u>

<u>Wheat</u> per bushel –	1828	11s.7 p
	1833	4s.3 p
	1838	1.0 p

<u>Bread</u> per loaf	
1828	6 p
1833	4 p
1838	5 p

<u>Butter</u> –per pound	1828	2s.4 p
Salt Butter		1s.7.5 p
Cheese per pound		4.5 p

<u>Turkeys</u> –	1840	25s.0 pair
Geese – pair		12s.0 pair
Ducks – pair		8s.0 pair
Chickens –pair		6s.0 pair
Eggs –each		4 p
Butter –pound		4s.0p
Milk –quart		1s.0p
English Ale –glass		6 p
Flour––pound		4.5p
Tea – pound		4s.9 p
Sugar –pound		5.25p
Meat–pound		4.75p
Salt – pound		2.25p
Soap–pound		9.25p
Tobacco – pound		4s.10p
Clothing	**1842**	
Men's shirts		3s.3p
Straw hats		5s.0p
Coats		30s.0p
Socks		1s.6p
Handkerchief		1s.0p
Petticoats		10s.0p
Shawls		10s.0p
Aprons		2s.0p
Dress		25s.0p
Stockings		2s.6p

<u>General Statistics</u>

- In 1843 there remained only 3532 convicts in assignment, and these became free during the next five years, so that in 1848 there were no convicts in private employ.
- In 1839 wages were high and employment was good in all parts of NSW. In building trades there was a great demand for workmen, especially in Sydney; masons could earn 48s per week; bricklayers 42s and carpenters 39s.
- By 1841 masons had advanced to 54s per week; carpenters 45s and bricklayers 42s

- The 1841 census shows 15,329 houses as completed whilst 16,455 were occupied – such was the demand for housing that over 1,000 were occupied prior to completion.

Info layout

Year
Industry
No. operators
Employment
Population reconciliation
country,
metropolitan
convicts,
men,
women,
military,
government service,

CHAPTER 38

NEW INDUSTRY &
COLONIAL PAY RATES

Pay Rates

Colonel Foveaux negotiated a pay rate between government and free labourers employed in building the new stores.

James Doran, to be fully victualled (and his family) and paid ½ gal. of rum for every 100 feet of stone cut.

William Walsh to be victualled and be paid 1 gal. of rum if he cuts 100 feet of stone.

Barney Dennison to be victualled and paid 20 shillings per week for 7 full days work

On 18th May 1811 Lt.Colonel Gordon (Commissary-in-chief's office wrote to the Colonial Office in London recommending the replacement of John Palmer as the NSW Colonial Commissary on the grounds he had been involved for 20 years and that was long enough in the one job. As an attachment to his letter, Gordon attached a list of people (and their pay rates) attached to the NSW Commissary.

- John Palmer 1 pound per day
- Deputy Commissary Broughton 5s. per day

- Super. of Govt Livestock –100 pound per annum
- Storekeepers –5s. per day
- Superintendents of:
  - Convicts
  - Blacksmiths
  - The Factory
  - Carpenters
  - Agriculture
  - Constables
  - Government Mills

All received 50 pound per annum.

Macquarie re-establishes the Police & Orphan Funds

On the 31st March 1810 Macquarie appointed the Lt-Governor and the Judge Advocate to form a committee for conducting and regulating the 'Police Fund. D'arcy Wentworth was appointed Treasurer. Money arising from the duties levied on public house licenses is to be paid to the Police Fund. In future the Orphan Fund will be regulated in the same way as the Police Fund – both funds will furnish quarterly accounts of receipts and disbursements and be published in the Sydney Gazette.

On 30th April 1810 Macquarie advised Viscount Castlereagh of his intention to change the revenue sharing of these two funds. 'It has hitherto been the practice to appropriate the whole of the duties and customs collected to the Orphan School and Gaol Fund. I have deemed it adviseable to now divide 3/4th of the customs and duties to the Police Fund, and 1/4th into the Orphan Fund. The Police Fund is to defray the expenses of jail and police establishments, the erection of wharfs, quays, bridges and the making and repairing of the streets and roads within the town of Sydney. The Orphan Fund will defray the expenses of the female orphan school and other charity schools to be established here (in Sydney) and other principal settlements 9in the colony. By increasing the duty on spirits to three (3) shillings per gallon and raising a license fee to publicans, there will be sufficient funds to carry these measures to complete effect'. Later, on 17th May, Macquarie appointed Marsden as Treasurer, and Marsden, Cowper and Lt-Gov. O'Connell to be the Board of the Orphan Fund.

Macquarie's goals were not fully met and he appealed to families to support the schools by cheerfully and liberally subscribing to the erection of schoolhouses within their respective districts, similar to those people of Liverpool and Richmond. The Government contribution will be limited to 25 pound per building per district.

On 30th March 1811 Macquarie proclaimed that ' from the 10th April next, the high road between the towns of Sydney and Parramatta is declared a toll—road, and all persons riding, leading, or driving horses, mares, geldings, cattle, sheep, swine, mules, asses, gigs, chaise, cart or wagon on the road shall pay to the gatekeeper a fee.' The fee ranged from .02 p to as much as 3.0s for a carriage with four horses. Tolls were payable only once in any 24 hours, and only if traveling in excess of three (3) miles along the road

New Industry

King George's instructions to Macquarie included the request to make the best use, for the establishment of the colony, the product of the convict's labour. He was told to use what was available to first serve the needs of the colony, but the 'remainder of such productions you will reserve as a provision for some further number of convicts as you may expect from time to time, to be sent from hence, to be employed under your direction.

Thus Macquarie set to very early in his role to review the overall condition of the colony. He found the housing, streets, military and even Government House conditions to be poor. He found the colony without a treasury; he found the children to be neglected and uneducated. He found no employment opportunities and the former military officers having controlled trade both within the colony and coming to the colony. Prices and costs were inflated, the commissary was 'empty' and religion was just about non-existent. His was a large role and he started with a master plan. The farmers and graziers would have to do without their assigned convicts; the convicts were all to be reassigned to Government service and the commissary would control trade and supplies.

Postal Service

Macquarie announced on 23rd June 1810 that he had appointed Isaac Nichols to be postmaster for the colony. The home of Nichols is to be made into the post-office. He is authorized to charge for delivery and to accept letters and parcels from the Captain of each incoming ship.

Policing

David Collins records, in 'Account of the English Colony of New South Wales', that the proposal to form a night watch was first made to him, as Judge Advocate, by a convict named Harris. Harris suggested that twelve reliable men should be selected from among the better-behaved convicts to patrol the settlement by night and detain 'stragglers' (those out after the curfew hour) and other persons acting suspiciously. Governor Phillip approved of the proposal and placed Collins in charge of the night watch. The Watch paraded immediately after the evening stand-down or tattoo was beat. They were to prevent gambling and the sale of liquor or slops, and report to Collins each morning.

Collins wrote, some time later, that: 'the night watch was found of infinite utility. The commission of crimes, since the institution of the watch, has been less frequent, and they were instrumental in bringing forward for punishment several offenders who would otherwise have escaped. The fear and detestation in which they were held by their fellow prisoners is ample proof of their assiduity'.

Schooling

Macquarie announced his policy of 'instructing' the rising generation on 24th February 1810. He wanted this new generation to receive instruction, which would make them 'dutiful and obedient to their parents and superiors, honest, faithful, and useful members of society and good Christians'. He had witnessed around Sydney a number of children who appeared to be neglected in their education and morals. He proposed establishing a 'public charity school' for the education of poor children, open to all wishing to attend. The Rev'd Mr. Cowper, the chaplain, would register them.

A Mr. John Eyre was appointed to be schoolmaster and was to take charge of the charity school in Parramatta. He would take his instructions from Rev'd Samuel Marsden. A John Davies was appointed to be master of the charity school in Sydney . . . Until a proper building can be completed they were to assemble in the Sydney church. Macquarie advised Viscount Castlereagh on 30th April 1810 that 'it is likewise my intention to establish schools at all principal districts and settlements, similar to those I established in Parramatta and Sydney'. Having encouraged the establishment of charity schools at Government expense via the Orphan Fund, Macquarie in early 1811 reversed himself and offered only limited official funding (25 pound) with the balance to be made up by subscription of parents and families. He started this program in Liverpool and Richmond, and wanted it done in every principal settlement. As a means of coordinating and controlling these various schools, he appointed a colonial schoolmaster at 100 pounds salary per annum. William Wilberforce backed this proposal to Under-Secretary Peel.

Burial Grounds

Macquarie proclaimed (11th May 1811) that only consecrated sites in Liverpool, Windsor, Richmond, Pitt Town, Castlereagh and Wilberforce were to be used as burial grounds, and the practice of burying the dead on farmland was to stop. The Government would contribute 10 pound per burial site for fencing, by a good wall or 'pallisadoes'.

Wharfs and Markets

Regulations for the use of wharves were made in February 1811. The Cockle Bay Wharf leading to the new George Street Market-place have recently been finished and this wharf facility was only available to small craft arriving laden with livestock, wheat, barley, oats, fruit, potatoes or other vegetables, discharge their load, remove all goods from the wharf to the market place and moor their boats away from the rails at the wharf except that the rings placed in the wall may be used to secure small vessels. The Hospital Wharf (at Sydney Cove-Circular Quay) is no longer accessible to vessels from Hawkesbury, Parramatta, and Kissing Point, laden with livestock or vegetables.

Cloth Making

William Broughton (acting Commissary during John Palmer's absence overseas) announced on 14th July 1810 that 38 named providers of wool to the Parramatta Commissary could come and receive payment. Those named included Macarthur, Marsden, Kemp, Lawson, Riley and Cox

Banking

Macquarie asked Earl Liverpool on 27th October 1810 to approve his (Macquarie) establishing a Government bank in the colony, similar to the one at Cape of Good Hope. He pointed out the need for a copper coin 'to circulate in the lower branches of trade' and requested Liverpool dispatch 5,000 pounds in copper coins to be placed into circulation at double its British value.

Coal Excavation

The instructions for the guidance of Lieutenant Purcell as the Commandant of the 73rd Regiment at Newcastle includes:

The principal objects of the establishment of a port or military station at Newcastle are to procure regular supplies of coal, timber and lime for use by Government. You are instructed to make sure that supplies are ready to load any boat entering Coal River, 'taking care to dispatch said vessels immediately on their being loaded. Purcell's instruction also included a caution to protect the safety of the miners, because 'much injury has been done to the coal-mines by persons destroying the pillars which support the roofs of the pits

The Races at Hyde Park

The Governor in anticipation of the first race at Hyde Park on 6th October 1810 issued a general order. There was to be 'no gaming, drunkenness, swearing or fighting, quarrelling or boxing taking place on or near the race-ground'.

Brick—and Tile-Making

Macquarie's instructions from King George in 1809 admonished the Governor-elect to carefully account for all tools provided by the commissary to the convicts. Likewise, he was to account for every item of clothing and provisions for the convicts, and make regular 'returns' of usage to the Commissioners of the Treasury. It was unfortunate that much of the equipment sent in the first, second and even subsequent fleets did not meet the needs of the colony. For instance the earliest shovels and picks were unsuitable fore the crusted soil; the axes were of no use against the high-sap hard wood found around Sydney Cove; the saws were easily blunted on the gum and box-wood trees, before the dried; there were no sickles to use to bring in the first wheat crop when it arrived in late 1788. Such implements had to be made by the local blacksmiths from scrap iron and steel pieces found on the ships. No different was the shortage of suitable equipment to mould and fire bricks. The first bricks were made nearby to Sydney Cove from a clay seam found within the present Hyde Park area. The quality of these 1788 bricks was much superior to the bricks made shortly thereafter in Brickfield Hill, Rose Hill and on the North Shore of the township. Brick making was so necessary to the fledgling colony, since for some years the authorities were unsure how to successfully dry and work the local timber, that one of the first issues to locate a settlement was 'is there a suitable clay seam available e.g. the location of Windsor, Newcastle, Liverpool all revolved around this elemental decision. Macquarie created a line of demarcation between the entertainment based Hyde Park (a successor by name change to 'The Common', 'Exercising Ground',' Cricket Ground' and Racecourse' and the brickfields site. 'His Excellency commands', said the proclamation of October 1810, ' that none of the persons who obtained permission to make bricks shall cross the ground beyond the line of demarcation.

Commissary, Granaries & Supply Operations

    a.   Education 1788-1833

CHAPTER 39

MORE THOUGHTS ON EDUCATION, IMMIGRATION 1788-1838

A.G. Austin in Australian Education 1788-1900 offers an explanation as to the lack of interest in educating the lower classes.

"Nowhere in Phillip's Commissions or instructions was any mention made of the children accompanying the First Fleet, or of the child convicts whom the British Government saw fit to transport, for it was alien to the official mind of the late 18th century to feel any interest in the welfare of these children. By 1809 the War Office had been persuaded to appoint regimental schoolmasters, but in 1788 the education of these children formed no part of the business of any department of state.

The conservative opinion in Britain was convinced that education was exactly the wrong remedy and agreed with the Bishop of London's conviction that it was 'safest for both the Government and the religion of the country to let the lower classes remain in that state of ignorance in which nature has originally placed them'.

In this atmosphere anyone who undertook the education of the poor became an object of suspicion. Even the devout Hannah Moore had to defend her schools against charges of Methodism, Calvinism and subversion. Ms. Moore wrote: 'they learn such coarse work as may fit them as servants. I allow no writing for the poor. My object is to train up the lower classes in habits of industry and piety'. Nearly a century later John Stuart Mill still thought it necessary to warn his readers that 'a general state education . . . established a despotism over the mind'.

The Pitt Tory Government resisted those favouring State intervention in education. They saw no reason to meddle in the upbringing of other people's children, and no reason to suppose that the new Governor of NSW would presume to dispute their opinion.

The early governors of NSW soon found it necessary to change their adoption of British policies, especially regarding education in the colony, since Britain was not a fragment of English society transplanted, but a military and penal garrison in which the governors were responsible for every detail of daily life. In a settlement where the maintenance of discipline, the regulation of food production, the rationing of supplies, the employment of labour, and the administration of justice were necessarily committed into one man's hands, there was no room for that laissez-faire indifference which characterized the conduct of public affairs in Britain.

Not only were the governors moved by the misery of the convicts' children but also they realized that the future of the colony had to built upon these children. In a colony where there was three times the number of men as there were women, a deplorably high proportion of illegitimate and abandoned children required some measure of protection and supervision. In 1807 on Bligh's testimony, there were 387 married women in the colony, 1,035 concubines, 807 legitimate children and 1,024 illegitimate children.

Phillip had set aside, near every town, an allotment for a church and 400 acres adjacent for the maintenance of a minister and 200 Acres for the schoolmaster. However the governors were not really concerned to assert the supremacy of either Church or State. All their actions were matters of expediency. To finance schools, they made direct grants of land, assigned convicts and issued rations. To staff schools they had used soldiers, convicts, missionaries and other literate person they could find. To accommodate the schools, they used churches, barracks, storehouses and private buildings. It was Macquarie who first set down the staging order of divinity. All clerics would be, for the first time, from 1810, responsible to the principal chaplain.

By the end of the Macquarie era, many changes had been made to the social order in the colony, including education, and most of these changes were in principal accepted by J.T. Bigge in his reports to the British Commissioners. Bigge's reported that ' the flow of immigrants and the increasing number of emancipated convicts has so increased the population of free settlers that the prosperity of the settlement as a colony has proportionately advanced, and hopes may reasonably be entertained of its becoming perhaps at no distant period a valuable possession of the crown. This makes me think that it is no longer fit for its original purpose'.

For public education to be considered as a government responsibility and controlled by a cleric meant that part of the cost could be defrayed by public revenue. The suggestions made by the new Archdeacon of the colony were that public education be controlled by a cleric who was also placed at the head of the Church Establishment. The costs could be defrayed, was the suggestion, by the parents contributing, annually, a ' bushel of good clean sound wheat, or equivalent value in meat, or 1/8th of the colonial import duty could be diverted to education; governments could subdivide its land at Grose Farm, Emu Plains, Rooty Hill and Cabramatta into small farms and apply their rents to the endowment of schools in general'. The last suggestion and the one that attracted Lord Bathurst's ear was that a 'new land reserve of some 25,000 acres should be established near Bathurst or Newcastle'.

The British Government ultimately decided in 1825 to direct Governor Brisbane to form a 'corporation and invest it with clergy and school estates, and from the proceeds it should support the Anglican Church and schools and school masters in connection with the established church' The territory of NSW was to be divided into counties, hundreds, and parishes as a result of a survey of the whole colony. The Corporation was not a success largely because it was never properly funded the way it was expected, nor did it enjoy the high enthusiasm or interest of the governor.

Macquarie 'reported' to Viscount Castlereagh on 30th April 1810 on the progress in carrying out British instructions

'In pursuance to your Lordship's instructions, I lost no time in directing my attention to the principal object pointed out in them, namely, to improve the morals of the colonists, to encourage marriage, to provide for education, to prohibit the use of spirituous liquors, and to increase the agriculture and livestock so as to ensure a certainty of supply to the inhabitants under all circumstances'. In his next dispatch Macquarie reported that 'with a view to the decent education and improvement of the rising generation, I have established several schools at head quarters and the subordinate settlements, which I trust will not fail of being attended with very desirable effects'. He also requested 'a few more chaplains and some additional schoolmasters which are very much required, and it would be very desirable if some should be sent out as soon as possible'.

Alan Barcan in his imaginative work 'History of Australian Education' notes that, in line with regular military policy the NSW Corps brought their own tutor with them for teaching the children of military personnel. No such luxury was available for the residents of Norfolk Island. In 1793, Lieutenant King (Governor of the island) established an import duty on liquor in order to raise funds for education. King built the first stone schoolhouse in 1794 and a second in 1795. Collins records ('An Account of the English Colony in NSW') that 'the first school was for young children, who were instructed by a woman of good character; the second was kept by a man, who taught reading, writing, and arithmetic, for which he was well qualified, and was very attentive'.

King also opened an Orphan Institution in 1795 when by this time there were 75 destitute children. These children were taught, fed, clothed, and given vocational training.

In Sydney Governor Hunter met with the school children each year, and as David Collins records, in 1797, Hunter inspected the children from three schools and 'was gratified with the sight of 102 clean and decently—dressed children, who came with their several masters and mistresses'.

In 1798, the Rev'd Richard Johnson (the first cleric in the colony, who had arrived with the First Fleet) amalgamated the three schools in Sydney and the three joint teachers held classes in the church. They had 150 to 200 children enrolled of 'all descriptions of persons, whether soldiers, settlers, or convicts' (/Johnson's Rules). After the Church was burnt down on 1st October 1798, it moved to the courthouse and then to a disused warehouse, but enrolments halved.

When King arrived to take over as Governor in 1800, he continued his deep interest in education and 'education expanded significantly'. (Barcan). There were three main reasons for this expansion.

    a.   King himself took a deep interest in education and brought with him the experience gained from his Norfolk Island success

    b.   Increased colonial prosperity and better financial provision. King imposed an import duty on goods to establish a fund for education. When the Female Orphan Fund opened in August 1801, there were 54 girls aged from 7 to 14 in the school. In August 1804, King gave it an endowment of 13 000 acres to secure its economic stability. Samuel Marsden, its Treasurer and religious guardian commented that the Orphan School is 'the foundation of religion and morality in this colony'

    c.   The growth of population, which produced both the need for and the ability to sustain schools. By 1800 Sydney was a town of 2 000 and the colony had some 5 000 inhabitants. Significance could be seen in the:

- Growth of a small commercial middle class,
- The publication of the Sydney Gazette, which offered an avenue for expression of opinion
- A 'distinction' between state-aided 'public schools' and 'private' education

Vocational training was possibly the most important challenge and target of the education system. In 1798, Hunter reported that young male convicts had been assigned to an 'artificer's gang in order that they may be useful mechanics'. In 1805, King developed a system of apprenticeships for boys. In the same year advertisements appeared in the Sydney Gazette for apprentice seamen. The Female Orphan School developed some vocational training for the girls by offering 'needlework, reading, spinning and some few writing'. A few of the girls became servants with them being 'bound as apprentices to officer's wives'.

The overall shortage of labour in the colony caused vocational training to make only slow progress.

Immigrants and Free Settlers

Collins records that on the 15th January 1793, the Bellona transport ship, arrived in Sydney Harbour with a cargo of stores and provisions, 17 female convicts and five settlers one of whom was a master wheel-wright employed by the governor at a salary of 100 pound per annum. A second was a returning skilled tradesman who had been previously employed as a master blacksmith. All five settlers had brought their families.

Collins conjectures that these first three settlers had received free passage, a promise of a land grant and assistance with farming, as the incentive for becoming the free settlers,

Manning Clark (A History of Australia) records that in 1806, 'a dozen families from the Scottish border area arrived as free emigrants and each received 100 acres of land on the banks of the Hawkesbury River in a place they called Ebenezer. They were devout Presbyterians, and were allowed to worship in the colony according to their own lights'. However the authorities were not prepared to tolerate the practice of the catholic religion, because they saw it 'as an instrument of mental slavery, a threat to higher civilization, and a threat to liberty' (Clark Vol 1)

Free Immigrants 1788-1810

Developing Immigration

Even by the census of 1828, NSW had fewer than 5,000 people who had come out voluntarily, in a population of 36 598. The colony had the attractions unavailable in the USA, free land and convict labour. Settlers were given land for agriculture and pasture usage. This meant freehold land, and it only applied to men who had immigrated as private citizens, to military officers who had decided to stay and to pardoned convicts who had been granted land.

In 1831, the British Government, against the opposition of many in the colony decided to stop giving away land grants to settlers and chose instead to 'sell' the land and use some of the proceeds to sponsor migrants to the colony. The initial sales price was 5 shillings an acre. It was a way of inducing poor families to leave the country, but as well of relieving the labour shortage. Between 1831 and 1840 about 50,000 prisoners were transported and about 65,000 free men and women chose to emigrate

The battle of the sexes was more equal amongst emigrants than among convicts: but even South Australia, which was wholly an emigrant's colony, had only 8 females for every 10 males by 1850, and in Australia as a whole there was fewer than 7 in every ten. The resulting challenge was only partially met by Caroline Chisholm who met every convict and emigrant ship to stress the dangers to young unmarried women. Her main accomplishment was to convince the Colonial Office, in 1846, to offer free passage to all families of convicts resident in the colony. Her detractors suggested that the result of her efforts towards convict families and emigrating poor families would be to create an imbalance of Catholics in the colony, who were already twice the proportion of the Australian population as they were in England.

Needs for Labour

    a. Timber
    b. Housing components
    c. Building items
    d. Blocks & bricks
    e. Drays & carts
    f. Furniture – household and 'official'
    g. Clothing items
    h. Cooking ware
    i. Roofing material
    j. Creating a market place
    k. Establishing the commissariat operations

l.   Boat building
m. Blacksmithing operations
n.   Coaches
o.   Road building
p.   Bridge building
q.   Trading operations

CHAPTER 40

TIMELINE OF SIGNIFICENT EVENTS

A. Farming & Grazing:
*   Feb 1788 Phillip established a 3.6 ha farm where the botanical gardens now stands. It was expanded to 6.5 ha by end of 1788.
*   June 1789 Phillip established a government farm at Rose Hill, which produces 200 bushels of wheat, 35 bushels of barley, oats, maize and flax.
*   By 1790 over 80 ha of land had been cleared and opened up at Rose Hill. The crops used were wheat and barley.
*   In 1797 Gov. Hunter planted the first grape vines. The plantings were expanded from the initial 8 acres to 12,000 vines in 1802. The first cuttings had arrived in 1788.
*   In 1803, 6 bags of hop plants arrived in the colony and were used to support the government owned brewery at Parramatta
*   In 1813 the Blue Mountains were successfully crossed and this opened up new pastures for sheep and cattle. Gov. Macarthur provided roads, a stable economy and further exploration. The livestock herds flourished.

B. Fishing & Whaling:
*   In 1788 the British ship Emilia commenced whaling in the South Pacific. It returned to England in 1790.
*   The first whaling ships were convict transports, which returned to England with whale blubber after dropping passengers off.

- Smaller vessels commenced hunting for fur and elephant seals in 1797 in Bass Strait
- Gov. King in 1802 advised Joseph Banks that 7 whaling ships were operating from Port Jackson
- By 1804 half of the 22 privately owned ships based in Australian ports were engaged in the Bass Strait sealing industry. Over 100,000 skins were landed in Sydney between 1800 and 1806.
- In 1805, the first Australian built whaler, King George, was launched. The Lady Barlow owned by Robert Campbell, sailed with sealskins and seal oil to establish a direct trade with Britain.
- In 1808 Lieut. David Collins was sent to establish a whaling station on the Derwent River.

C. Manufacturing

- In Nov 1788, the bricks, made at Darling Harbour, were used to build the first permanent government house on the corner of King & Bridge Street.
- The brickfields were located to Brickfield Hill, Rose Hill, Gore Hill and St. Peters, but the clay quality was generally inferior.
- The first windmill was erected in 1795 on Observatory Hill (The Rocks). It ground 6 bushels of flour an hour.
- In 1796, the naval dockyard was established
- In 1799 one convict was employed to make 6 dozen brooms each week.
- In 1800-1801 linen manufacture began on the Hawkesbury River area. In 1802 this activity was transferred to the Female Factory at Parramatta
- In 1811, Blaxland advertised local salt for sale.
- By 1814, the Female Factory was using more than 17,000 kg of wool.
- In May 1817, the first steam-powered windmill was in use making 70 bushels of flour each day. By 1840 there were 220 windmills in the colonies.
- In July 1820, a local paper mill was supplying all—Australian paper to the Sydney Gazette.
- By 1820 the Harness and carriages works were in full production. The government had built a lime kiln and brickworks in Newcastle

The Economic Setting for the Colony

Some Special Economic Events

A number of 'special' events have influenced the course of the early economy and impacted on the extent and rate of economic growth and these have been nominated for further outline. The list of events is not extensive but indicative of sometimes more obscure events which can impact on economic growth eg education.

Although it may be suggested that the Report by Commissioner Bigge did not largely influence the Colonial economy, it must be stated that his recommendations to continue with the new Bank of New South Wales, which had been chartered incorrectly by Governor Macquarie, moved the economy along, as did his support for the continuation of the transportation of convicts to the Colony. His lack of support for land grants and early release of convicts may have slowed the economic growth until the consequences of his recommendation that the sale of Crown land be made, was considered in London. After the decision was made in , to replace the system of land grants with its outright sale, the revenue from the Sale of Crown land became considerable and kept the economy afloat, even if it was being badly managed in terms of food production ,until 1810, and the arrival of Macquarie.

Other special events fed on each other. Exploration across the mountains and uncovering the mystery of the rivers opened up huge pastoral areas and fostered the growth of the sheep and wool industries. The continued growth of the pastoral industries all through the 1800s was eclipsed as the prime exporting commodity only upon the 'official' discovery of gold. The discovery of gold once again filled the Colonial coffers and set into motion the most remarkable of special events , the expansion of the rail system across the Colony of New South Wales and between the Colonies. Instead of relying on sea transport, the very reason that the major cities were initially located on harbours and bays, the cities were now connected by rail. The senior colony of New South Wales, could now diversify its population, move livestock and produce from Tamworth and Albury to the populace of Sydney. The most powerful benefit of the advent of the rail system is the most simplistic one. The Colonial labour-force learned how to engineer bridges (the Hawkesbury); how to construct gradients (crossing the Blue Mountains); and engineer the iron horses themselves for local conditions. This new knowledge led directly to the coming engineering shops and the likes of business adventurers such as Thomas Mort, whose remarkable drive, ingenuity and entrepreneurial ability led to the formation and operation of The Mort Dry Dock & Engineering complex in Balmain; The NSW Fresh Food & Ice Company, the development of refrigeration and the opening of abattoirs in remote locations rather than in Sydney town. Neither can we overlook the value of education in and to a largely illiterate economy. Finally the growth of the free trade movement brought to the fore the likes of Parkes, Reid, Wise and Pulsford—politicians who stood for a sound forward-looking, progressive party, whose policy suited the peoples of the Colony and led to the formation of the first 'party' ticket in the country. Federation took centre stage in the second half of the century and again changed the face of the country and whilst our analysis of the fiscal considerations of Federation and the post-Federation relations between the Commonwealth and the States will set the stage for review as to whether the Federation movement was successful.

- There may well be more 'special events' than those discussed but it seems that these interlinking events boosted the Colonial economy in a remarkable way: the crown land policy and reform the growth of education_the Report by Commissioner Bigge exploration_pastoral expansion_the expansion of the rail system the Fiscal impact of Federation
- Commonwealth-State Financial Relations

The results of all these events, led to a growing population, increased productivity and production; an amazing increase in both exports and imports, leading to an improved quality of life for all and the climate to keep the momentum going in the right direction.

The transportation of convicts seemed to have settled into a workable routine by the time of the arrival of Governor Lachlan Macquarie as Governor Bligh's replacement. The Report of the Select Committee on Transportation of 1812—records that

'The convicts who were distributed amongst the settlers, were clothed, supported and housed by them; they either work by the task or for the same number of hours as the Government convicts; and when their set labour is finished, they are allowed to work on their own account. The master has no power of corporal punishment over them as this can only be inflicted by the interference of a magistrate. The convict, if he feels abused by his master, can complain to a magistrate who, if justified, can deprive the master of his servant.

It is to be found in the written evidence of Mr Commissary Palmer to this inquiry that the expense of each convict in the service of the Government was about 40 pound per annum, made up of food—about 24 pound; clothing—about 10 pound and the equivalent value of rental accommodation at 6 pound, and that a free labourer at Sydney could be hired for about 70 per year, but would do twice as much work. Palmer reports the annual expense of a convict is 30 pound(24 + 6—with clothing being furnished by the Commissary, compared with the cost of holding them in a prison hulk on the Thames at 24 pound, and with the value of their work being about 8 pound or 1/3rd of the cost of keeping them."

The system was fundamentally changed in 1836, and the 2nd Select Committee of Inquiry into Transportation in 1837-38 recorded that " All applications for convicts are now made to an officer—'Commissioner for assignment of Convict Servants' who is guided by Government Regulations. Settlers to whom convicts are assigned, are now bound to send for them within a certain period and pay the sum of 1 pound per head for their clothing and bedding.

Each assigned convict is entitled to a fixed amount of food and clothing—in NSW of 12 lb of wheat, or equivalent in flour and maize meal, 7 lb of mutton or beef or 4 ½ lb of salt pork, 2 oz of salt and 2 oz of soap each week. 2 frocks or jackets, three shirts two pair trousers, 3 pair shoes and a hat or cap, annually. Plus one good blanket, a palliasse or wool mattress which remain the property of the master. Obviously they are well fed, well clothed and receive wages of between 10 to 15 pound per annum."

The 2nd Select Committee also heard evidence on convicts who have been emancipated or their sentence has expired.

"These people find no difficulty in obtaining work at high wages; and having acquired experience in the Colony are generally preferred to new arrivals. They fill many positions of trust for instance as constables, overseers of pastoral properties and road or building gangs, as superintendents of estates , clerks to bankers, lawyers and shopkeepers, and even as tutors in private families. Some have married free women and have become prosperous."

Introduction

The discovery of gold on the mainland, in all states, had so powerful an effect that a special analysis of its benefits, must be made. We observe that the main bonuses to the Colonies was population and wealth. By-products became an increase in exports, offset by an increase in consumption goods, all designed to improve the quality of life, the dramatic growth of the railways system which brought with it extensive overseas borrowing, additional employment and new skills.

This section will review each of these benefits and explore the race problems that arose in the Colonies and the Commonwealth (originating with the gold rush), and see if this was limited to politician's minds or if it pervaded the lives of the peoples. Edward Pulsford claimed, as a rabid open-immigration supporter that the people of Australia supported the right of the Chinese and the Japanese to migrate to this country, the same as the majority of them had, not too many years previously.

Another by-product became the exploration for other minerals such as silver, copper and silver-lead, which became important export items from 1884.

Background

An extract from an address to the New South Wales Legislative Council by Governor Fitzroy on 11th May, 1853 gives an interesting insight into one aspect of the discovery of gold in the Colony and the improvement in the prosperity of its settlers.

"I desire first to acknowledge, with gratitude to Divine Providence, the general prosperity presently enjoyed by all classes of the community. At no former period of the existence of the colony has the material condition of its inhabitants been in a more satisfactory or progressive state. Although the prices of the necessities of life have been very considerably advanced, I am happy to say that they still continue abundant; whilst the increased means at the disposal of the people generally have enabled them without difficulty or inconvenience to meet the additional expenditure to which they are subjected. I must except from this satisfactory state of things, the paid servants of the crown, whose incomes, fixed with reference to former prices, now prove inadequate to their proper position and reasonable support. It will be my duty to invite your concurrence in such an advance in their present remuneration as the altered circumstances of the Colony may appear to render just and expedient.

Whilst in the enjoyment of so large a measure of material prosperity, we must not forget the duty which devolves on this Legislature to make some corresponding provision for promoting the intellectual and moral advancement of the community. Measures are being prepared for augmenting the amount allotted for education, with a view to extension of primary schools, as well as the encouragement of institutions destined to promote the higher branches of literature and science"

The British Colonial Secretary commissioned a report on the subject of the effects of gold discovery in 1852, and the report noted:

"assuming there are 30,000 men engaged at the gold mines in Victoria alone, then 15,000 of that number have been diverted from their previous occupations in that province, along with a further 5,000 from South Australia. To supply the places of these 20,000 , there would be required, under the regulations of the commissioners, 100,000 persons and these would only restore the labouring population to the state it was before the discovery of gold. Thus the immediate need is for a regular and uninterrupted supply of labouring immigrants, because every careful servant soon becomes an employer".'

In real terms, most of the gold was 'sold' overseas, rather than treated in the Colony..

In what well may be the first legislative statement of fiscal and monetary management in the Colonies, the South Australian Bullion Assay Act of 1852 heralded significant changes in the currency management of the Colonies. The Act enabled rates of exchange to be fixed, which prevented further speculation of gold in Adelaide, it stopped the drain on the Banks of coinage, encouraged former South Australian Colonists to return 'home' from the Victorian gold-fields, with their gains, and enabled the three banks of the day to survive the panic, namely The South Australian Bank, Bank of Australasia and the Union Bank of Australia. These banks were formed following the success of the Bank of New South Wales (founded in 1817 for the purpose of keeping the public account).

The discovery of Gold was kept secret whilst convict transfers were still being undertaken, lest the 'dream' of great wealth became stronger than the requirement to work out a penal service.

The discovery of large tracts of good grazing land and its associated export development of wool, and the discovery of large gold deposits rapidly boosted the fortunes of the Colony.

a. Gold Production & Value

The Wealth and Progress of New South Wales, published by the Colonial Statistician (Mr T. A. Coghlan) in 1900 records the value of gold produced in the Colony between the years 1851 and 1901, as being close to 50 million pounds. For the Australia wide production, this figure becomes close to 450 million pound, with the largest value being attributed to the State of Victoria at 210 million pound or close to half the total Australasian value of production.

Another side effect of the discovery of gold in the eastern states was the emigration of population from South Australia to the eastern states. In January 1852, the South Australian Parliament passed 'The South Australian Bullion Act' with the major background speech by the Premier observing :

"Throughout 1851 and 1852, South Australia has rapidly lost population to the adjacent Victorian goldfields. Worried bankers ,merchants and shopkeepers

wonder what they ought to do about the situation, as it looked as if they might all be heading towards bankruptcy."

The Burra Burra copper miners had been amongst the first to leave for the El Dorado, and soon most of the towns in the country districts were nearly cleared of their menfolk. There has been a general depreciation of land and property values. Every emigrant took whatever money he had in gold, thereby reducing specie to the banks, but diggers who returned with gold could not find buyers for it. The Chamber of Commerce and the Bank Managers conferred, and in January 1852, George Tinline, the Manager of the Bank of South Australia, had the idea of assaying gold into stamped ingots and then allowing it to pass as legal tender.

A hurried meeting of the S. A. Legislative Council was called and a special act was passed on January 28, 1852 to 'provide for the assaying of uncoined gold and to make banknotes, under certain conditions, a legal tender for the next twelve months' .

Owners of the ingots were authorised to convert the gold for bank notes at the rate of 3 pounds 11 shillings per ounce. The Bullion Act should not have been assented to by the SA Governor as it interfered with currency but the Act restored confidence in trade, and helped save the Colony of South Australia from insolvency, and it led to the importation of 1,500 million pound of gold from Victoria.

b. Population Growth

The statistician's figures of population on the goldfields are probably not very reliable because of the difficulty in collecting such information but the estimates for December 1861 shows there were over 17,000 miner's rights and business licenses on issue and an estimated working population of over 28,000. This compares to an estimated working population in the Victorian goldfields in April 1854 of 67,000 (there were 40,000 licenses on issue in 1852), including approx 2,000 Chinese. The Ballarat District had 17,000 workers, The Bendigo/Sandhurst District had 16,000 workers, and the Castlemaine district had over 23,000 workers. There was estimated to be, in total, nearly 7,000 itinerant travellers at any one time in the 5 goldmining districts in Victoria.

c. Government Revenue

MAIN SOURCE OF GOVERNMENT MINING REVENUE—(1885)
'000

Year 1885

Mineral Leases	20,750
Mineral Licenses	2,311
Miners Rights	4,143
Leases of Mining Lands	4,510
REVENUES—MINING	31,714

This compares with Revenue from General Fines and forfeitures of 20,171 pounds for 1885.

Dr. G. L. Buxton (The Riverina 1861-1891) submitted that ,

"influx of population during the gold-rush years would, as a result of natural increase, have generated substantial pressure on existing resources, including land, and that this may have inevitably led to a struggle for redistribution of wealth."

But that is when he then goes on to say

"recently N. G. Butlin has suggested in 'Investment in Australian Economic Development" that the selector-squatter struggle has been over-emphasised by historians, but an adequate knowledge of this struggle is necessary for any real understanding of the course of pastoral investment in New South Wales and the development of Australian rural society and its politics."

That the British overlorded the Colony for the first 112 years and imposed their own ways, standards and conditions, might well be considered another significant step in our economic history, and then the growth of the rural economy and the definite boost thereto from the coming of the railway system should be another .

Customs revenues peaked in 1842 at 182 thousand pound, at a time when, for the first time, the Colony's total revenue leapt to 700 million pound. These spikes were on account of the gold discovery and the importation of goods and the inflow of people to the gold fields.

The discovery of gold and the burgeoning wealth of the Colony prompted the Legislative Council in 1852 to seek the British Government's acceptance of an offset arrangement whereby the Colony of New South Wales would accept responsibility for all civil (ie official) salaries, provided the British Government surrendered all Colonial revenues to the discretion (under a proposed new constitution) of the Legislature.

The verification that the British authorities accepted Colonial funds, raised from the earliest sale and lease of Crown Land, and to be used for the funding of 'free immigration' to the Colony.

a. The concurrent Napoleonic wars being undertaken by the British, as well as the ongoing American War of Independence placed a substantial burden on the public purse, and the British Treasury was seeking every opportunity to limit, defray or offset expenses relating to the Colony in the Great South Land.

N. G. Butlin in the introduction to Chapter 7 of Historical Australian Records—Statistics—'The Economy before 1850', suggests there is a great deal of statistical data available on the new settlement before the discovery of gold. 'It represents some indication of the nature of the workforce of the settlements, the arrivals of convicts and free settlers, the economic activities they developed to support themselves and the heavy expenditure by the British Government to make the settlement a success. The Colony was supposed to support itself, increasingly so as pressures for public economy grew in post-Napoleonic Britain. The tables on Colonial Fund and Land Fund Revenues show this increasing shift to local self-support'. Butlin, by implication, is suggesting the financial pressures on Britain by the Colony would have caused the use of Crown Land sales to become a relief in the homeland Budgets.

The gold 'rush' brought great wealth not only to many individuals but also to each of the Colonies of Victoria, New South Wales, Queensland

and Western Australia. A great leveling followed also immediately when the depression of 1890-3 came about.

The use of all this gold extracted in such a relatively short-period is interesting, and the Colonial Statistician records that ' Gold is coined only at the Sydney mint, and the weight of gold sent for coining in the period 1885 to 1886 was 15,005,884 ounces, and valued at 56 million 880 thousand pound(56,880,142); but of this amount New South Wales produced only 6,994,135 ounces or 26,716,196 pound. Queensland was the second largest contributor followed by New Zealand and then Victoria. The greater part of the gold extracted in New South Wales, Queensland and New Zealand came to Sydney for coinage, but by far the largest portion of the balance of gold extracted goes to Melbourne. Of the total gold extracted, some 317,312,707 pounds value, nearly 18 percent passed through the mint of the Colony, being sovereigns and half-sovereigns.'

Gold produced in the Colony of New South Wales peaked in 1862 at 620 thousand ounces but fell away consistently until in 1886 less than 100 thousand ounces was produced. This decrease is explained by the Colonial Statistician's office as being:

"the fact that the rich alluvial deposits discovered in the early days had been exhausted, and other resources of a more permanent nature are being developed. These ventures offer more regular employment to the labouring classes, perhaps without the chance of accumulating rapid fortunes but with more security against loss. The key New South Wales gold production areas were Bathurst, Mudgee districts, Tumut and Adelong, Temora, New England District. In the early days many mines were abandoned by reason of the want of proper appliances for the saving of gold. Now these mines have been re-opened and a revival of mining in these various districts is being seen. However the dry weather over the last few years has had an important influence on alluvial gold-mining, and large areas of payable ground are now deserted, owing to the want of water for sluicing purposes.

The economy was strengthened because it added gold to the powerful list of woollen exports. Wool temporarily lost its number one export title to gold from 1856 to 1870 but then returned to the top of the list.

The discovery of gold strengthened the Australian demands for the introduction of responsible government. By the end of 1852 the British Government had accepted these arguments, and invited the members of the legislatures of New South Wales, Victoria, Tasmania and South Australia to draft new constitutions. This request drew two events to the fore. Firstly a split occurred in Australian politics between the conservative constitutionalists and the liberal constitutionalists. Secondly, responsible government became the architect of chronic instability of governments that followed. The Australian delegation to London had accepted uncritically that responsible government—governing for one's own people—was the one way of ensuring control over domestic questions. But it was soon learnt that responsible government assumes two main parties, and to have two main political parties you need groups with clearly defined principles and interests. 'Between 1856 and 1878 it was found that there were differences of 'interest' but no serious differences of principle' (Clark—Select Documents in Australian History Vol 2 P.321)

The rest of the world watched change take place over centuries whilst Australia abbreviated all those same changes into less than 100 years. During that time Australia grew in monetary, population and self reliant terms. The changes in Australia were compressed into a shorter period but driven by the need to catch the rest of the world and make a mark.

At the time of the first gold rush in 1851, only 4 out 10 children attended school. By 1861, education was free, compulsory, secular and schools were well attended.

At the time gold was discovered, license fees and duties on exports of gold and duties on the domestic conversion of gold were applied and this revenue helped fill the Treasury coffers.

A short time before had come the first Appropriation Bills and 'Ways and Means' through the Legislative Assembly in 1832 under Governor Bourke. This was a major step forward in Government economic planning, as was the limited deficit budgeting that commenced at this time. The improvement in Government economic planning simplified the analysis of and planning for the dramatic increase in revenues and thus availability of funds for improving social infrastructure such as railways, roads, new inland settlements, schools, law courts, mechanics institutes and libraries, cottage hospitals. Government played a different role in those early days, when development of government and community assets was a much higher priority than maintenance of those assets, as is the case today. The Treasurers of the 1850s were in demand to understand and carefully formulate priorities that served their colony, rather than the select few.

Effects of Gold Discovery

    a.   A number of immediate results came from the discovery of gold: it assisted in terminating transportation it assisted in bringing responsible government forward land and political reforms came about as a result of the digger's demands for such reforms a general consequence was a rise in prices, wages, rents and charges

    b.   A shortage of general labour supply.

Self-Government

It is pointed out above that the discovery of gold was hidden and suppressed for many years. It was recorded in 1896 by the Colonial Statistician that the existence of gold had been known to the authorities during the early days, when the Colony was a convict settlement, but for obvious reasons of State, the matter remained secret. The first authenticated discovery of gold is contained in the field notes of Assistant Surveyor McBrian bearing the date of 16th February, 1823, with the reference being to a location on the Fish River just out of Bathurst, where Edward Hargraves made his big and public find twenty-eight years later. In 1839, Count Strezlecki , the namer of Mount Kosciusko, found gold in the Goulburn area, and was asked by Governor Gipps to keep the matter secret. The Rev. Clarke found gold in 1841 in the Macquarie Valley and expressed his belief publicly that 'the precious metal would be found abundantly dispersed throughout the Colony'. Edward Hargrave's discovery in 1851 was the first officially recognised find and led to the 'Gold Rush'.

Finding a Place for Gold

Gold occupies a foremost place in the country, both on account of the quantity found and the influence which the discovery had on the settlement of the country.

Coghlan, T. A. (Wealth & Progress of NSW-1900-1901) expresses a concern over the actual discovery date.

"The date of the discovery of gold in New South Wales was, for a long time, the theme of much controversy, and the question as to the original discoverer was long disputed. It is now agreed, that the existence of gold was known to the authorities during the early days when the state was a convict settlement, but for obvious official reasons the matter remained secret. As set out previously, the first authentic record of its discovery is contained in an extract from Assistant-Surveyor McBrian's Field-book, bearing date 126th February, 1823, in which the following note appears.—'At 8 chains 50 links to river, and marked gum-tree—at this place I found numerous particles of gold in the sand and in the hills convenient to the river.' The river referred to is the Fish River, at about 15 miles from Bathurst, not far from the spot to which the first gold rush was made twenty-eight years afterwards. "

In 1839, Count Strzelwcki found gold in Clwydd and communicated the discovery to Governor Gipps, but was requested to keep the matter secret, lest the existence of gold should 'imperil the safety and discipline of the Colony' (Coghlan P371). The Rev'd W.B. Clarke found gold in 1841 in the Macquarie Valley, but it was not until 1851 (the last convict had been shipped to the Colony some years previously in 1840, and by 1850 most had been released) that payable deposits were proved, by Edward Hargraves, a British immigrant and a recent traveller from California, in the area of Bathurst, on the banks of the Macquarie River. Only a few weeks later, deposits were found in Ballarat and Sandhurst (Bendigo) and Mount Alexander, all in the Colony of Victoria. For his find and public announcement in the SMH of 15th May, 1851, Hargraves was awarded 10,000 pound and appointed a Commissioner for Crown Lands.

The finds were all located in easily worked alluvial deposits, and therefore without costly diggings or appliances. Coghlan suggests "Rich they may be (and thus attracting the greater number of miners), alluvial deposits are very soon worked out, their area generally being of limited extent."

In July 1851 a 'mass' of gold was found in the Maitland area gold-fields which weighed 106 lb or 1,272 oz. Coghlan clarifies the description and says although called a 'nugget, it was really a piece of reef gold.' Another nugget in 1858 was found near Orange, which was melted at the Sydney mint and weighed 1,182 oz with a value of 4,389 pound 8 shillings and 10 pence. Numerous other large nuggets were found around the Colony, including Temora, Maitland, Mudgee, Hargraves and Delegate (via Cooma).

From 1851 to 1901, a quantity of 13,475,633 ounces was produced in New South Wales with a value of 49,661,815 Pound. Values increased during this period and although 1862 produced the most quantity (640,622 oz worth 2467,780), 1899 exceeded the value of any other year (496,196 oz worth 11,751,815).

The quantity of gold produced in 1901 fell from 345,650 to 267,061 whilst the number of miners employed dropped 5,894 for that period.

The Gold Dredging Act validated all leases and applications until 1899, and authorised a system of sluicing and dredging which has 'awaked considerable activity in certain districts where gold is being saved from the beds of rivers and creeks, as well as from wetlands which the ordinary miner experienced considerable difficulty in working.' (V & P NSW LA 1899)

Coghlan comments on the irregularity of gold-mining (P376)—"It is a well known fact that in years of prosperity, when employment of all kinds is easily obtainable, people are attracted from gold-mining to other pursuits, which, while offering smaller chances of rapidly acquiring wealth, nevertheless gives steady employment, and when working in steady occupations is scarce, these persons again give their attention to gold-mining. The depression in trade experienced during the last few years had the effect, therefore, of largely increasing the seekers after gold, many of the unemployed being supplied with Miner's Rights and with railway passes to take them to likely spots where a living could be made by fossicking, on the condition that the cost could afterwards be refunded, when the men were in a position to repay the money." Another benefit to the Colony of this process was that, in addition to the miner's right, the government hoped many men, and their families would take up residency in the area, on the gold-fields. The benevolence of the state was masterful in its manipulation for the betterment of all!

When the names of the districts where alluvial ,quartz and gold were found in the late 1800s is listed, one finds the areas where new population growth was taking place at increased rates.

Armidale, Bathurst, Orange, Parkes, Wyalong, Cobar, Peak Hill, Gundagai, Wellington, Forbes, Nowra, Gulgong, Temora and the Lachlan District. Discoveries covered much of the State, and even as late as 1894, the discovery of riches in the Lachlan District attracted more than 10,000 men of whom 4,600 were still there in 1901. However much gold was discovered, the average gold won per miner was 17.24 ounces, valued at 62.1.10 pound.

There were growing factors, other than just the population. There were 318 steam engines used in mining in 1899, 1762 crushing machines and 1,986 stamp heads. All this equipment was made in the Colony and valued at 975,000 pound. It also required skilled workers to maintain and operate the equipment.

Coghlan records (P381) that "from the date of the first discovery of payable gold, in 1851, to the end of the year 1900, the quantity of gold produced in the Commonwealth and New Zealand represents a total of 443,550,310 pound, extracted in the short space of 49 years. The share of each state is as follows:"

NSW	48,740,533	11%
VICTORIA	257386448	58%
QLD	50209783	11.3%
SOUTH AUST	2294975	0.5%

WESTERN AUST	22914059	5.2 %
TASMANIA	4598412	1.0%
COMMONWEALTH	386144210	87%
N.Z.	57406100	13%
AUSTRALASIA	443550310	100%

Compared to the world's production of gold, the Commonwealth of Australia only produced, in 1900 about 26%, with NSW only being 2.3% and Victoria being 12%.

Population of Gold Towns in 1900

Armidale	4,249	Bathurst	,9,223
Orange,	6,331	Parkes	3,181
Wyalong,	1,510	Cobar,	3,374
Peak Hill,	1,107	Gundagai	1,487
Wellington,	2,984	Forbes	4,294
Nowra,	1,904	Gulgong	1,579
Temora	1,603		
the Lachlan District		10,000	

The Chinese Problem

Timothy Coghlan, a close friend and admirer of our Federationist Senator Edward Pulsford, made a controversial observation on the Chinese question.

He wrote " The unanimity with which the Australian states have passed laws restricting the immigration of Chinese may be taken as some evidence of the un-desirability of the race as colonists. At the census of 1861 there were , in New South Wales, 12,988 Chinese. In November , 1861 , a duty of 10 pound per head was imposed upon Chinese male immigrants. This continued until November 1967, and led to a decline in the number of Chinese in the State to 7,220. By 1881 the number had risen to 10,205 and to 15,445 at the end of 1888. Numerous departures followed and only 12,156 were found in 1891 and less than 11,000 in 1901. For many years New South Wales offered little inducement to the Chinese as a place of settlement, the superior attractiveness of Victoria and other States as gold producers claimed their attention. During the riots at Lambing Flat in 1860, large numbers of Chinese came across the border from NSW and established themselves in Victoria, their strength being constantly supported by new arrivals, but they did not remain in NSW as is shown above. The violent anti-Chinese attack on the Burrangong goldfield near Young NSW ('Lambing Flat')on 30th June, 1860, by 3,000 diggers led to many Chinese being beaten and their camps destroyed. Tensions were reduced by the departure of many of the Chinese and the passing of the Chinese immigration restriction bill in November 1861.

From 1878 to 1888 over 27,000 Chinese arrived in New South Wales whilst 16,000 departed."

This second rush in 1878 caused the introduction of the 'Influx of Chinese Restriction Act' in 1881, re-imposing the poll tax of 10 pound. The next measure by the Parliament followed a meeting of all state representatives where it was agreed that they were witnessing a 'growing danger'. The new Act came into force on 11th July 1888 and prohibited any vessels from carrying into the State more than 1 Chinese passenger to every 300 ton of cargo, and each Chinese landed are required to pay a poll-tax of 100 pound; they were not to engage in mining except with the permission of the Minister for Mining, nor were they permitted to take advantage of the Naturalisation Act. Any Chinese that come as British subjects (from Hong Kong) had to pass the educational test prescribed by the Immigration Restriction Act of 1898.

The penalty for breach of the Chines Restriction Act was 500 pound. The Act had greatly reduced Chinese immigration, but it was believed that a large number of Chinese found their way into NSW through the other States.

The 'History of the Australian Gold Rushes' edited by Nancy Keesing records an extract of an unpublished manuscript by the Manager of the Robe branch of the Bank of South Australia (Thomas Drury Smeaton) written in 1865.

"in 1858 there were 33,000 Chinese on the Victorian gold-fields, whilst in 1853 there were fewer than 2,000. The Chinese coolies were highly unpopular among the miners often for reasons based on ignorance and prejudice. In 1855, Victoria passed an Act imposing a poll-tax of ten pound on each Chinese immigrant and forbidding ships to carry more than one Chinese passenger for every ten tons of the vessel's tonnage. The shipping masters promptly evaded the tax by landing coolies at South Australian ports, from which they travelled overlands to the goldfields. The town of Robe on Guichen Bay in South Australia was a favoured port. In all about 16,500 Chinese passed through Robe on their way to the diggings. Of this large number all were males"

Conclusion

Our goal was to determine the quantity and value of gold extracts in the Colony of New South Wales and the country as a whole. Another purpose was to determine which areas of the State were most influenced and how the proceeds were utilised. What labour was involved and what by-products were advantaged?

In summary then we learnt that New South Wales produced 12,862,922 ounces of gold valued at 48,740,533 pound, whilst the Commonwealth produced 63,464,717 ounces valued at 443,550,310 pound. Of this amount 96,676,500 pound was put into circulation as coinage and over 2 million ounces were exported, valued at about 16 million pound.

Over One million pounds worth of equipment was employed, including the steam engines valued at 970,000 pound.

New businesses flourished on the gold-fields—sale of stores and provisions, prostitution, tent-makers, log houses, basic furniture, firewood cutting and sale, tool making, Cobb & Co. coaches—and gold escort services, sly grog production (officially alcohol was not allowed onto the gold fields), policing, licensing and clothing makers.

The biggest benefit of the gold discoveries was the move by the British Government to provide responsible government to each of the Colonies.

Edward Pulsford in 'Trade and Commerce in New South Wales' (1892) writes

"The most important event which occurred in the decade 1850-1860 was the discovery of gold, which will for ever stamp 1851 as the most remarkable year in the commercial history of New South Wales, from the foundation of the Colony to the present. Volumes could be written to record the successes and failures of gold-mining, the way in which new towns are settled, and development both retarded and promoted.

On 22nd May, 1851 the Governor of New South Wales had proclaimed the Government's right solely to sell all gold removed from the Colony's diggings. And then provided that a license fee of 30 shillings per month was to be paid to dig on Crown lands. From the first find, the Government had been determined to have a two-way control over the gold successes, so that the Government received its share.

Frank Crowley in Colonial History—Volume 2, 1841-1874 records(P206) a detailed report, dated 10th October, 1851 by Lieutenant-Governor Latrobe to the Colonial Secretary (Earl Grey) in London :-

"The immediate effect of the gold discoveries were a sudden increase in the size of the population in Eastern Australia and the export of large quantities of gold bullion to Britain. At first, wool growing and cattle raising suffered from loss of workmen, but squatters quickly adapted to the new situation. There was a large meat-market on every goldfield, and mass production of cheap galvanised fencing wire enabled a small number of boundary riders to replace the army of shepherds. Freight costs were greatly reduced by the keen competition between shipowners, at a time when wool prices were steadily rising. Farming was at first disturbed and then stimulated by the rising population and the increased demand for food. Many small industries in and around Sydney were adversely affected by the shortage of labour, rising wages and competition from the flood of cheap imported goods from Britain. Every ship that brought immigrants and gold-finders had its holds jammed tight with pots and pans, picks, shovels, shop clothing, lanterns and cheap furniture. The commercial boom in Sydney and Melbourne lasted until 1855 and the sudden increase in capital available for investment and speculation resulted in a building bonanza, especially in Melbourne City and the towns centred around the goldfields such as Bendigo and Ballarat. "

The associated boom in trade and commerce also brought fortunes to Melbourne merchants as well as to the farmers and squatters who were close to the diggings. Store keepers on the fields made a great deal of profit from their buying and selling. Flour resold at 3 d per pound, mutton at 3.5 d per lb., sugar was 2s 6 d per lb.; tea was 4 shillings/lb, boots 2 pound; blankets 2 pound.

The Sydney Morning Herald of 4th August, 1852 announced 'Steam Communication with England at last' and reported that steam powered ships were now running between Britain and Australia on a frequent basis.

In the middle of 1852 the diggings at Bendigo held about the same number of workers as did the Ballarat diggings—30—40,000 people at each. It was reported that about 2,000 carts and drays were on the road from Melbourne at any time of the day.

An ex-convict writing in the Melbourne Argus questioned the acceptance of the ill-effects of the gold fever—the increase in crime, the high price of labour, the stopping of the public works, in particular the unfinished sewerage system in Melbourne and other burdens of the 'root of all evil'

Another less obvious problem with the gold-fever came from the society ladies of Sydney, who claimed that' the town had gone downhill rapidly during the last two years, mainly because of the extortionate prices being charged and the scarcity of domestic servants'. (SMH 10.7.1853)

Because of the local shortage of coins in Sydney, and fluctuations in the price of raw gold and in the exchange rate between Australia and Britain, the Royal Mint was invited to and accepted the opening of a mint in Sydney on 14th May, 1855.

The goldfields , concludes Crowley (Vol 2, P404) in a very short time contributed a major economic boost to the Australian Colonies that had only received sixty years of Imperial Expenditure from the convict system.

The Albury Border Post of 22nd February, 1860 waxed poetic in its article on the value of the goldfields.

"The traffic from Sydney to Melbourne will bring a population to the fine port and district of Twofold Bay. In this manner are the gold discoveries utilising themselves, and we imagine that each unoccupied portion of this vast continent will in its turn be visited by the wave of population, the flowing and ebbing of which will leave there a deposit, turning the wilderness into a fertile valley, and bidding the desert to bloom as the rose."

So we conclude with the recognition of some of the essential gains from the discovery of gold and can say that the country was much better off having discovered the riches under the ground, and transferred some of them to the top of the ground.

CHAPTER 41

THE PASTORAL SYSTEM AND LAND REFORM

Edward Pulsford, the doyenne of Free Trade wrote in a learned work on 'Trade & Commerce in NSW'(1892) that

"New South Wales is not great in agriculture, unless the term be used in the wide sense accepted in Great Britain and the United States, where it includes the pastoral industry. It is difficult to say why the distinction should be made in Australia, but at all events it is made. 'Agriculture' in Australia is divided into (1) the pastoral industry (2) agricultural farming and (3) the dairying industry

Agriculture in New South Wales has yet (as of 1892) to achieve great distinction, but steady progress is being made. In 1871 only 417,000 acres were under cultivation; by 1881, it had increased to 710,337, and by 1891 it had grown still further to 1,241,419 acres; about ¼ of the area is under artificially grown grasses. During the last harvest a little over 10 million bushels of grain was grown in the Colony . Maize was the largest grain at 5 million bushels , a little more than sufficient to meet local needs and so a small inter-colonial export trade has commenced; wheat stood at 4 million bushels; hay at 210,000 tons; potatoes at 62,000 tons, and the rest of the acreage is in sugar cane and a small acreage in tobacco.

There is potential for great diversity and the future should hold plenteous bounty for the inhabitants of the Colony and certainly self-sufficiency in food production."

'Wool remains and should continue to remain', wrote Pulsford, in 1892, 'the backbone of our commerce'. Since 1871 the number of sheep has risen to thirty-six million, from sixteen million in that earlier year. in 1871 one-third of the sheep were in NSW, in 1881 there was one-half , in spite of bad seasons. The losses from 1876 to 1885 were twenty-eight million, not including the lambs not realised. The year 1884 was a horror and the biggest drought year seen since the Colony began. In 1871 wool production stood at 65 million lb. Full details are to be found in the Appendix of Statistics.

We consider the growth of the Education movement in the Colony in economic terms. Education achieved many goals: It created employment for builders, teachers, administrators, and dropped the illiteracy rate from over 70% to under 20% in a relatively short period of time. This in itself assisted economic growth by a declining crime rate, by offering better-educated workers to employers, and by bridging that generational gap and ensuring that illiterate parents did not restrict the opportunities for their children.

The earliest days

The First Fleet arrived in the Colony with 17 children belonging to the convicts and 19 children belonging to the Marines.

Nowhere in Governor Phillip's commission or instructions was any mention made of these children or their future, or of the child convicts whom the British Government saw fit to transport (there were 47 child convicts in Sydney and 36 at Norfolk Island—HRA I i, 203), for it was alien to the official mind of the late 18th Century to feel any interest in the welfare of these children. By 1809 the War Office had been persuaded to appoint regimental schoolmasters, and by 1833 the Colonial Office was prepared to sanction an experiment in the reformation of child convicts in VDL, but in 1788 the education of these children formed no part of the business of any department of state.

A. G. Austin in his work 'Australian Education 1788-1900' outlines the approach to education of all the Colonists, both the children and the adults.

"The early governors of New South Wales, soon found it necessary to contradict their masters in Westminster, for 'Botany Bay ' was not to be a fragment of English society transformed to the Antipodes, but a military and penal garrison in which they (the Governors) were responsible for every aspect of daily life. In a settlement where the maintenance of discipline, the regulation of food production, the rationing of supplies, the employment of labour and the administration of justice were committed to one man's hands, there was no room for the laissez-faire indifference which characterised the conduct of public affairs in the Mother Country. Not only were they moved by the misery of the convict's children, but also they realised that the future of the Colony had to be built upon these very children. In a colony where there were three times as many men as there were women, and where the distribution of female convicts were never properly supervised, there was, as might be expected, a high proportion of illegitimate and abandoned children. In 1807, on Bligh's testimony, there were 397 married women in the colony. 1,035 'concubines', 807 legitimate children and 1,024 illegitimate children; something as Governor King had already pointed out, had to be done to rescue these children' from the future misery to be expected from the horrible examples that they hourly witness from their parents' and those they live with. "

Phillip had been instructed by the King that ' a spot in or as near each town as possible be set apart for the building of a church, plus land there for a Minister and for a school-master.' (HRNSW 1 Pt 2)

In all this the Governors were not concerned to assert the supremacy of either Church or state. All their actions were matters of expediency. To finance schools they had made direct land grants, assigned convicts and issued rations; they had accepted Special Purpose Grant funds and subscriptions from the public; they had diverted money from fines and impositions and had made grants from public revenue. To staff the schools, they had used soldiers, convicts, dispossessed missionaries and any other literate person they could find; to accommodate the schools they had used churches, barracks, store-houses and private buildings, and to supervise them, they had used the colonial chaplains.

The first Governor to actually make real progress as opposed to the lazy ideas put forward by Richard Bourke (Governor 1831-1837) was Sir George Gipps (Governor 1838-1846); from the outset Gipps clearly defined the educational problem and with great clarity wrote a report and recommendation to the Colonial Office Secretary—Lord Stanley.

"The great dispersion of the population of New South Wales renders a system of education necessary, that shall be as comprehensive as possible. In large towns, or in a densely populated country, separate schools for each Christian denomination can be established, and in a qualified manner may answer the object of their Institution; though if in NSW each separate denomination shall have its separate school, then a large portion of the population shall remain uneducated and out of Sydney, or for the poorer classes of society the shall be scarcely any education at all. Schools are springing up in many of our country towns, but unless they combine they will be but ephemeral."

Establishing the Government System

This period of educating the populous was purely denominational and left to the churches, but as Gipps foresaw, the growth of educating the people should lay with the Government, not the Church, because the Colony was too diverse and sparse, and the cost of education would easily blow out their budget, as could happen to the Colonial budget unless certain limitations were imposed. There had been no provision made for the establishment of schools under State control.

In 1834, the first attempts were made to modify the system in force and by 1839 the first grant was made for the purpose of 'imparting instruction', free from sectarian influences to the children of those who objected to denominational education. It was not until the time of Gipps that any definite steps were made to the educational policy of the State. In that year a committee recommended the adoption of the Irish National School system, and in 1848 an Act created two school boards, and to each respectively was passed the denominational and non-denominational (or National) administration.

This progress commenced the second period of primary education in the Colony. The anomaly of two Boards was abolished in 1866 (the Public Schools Act), after 18 years of operation, and so all schools receiving aid from the State under the control of a Council of Education board. The public schools were totally administered by this board whilst the denominational schools were jointly administered in conjunction with the various religious bodies. Education commenced making considerable progress during this administration. This eventually proved impossible to maintain, because the majority of the people in the Colony were opposed to granting State aid to religious schools, and in 1880 State aid to denominational schools was abolished by Sir Henry Parkes, who had long advocated 'Free, secular and compulsory education'.

Under the Public Instruction Act of 1880, the entire educational system of the state was remodeled. The Council of Education was abolished and all educational matters placed into the hands of a Minister for Education. Provision was made for the establishment and maintenance of public schools, to afford primary instruction to all children without sectarian or class distinction; of superior public schools, in which additional lessons in the higher branches might be given; of evening public schools, with the object of instructing persons who had not received the advantages of primary education while of school age; and of high schools for boys and girls, in which the course of instruction should be of such a character as to complete the public school curriculum, or to prepare students for the university.

Although it was designed to be strictly unbiased it was decided that four hours of tuition each day would be sectarian whilst one hour could be devoted to religious instruction, to be given in a separate classroom by a clergyman or religious teacher.

It was compulsory for parents to send their children to school for at least 70 days in each half-year, unless exemption was approved Penalties were provided for breaches. Although considered 'free', parents are required to pay a weekly fee of 3d per child but not to exceed 1s per family. These fees are paid into consolidated revenue. Children were allowed to travel free each way by train. Provision in the Act was also made for training schools, and for regular inspection of school by Local Boards. These boards were designed to review facilities, suspend teachers not performing, and take action on absentee children.

Illiteracy

At the census of 1881, out of the 751,468 people listed, 195,000 were illiterate or 26%. Included were 154,000 children under the age of 4, so there were 41,000 people over the age of 5 who were unable to read (or under 6%).

Of the 5,800 people married in 1857, 28% were illiterate while by 1900 only 1.5% were illiterate.

As of 1901, the number of school age children was 263,835 of which 172,352 were receiving instruction in State schools 12,755 were instructed at home and the rest by church schools. There were 583 students at the University of Sydney, which had been commenced in the 1850s.

The cost per child in attendance in NSW was 4.6.7, compared with Victoria at 4.12.2.

In a debate in the Victorian Parliament (Legislative Assembly) of 12th September 1872, Attorney-General Stephens introduced a Bill into the House in which the NSW concept of 'free, compulsory and secular' education was adopted for Victorian schools. Stephens stated:

"The political desire to avoid sectarian conflict has always been paramount, but it is not the sole cause of the system; voluntarism, liberalism, and even agnosticism are all influential at a time when the fundamental beliefs of the Christian are being questioned. However, religion is not being driven out of schools. The new policy is to stop taxpayer's money being given to Church schools, to educate voters, and thereby build up prosperity, at a time when the population is increasing rapidly and also dispersing widely in the rural areas. Victoria is to lead the way."

The other Colonies were to follow over the next twenty years.

The Churches, in particular the Catholic Church reacted strongly to these bipartisan moves towards secular education and in a Pastoral Letter in New South Wales the Archbishop reminded his flock that " it is self-evident that education without Christianity is impossible; you may call it instruction, filling the mind with a certain quantity of secular knowledge, but you cannot dignify it with the name education; for religion is an essential part of Education, and to divorce religion or Christianity from Education is to return to paganism, and to reject the Gospels."

So the story of education in Australia is essentially one of neglect for the first One Hundred Years of settlement, during which time it appeared that the challenges of the wide open space of the rural colony and the internal conflicts between Church and State were just too much for the Administrators to handle. In Victoria where the conflict between Church and State ran deeper than any other Colony, the rival claims of denominationalism and secularism to dictate the nature of the education system dominated the debate. State aid to education had increased from 6,000 pound in 1851 to 30,000 in 1853 and despite bitter dispute to 50,000 in 1853, a considerable portion of the Colony's tiny 2 million pound budget of that year.

The debate would continue on in each Colony, even until Menzies in 1964 re-introduced Government contributions to private schools. At least Henry Parkes, in New South Wales, cooled the ardor of the senior churches in the debate and rationalised religious instruction in government schools sufficiently for the children in attendance to get some learning'

The Financial Economy

Public Finance – Sources of Revenue

One goal of the Governor of the Colony of New South Wales in 1788 was to achieve self-sufficiency for the colony even though it was a penal Colony. By 1823, the British Government had taken the approach it would be limiting its direct expenditure to the transportation of the convicts and they're travelling food and supplies. The Colonial Administrators would be responsible for the convict's security, food, clothing and accommodation in the Colony. The proceeds from the sale of Crown land were to be the exclusive reserve of the British authorities, and not that of the colonists. The Governors commenced working the convicts for creating food, minerals (eg coal production), roads, housing and public buildings, and generally paying their own way. By 1796, other convicts had been assigned to landowners on a fully maintained basis, thus saving the British Treasury a great deal of money.

Such policy, of the Government maintenance of convicts, created the need for an accounting by the Colony to the British Parliament with the appointment of a Treasurer acting as a Financial Controller, who could prepare monthly and annual despatches to the British Colonial Secretary. Following self-government in 1856, the procedures changed, as the Colony became fully responsible for their own economic planning and fiscal management.

Colonial Accounting in New South Wales

The Colony went through two stages before adopting the standards recommended in the 1823 'Blue Book', which replaced the 'gaol' and orphan funds. These two phases were the Gaol and Orphan Funds pre-1810, and the Macquarie promoted Police and Orphan Funds of 1811-1821, which results were published quarterly in the Sydney Gazette. The 'gaol' fund was a record of funds raised by a surcharge on the citizens of Sydney town, as a means to complete the construction of the Sydney 'gaol'. The voluntary collections fell far short of the funds needed and a part-completed gaol required official support. Customs duties were imposed on imports, and the gaol was completed with Government monies, the fund was renamed the police fund. The orphan Fund started in 1802 accepted as its revenue the customs duties on spirits and tobacco and was later (1810) named the Orphan School Fund with the intention of creating a fund to erect the first school building in Sydney town. The advisory Legislative Council were appointed in 1823, and the first Appropriation Act was passed in 1832, even though, in the interim, the Governors were passing 'messages' of the financial condition of the Colony to the members of the Council.

Upon self-government in 1855, the government accounting procedures were again revised, since the Colony was now fully responsible for all its fiscal matters.

About this time, gold was discovered and license fees, duties on exports of gold and duties on the domestic conversion of gold were applied and helped fill the Treasury coffers.

This was a major step forward in Government economic planning. A limited deficit budgeting commenced at this time. Deficits were short term and recovered usually within 5 years, although the Colonial debt, mainly to overseas bondholders was kept very much in check after the surge of investment in railways and telegraph services.

The formal Federation debates commencing in 1888 were based around the role and adjustment to individual Colonial tariffs, their discussion in the Finance Committee of the National Debates, and their incorporation into the final Constitution of 1901. These trends from 1856 are to be discussed and analysed

Federation installed a new system within the structure of the new Commonwealth Treasury whilst the States revised their reduced revenue collection procedures and accounted for the grants (return of surplus) of revenue from the Commonwealth.

Federation brought further changes to the raising of revenues, whilst the largest expenditure of the Commonwealth became the return of centrally collected funds to the States. The advent of the Commonwealth Treasury improved once again the quality of recording keeping and brought into being the first Commonwealth estimates and National budgets. By 1901, the public finance mechanism had grown from a colonial exercise by appointed settlers to a fully charged Government instrumentality.

From the earliest records (HRNSW), certain conclusions can be drawn, and these can be set out as follows:

a. There was a wide range of duties and taxes imposed on the early settlers, especially on alcoholic beverages. The general rate of duty on spirits was 10 shillings per gallon, and on wine it was 9 pence per gallon. On tobacco the rate was 6 pence per pound, while timber attracted a rate of one shilling per solid foot. General Cargo attracted an ad valorem duty at a flat 5% rate.

b. There were also licenses and tolls. Hawker's Licenses sold for 20 pound, and it cost a settler 2 pence (tuppence) to go from Sydney town to the settlement of Parramatta. A country settler (in the Hawkesbury) paid One penny to cross the Nepean River Bridge at Windsor.

c. References to crown land sales were recorded in the 1825 'Blue Book', and based on the decree by George 3rd in a Proclamation on 25th March, 1825, that there was to be imposed a new charge on crown lands at the rate of One shilling for every 50 acres, to commence 5 years after the date of the original grant. To that date all crown lands had been disposed of by way of grants, and this rent was a form of back door compensation to the crown. In the official grant documents, the receiver of the land grant was given notice that further costs may attach at some future time to the land, and it was this opportunity that provided the Crown to raise this 'rent' charge on the land in 1825.

d. There was to be a Land-holders fee of Fifteen shillings per 100 acres of crown land reserved for each three years for free settlers, followed by a two shilling fee per 100 hundred acres redeemable after twenty years from purchase.

e. On the 18th May 1825, the 'rent' was changed, by order of Governor Sir Thomas Brisbane, to a flat rate of 5% of the estimated value of the grants, without purchase (as opposed to purchased land), to commence 7 years from the date of grant. 'Rents' on any 2nd and subsequent grants were payable immediately, without the benefit of the 7 years grace period.

f. The Table of Land Grants between 1789 and 1850 shows the substantial number of acres granted to settlers and we can conclude that the revenue sourced from 'rents' on Crown land grants could build into a considerable sum for the Crown in the future.

g. By Proclamation, also dated 18th May 1825, George III authorised the sale of crown lands at the rate of 10 shillings per acre, to a maximum of 4,000 acres per individual or a maximum of 5,000 acres per family. Payment was by way of a 10% deposit and four equal quarterly instalments.

h. The title pages to the 1822 'Blue Book' are entitled ' Abstract of the Net Revenue and Expenditure of the Colony of New South Wales for the Year 1822', which indicates (and as the detailed records also reflect) that all Colonial revenue and expenses were consolidated in the 'Blue Book'.

i. The Table of Civil List Salaries for 1792—1793 sets out the Governor's Salary at One Thousand Pounds. But in the 1822 statement of expenditures on the Civil Salaries, the Governor's Salary had increased to Two Thousand Pounds. By 1856 the Governor's establishment was costing 15,000 pounds per annum.

j. In fact, the total of Civil List salaries in 1792 was only 4,726.0.0 pounds, but by 1822 the total had increased to 9,828.15.0 pounds, due to both individual salary increases as well as more people being placed on the Civil List.

k. The official 'Observations upon revenue for the Colony in 1828' (written by the Colonial Treasurer of New South Wales) makes an interesting point. It observes that the 'net colonial income' of the year 1828, as actually collected, is exclusive of sums in aid of revenue, which cannot be viewed in the character of income. This item is further defined as ' the proceeds of the labour of convicts, and establishments connected with them, being applied to the reduction of the amount of parliamentary grants for their maintenance'. In subsequent reports, 'receipts in aid of revenue' included items such as—'sale of Crown livestock; sale of government farms produce; sale of clothing and cloth made at the Female Factory at Parramatta; sale of wheat, sugar, molasses and tobacco produced by the convicts at new settlements such as Port Macquarie.

l. The total quantity of alcohol imported into and thus consumed in the Colony, even in 1828, and with a population in 1828 of only 37,000 people, of which adult numbers would be less than 25,000, was 162,167 gallons of spirits and 15,000 gallons of Colonial distilled spirits (distillation from sugar was prohibited in 1828, however, the high price of grain and the higher taxing of locally manufactured spirits became a natural deterrent). A final observation was made in the 'Blue Book' compilation of 1829 that the only duties imposed on spirits in that year was upon spirits imported directly from H. M. Plantations in the West Indies. So the British authorities received a double benefit in trading and duties.

m. The quantity of dutiable tobacco in 1828 was 136,748 pounds (compared to 91,893 pounds in 1825). The Government experimented with locally grown tobacco at establishments in Emu Plains and Port Macquarie with the result being 51,306 pounds produced. So the total consumption of tobacco in 1828 was over 4 Lb. Per head of adult population.

n. Shipping companies also paid lighthouse charges, along with wharfage. The growth of shipping, into the Port of Sydney, was so great that it meant that by 1828, the revenue from lighthouse dues, harbour dues and wharfage was over 4,000 pound.

o. In 1828, the postage of letters attracted fees, for the first time, and the official Postmaster collected 598 pounds for general revenue. This revenue grew rapidly so that by 1832 the amount of postage collected was 2,00 pound. Each colony imposed its own postage and printed its own stamps until Federation.

The commencement of sales of both crown lands and crown timbers increased general revenues to the extent that in 1828, the amounts realised were:

Sales of Crown Lands	5004.19.2
Sales of Cedar cut on crown land	744.15.11
Sales of other Timber	9365.11.4

The Governor imposed a fee of One halfpenny per foot for all cedar cut on crown lands. The 'Blue Book' makes the further observation that this charge 'has checked bushrangers and other lawless depredators by depriving them of ready means of subsistence by the absence of all restraint from cutting Cedar upon unallocated lands'. q. There was a major improvement in record keeping and reporting after self-government in 1855. The "Financial Statements of the Colonial Treasurers of New South Wales from Responsible Government in 1855 to 1881" provide a detailed accounting mechanism for recording classifications and compilation of budgets and reporting to the Authorities. They contain ' explanatory memoranda of the financial system of New South Wales, and of the rise, progress and present condition of the public revenue'.

The interest in this period (from 1822 to 1881) is that these records, of the 'Blue Book' and the printed Financial Statements of 1881, provide the first identification of the items included in the revenue and expenditures for the Colony. This historical data is relevant to understanding the social conditions in the Colony, the application of duties, tariffs, tolls and fees which embraced the essential revenue of a Colony that was designed to be self-sufficient and which was being given minimal economic support by the British Government, even though the opportunity cost of housing 'prisoners' in the Colony was a fraction of the cost of housing them in England

Developing Government Services

The economy, like most unplanned economies in the New World went through its two paces—boom and then bust. But the busts were essentially limited to two periods, the 1840s and the 1890s. The boom times came with the discovery of gold; exploration followed by the growth and expansion of the pastoral industry and the rise of the squattocracy. As the momentum gathered for Federation, Free Trade policies in the Colony of New South Wales set it aside from the protectionist and restrictive policies of Deakin, and his champion, David Syme of the Age newspaper, in the Colony of Victoria. However with the discovery of gold in the 1850s came other side effects such as the termination of transportation, introduction of self-government, along with further land reforms, a rise in wages, prices and rents due mainly to the shortage of a general labour supply.

The railway system underpinned the economic gains from the 1850s and set the pastoral industry onto a more comfortable plain. But mainly the railways allowed the policy of decentralisation to be formally adopted. The regions of Newcastle and the Riverina grew and developed rapidly. Newcastle had been an ideal of Macquarie but it developed slowly until the rail system allowed coal extracts from the region to be moved quickly and cheaply to Sydney and then onto Victoria, which area became a major user of New South Wales coal.

The Treasurers of the Colony knew only the advantages of balancing the books each year—there was no deficit financing undertaken until after 1856 when overseas borrowing commenced with the financial houses in the City of London, who had accepted the credit worthiness of the Colony and hastened to use this new outlet for surplus funds available for investment by Britain. The use of bank drafts for export commodities had commenced with the large wool exports to Britain and led to the creation of the Union Bank of Australia, the Bank of Australasia. This period also saw the rise of the great pastoral and financing houses—Brooks and Younghusband, Dalgety and Goldsbrough Mort. Shipping fleets grew rapidly for transporting convicts, then free immigrants and returning with wool, and other commodities. The P & O operators, with their One million pound of paid up capital won the lucrative mail contracts from the British Government and commenced regular monthly trips from London to Australia.

The published public accounts reflect an annual cumulative surplus (of revenue over expenditures) each year from 1822 to 1900. What this meant was that the Colonial Treasurers and their advisers had the flexibility of running into temporary deficit, for instance in 1838 (—164102 pound) and 1839 (—121464) knowing that the cumulative surplus of 314517 pound would allow them to do so without having to borrow long-term. In this instance the cumulative surplus was reduced to only 28951 pound. The ways of recording in the various periods varied and opened the way for considerable mistake and misinterpretation, as we will see. The periods (there are five distinct periods) we speak of are:

the goal and orphan fund period 1802-10
the Police and Orphan Fund period 1810-21
the 'Blue Book' period 1822-55
the self-government period 1856-89
the pre-Federation period 1889-99

Governor Macquarie had appointed D'Arcy Wentworth and Reverend Samuel Marsden to be Treasurers of the Police and Orphan funds and we find their monthly reports published in the Sydney Gazette of the period 1810-1821.

Clerical staff within the Colonial Secretary's office period recorded the Blue Book.

The Blue Book contains the comprehensive recording system of the times and the Consulting Accountant James Thomson introduced a new system after self-government, which was burdensome, intricate, and open to much abuse. After self-government, the ledgers were kept open until the funds appropriated to each line item in the budget were spent. This sometimes meant the ledgers could not be closed for upwards of three years, by which time the trail was cold in trying to keep track of annual revenues and expenditures. This problem was corrected in 1885, when a return was made to annual statements based on cash inflow and outflow.

Some Observations of Interest

The Marsden and Wentworth transactions created major conflict of interest situations. It is interesting to muse how a Reverend gentleman who was paid from the Civil List at the rate of 150 pound per annum, could afford to operate 4,500 acres of pasture land and build up a flock of 3,500 sheep in a span of less than twenty years. Even allowing that the land came about from grants, the sheep were purchased and although the convict labour assigned to him was unpaid, they had to be kept, with sleeping huts, food and clothing furnished. We might also ask why the monthly meat bill for the orphanage ran to over 60 pound even though the Orphanage owned and operated a farm, which regularly sold 'on the hoof' and then bought back, dressed meat. For its annual sale of livestock in 1811-1812, Marsden received only 127 pound, but from the same source purchased over 700 pound of dressed meat. The means were easy to share the spoils between those that could help him gain wealth and reach his target of becoming a large landowner and successful grazier. Marsden housed only female orphans aged from 5 to 14. On an average month, Marsden paid the butcher over 60 pound, being for an average of 2,500 lb of meat (the average price per pound was 6 pence. By the 30th September 1818, Marsden held 3,033 pound in the Orphanage account, and on average disbursed 550 pound each month from that account. The only 'admonishment' that Macquarie made if one can imply an act of admonition from a minor regulatory change, was that a lesser percentage of revenue from tariffs and duties was to be directed to the Orphan Fund.

Macquarie, at this time, chose to modify the basis of the Orphanage Fund revenue and deleted an item by redirecting that revenue to the Police Fund. In 1818, Macquarie also directed that 3,000 pound of the balance in the Orphan Fund be deposited with the new Bank of New South Wales.

Macquarie made no objection to the fact that Marsden was misdirecting funds from the Orphan Fund for the repair of St. John's Church, Parramatta, in July 1811 to the extent of 56 pound, nor to paying the Matron of the Orphanage a monthly stipend of 5 pound when the going rate would have been only 1 pound per month, nor of paying 4.5.0 for a bonnet for his wife from the fund.

Macquarie wrote approved on each monthly statement, when presented to him by Marsden, obviously without proper 'auditing' procedures being used.

The Orphan Fund, as published in the Sydney Gazette, quarterly between 181 and 1820, showed numerous arithmetic errors always on account of a shortage, and one may wonder why, no-one handling the accounts, such as the other Trustees, the Governor's secretary, or the Judge-Advocate, ever picked up these quite substantial errors. During the course of the years 1812-1818, the amount of shortage or error in addition came to a total of 997 pound.

Wentworth, as Treasurer of the companion 'Police' Fund also had his dubious methods. He built up large surpluses of cash and bills receivable rather than spend funds on road and bridge or wharf construction; he expended large amounts through the military for 'repairs' to the streets of Sydney and other questionable contracts, which were never commented on publicly by Macquarie. Macquarie's 'blindness' to any inconsistencies or abuses in the accounts, made it appear that he was only interested in outcomes, regardless of how they were achieved.

Wentworth was also the town Magistrate and Superintendent of Police responsible for fines, which were an important source of revenue to the Police Fund. Two items of regular expenditure, open to abuse, and which appear to be inordinately high were purchase of firewood and lamp oil and payment for the capture of absconding convicts. The Military personnel were fleecing the Government stores, operating the barter system in the Colony and were obviously monopolising the ample rewards in cash available if one found favour with Wentworth.

Legislative Councillor, Robert Campbell, recommended to the Governor on 25th August, 1835 that the British Treasury should consider paying a flat rate of 10 pound per head for each of the 20,000 convicts in the colony at that time by way of maintenance and support to the local treasury. He suggested that 'because the accumulated balances in the Treasury are evidences not of superabundant revenues but of defective financial arrangements whereby public buildings have fallen into disrepair or become unfit for the required purposes. Campbell suggested that 'because the large revenue raised is not the result of industry or creation of wealth but proof of the improvident and vicious habits of the community. He noted that 3/4 ths of the revenue of 157,300 pound arises from duties on spirits'. This whole proposition was rejected by Governor Sir Richard Bourke, but associate Councillors, John Blaxland wrote a letter also on 235th August, 1835, suggesting that the British Treasury had saved over 11000,000 pound by using New South Wales as a penal colony—he represented that 1,913,462.17.0 had been saved if hulks had been used or 11,008,837.5.6 if prisons had been built. He was basing his numbers on a saving of 30 pound per head for the 20,207 convicts in the colony at that time.

In response to this disagreement between Bourke and the Councillors, Bourke announced that 'the revenue of last year has been unusually productive. We are able to provide for such objects as tend to improve the morals, augment the wealth and procure the comfort and convenience of all classes of the community. These include supporting Public Schools and places of religious worship, the formation and improvement of roads and the repair and erection of public buildings'.

A. T. Yarwood in his biography of 'Samuel Marsden—the great survivor' writes that Marsden opened the female orphan house on Sunday 12th August, 1801 with a sermon followed by a visit through 'the best house in all Sydney (Rowland Hassall), and a feast. 'Thirty-one girls had been received into the house for learning, clothing, bed and board—and protection from parents and their associates (Yarwood)

At the other end of the time scale in 1899, the Federation debates also warrant a closer look at the figures furnished to Convention delegates. As the official Colonial Statistician for New South Wales, Timothy Coghlan was trying to make a name for himself in the Commercial world and was in regular disagreement with the Premiers and Treasurers of the Colony. He had been publicly accused by Edward Pulsford, the leader of the Free Trade Movement of 'playing games' with his statistics, but the greatest self-serving abuse must have come with the request to furnish official statistics to the Federation debates in general and the Financial Sub-committee in particular.

He provided, in 1892, statistics for the year 1889 knowing that the figures were out of date, and were to be used until 1899, and as such capable of misinterpretation and misuse. But these figures became the guiding hand for the Finance Committee's recommendation on the structuring of the financial clauses for the Constitution. The 1889 figures remained in use until 1899 even though Coghlan delayed the scheduled collection of new statistics (which was scheduled for 1896) until 1902. Revised interim figures would have changed the course of Australian history, especially the fiscal nature of the Federation debates. A set of figures which should have formed the basis of the Federation debates and the Constitutional clauses is included in the Appendix to this work and the reader may judge for himself whether Coghlan's self serving submissions made sense. That New South Wales, being a free trade state, got great benefit from the incorrect figures being used is not questioned but the three smaller colonies—South Australia, Tasmania and Western Australia, were all significantly disadvantaged, although Western Australia was the only Colony to get preferred treatment under the Constitution. One example is with the Colonial debt in New South Wales. In 1890 the debt was only 16 million-pound, but by 1900 the debt had burgeoned to over 150 million pound. This appeared to be a carefully planned exercise by the Premiers and the Treasurers to manipulate the proposed constitution for the benefit of that colony.

By also manipulating the figures presented to the Convention delegates, Coghlan's hoped to get appointed as Commonwealth Statistician and get recognition as a great Australian. Neither happened, but he did manoeuvre a knighthood in spite of a poor showing as Agent-General for NSW in

London. His writings, especially the four-volume work of Labour and Industry Growth in New South Wales are illuminating, mischievous in their conclusions, and self serving and misguided. His was a life spent on serving two masters. Himself and to a lesser extent the Government that paid him handsomely for many years.

Structural Changes

Treasurer—James Thomson) recorded that:

"The Financial System of the Colony of New South Wales is regulated chiefly by the Constitution Act of 1855 and the Audit Act of 1870, and in matters relating to Trust Funds and Loans by special Appropriation Acts of the local legislature.

The Imperial Act granting a constitution to the Colony of New South Wales was assented to on 16th July, 1855, and became effective on the 24th November 1855. This Act provides for a Legislative Council (Upper House) and a Legislative Assembly. The Upper House members were to be nominated by the Governor, while the Lower House members were to be elected by inhabitants of the Colony.

"Prior to the passing of the Constitution Act, the territorial revenues of the Colony belonged to the Crown, but on that Act coming into operation in 1855, these revenues were all placed at the disposal of the local Parliament, and together with the taxes, imposts, rates and duties, were formed into one fund, under the title of the Consolidated Revenue Fund. In lieu of the Crown Revenues thus given up to the Colony, an annual Civil List of 64,300 pounds was made payable to Her Majesty out of the consolidated revenues of the Colony.

The Constitution Act also provides that the legislature of the Colony shall have power to make laws for regulating the sale, letting, disposal, and occupation of the wastelands of the Crown within the Colony; and also for imposing taxes and levying customs duties. All Money Bills must, in the first place, be recommended to the Legislative Assembly by message from the Governor, and no part of the Public Revenue can be issued except on warrants bearing the Governor's signature, and directed to the Treasurer of the Colony.

The Audit Act of 1870 was passed to regulate the receipt, custody and issue of public monies, and to provide for the audit of the Public Accounts. The Treasury is the Department entrusted with the collection and disbursement of the revenues and other public monies of the Colony. It is under the control and general management of the Treasurer and Secretary for Finance and Trade. The permanent head of the Department is responsible to the Minister for the efficient conduct of its business.

The revenue of the Colony is now to be classed under the following general headings:

1. Taxation
2. Land Revenue
3. Receipts for services rendered
4. miscellaneous receipts

The main elements of the these four categories items consist of:

a. Taxation

1. customs duties
2. excise duties
3. duty on gold exported
4. trade licenses

b. Land Revenue

1. Proceeds from land auctions
2. sales of improved lands
3. rents and assessments on pastoral runs
4. quit rents
5. leases of mining lands
6. miner's rights

c. Services receipts, include:

1. railway & telegraph revenue
2. money orders
3. mint charges
4. gold escort fees
5. pilotage & harbour fees
6. registration of cattle brands
7. other fees of office

d. Miscellaneous

1. rents
2. fines
3. sale of government property,
4. interest on bank deposits
5. other general revenues

The revenue and expenditure of the Colony is increasing year by year in proportion to the prosperity of the people and the increase of population. This is naturally to be expected for as new lands are taken up and outlying districts occupied, demands upon the government for all those services which tend to promote the well-being of a community are constantly being made; and although these services when granted create an additional expenditure, there generally follows an augmentation of the revenue both from the sale and occupation of the waste lands of the Colony, and the larger consumption of dutiable articles"

When responsible government was established in 1855, the revenue amounted to 973,178 pounds (or 3.51 pound per head) and the population was then 277,000. In 1875, exactly twenty years after the introduction of responsible government, the population had increased to 606,000 and the revenue to 4,121,996 (or 6.80 pound per head)."

From the Government Gazette of 2nd January 1879, this condensed statement is taken:

REVENUE, 1878

Taxation		
Customs Duties	44,220	
Duty on gold	6,898	
Licenses	<u>109,851</u>	160,969
Land Revenue		
Sales	1,915,466	
Other	410,254	
Services	1183,582	
Miscellaneous	<u>172,907</u>	3,682,209
TOTAL REVENUES for 1878		<u>£3,843,178</u>

An interesting observation on latter day government finance and government involvement in entrepreneurial activities is made by Trevor Sykes in his book, 'The Bold Riders' 1994—Chapter 14, Page 438:

"The Savings Bank of South Australia was formed in 1848 and the State Bank of South Australia was formed in 1896. By 1984 they had led stolidly blameless lives for 136 and 988 years respectively. In 1984 they merged to form a new, larger State Bank of South Australia.

The chairman of Hooker Corporation, Sir Keith Campbell, headed the Campbell Committee, set up by Federal Treasurer, John Howard, in 1979. The Committee delivered its report in March 1981. The Report recommended deregulation of the financial system, a part of a worldwide trend, leading to deregulation in the federal sphere in 1984 by Paul Keating. The Campbell Report recommended that, once the banking system had been deregulated to make it more competitive, there would cease to be any justification, on efficiency grounds, for continued government ownership of banks, so that if government banks were to remain, should be no more fettered or subject to government interference than private sector institutions undertaking similar activities."

The State Savings Bank of South Australia foundered and failed in 1989, only 5 years after deregulation and 140 years after its opening.

GOVERNANCE OF PUBLIC FINANCE IN THE COLONY

GENERAL OBSERVATIONS

On the origin and nature of the New South Wales Colonial Revenue:—

"The Revenues collected within the Colony of New South Wales, from its establishment until the commencement of the administration of Governor Macquarie in 1810, were raised in support of the 'Gaol' and 'Orphan' Funds respectively. The Revenue thus levied for, and appropriated to the Gaol Fund consisted of a Duty of 1s. per gallon on Spirits, 6d per gallon on wine, 3d per gallon on beer, together with a wharfage duty of 6d on each cask or package landed. These duties appear to have been first established upon the authority of Governor John Hunter R.N. during his administration in 1795—1800 and were the earliest sources of local revenue in the Colony.

The Revenue raised for the Orphan Fund was derived from fees on the entry and clearance of Vessels, and for permits to land and remove spirits—both first levied in 1800; from licenses to retail liquor and from a duty of 1.5% on goods sold by auction (first collected in 1801); from a duty of 5% ad valorem on all articles imported, the produce of countries to the eastward of the Cape of Good Hope (first imposed in 1802); from fines levied by the Courts and Magistrates; from fees from grants of lands and leases, and quit rents on crown lands (Quit rents ceased in 1805). Other than quit rents and crown land fees, all revenues were levied upon Colonial authority.

The following is revenue raised in 1805 (James Thomson reports that the records from 1805 to 1810 are 'imperfect')

1805 Revenues in Gaol and Orphan Funds:

Duties on Spirits	1569.11.3
Fees on Vessels, licenses	595.13.7
Ad valorem duty	531.10.3
Fines by courts	86.5.8
Revenue raised in 1805	2783.0.9

In 1810, Governor Macquarie changed the designation of these two funds to 'Police Fund' and Orphan School Fund. The designated revenues were split 3:1 into each fund. The Act 3 Geo IV c.96 of 1822 gave further powers of taxation to the Governor.

UNDERSTANDING THE PUBLIC ACCOUNTS OF 1810-1818

In preparation for understanding the Public Accounts of the Colony as printed by the Sydney Gazette between 28th August, 1810 and the 28th November 1818, and published under the authority of the Governor (Lachlan Macquarie), we must understand firstly the nature of the two Treasurers.

The Orphan Fund, whose official nomenclature is 'The Female Orphan Institution Fund' (a successor by name—change to the Orphan & School Fund) was administered by the Reverend Samuel Marsden, an Anglican churchman, who, as an official (principal) chaplain was on the Civil List for receiving an annual stipend or salary, as well as being the principal trustee and administrator of the Orphanage, the rector of St. John's Church, Parramatta, livestock trader, a marriage celebrant, a large land and livestock owner and a pastoralist, as well as self-appointed moral censor of the Colony. Marsden was also a magistrate at Parramatta—'the hanging preacher'.

That a conflict of interest is perceived is acceptable but the nature of the accounting process allowed the distinct possibility of misappropriation of funds. For instance the orphan fund was designated as being used for the operation of the Female Orphanage within an existing building in Sydney town, with a larger building to be constructed at Parramatta. However, we find that the orphanage farm sold produce in the amount of less than 1,000 pound during seven years. Marsden also 'sold' the labour or services of orphans for 310 pound during that period, and deposited that cash as revenue to the fund, instead of either dropping fees from people having to place children in the orphanage (usually 3 pound per head) or giving the money (or its equivalent in goods) to the Orphans themselves. The governor shared the import duties between the two funds so that the Orphan Fund received 17,649 pound and the Police Fund received 77,600 in funds or bills receivable during this period.

But Marsden acted with impunity in expending over 1,000 pound on expenses, repairs and improvements to St. John's church. At least this amount was recorded.

The frightening thought is that some of the higher, unexplained expenditures could well have been going into the Marsden personal fund and assisting with the expenses of operating his 4,000 head herd of sheep and cattle or of paying farm expenses for his 4,500 acres. The small 30 acre farm attached to the Orphanage cost 1,268 pound to run for seven years so it is reasonable to expect that Marsden's broad acres were costing a goodly amount to operate. His stipend of 150 pound per annum would not have stretched to paying farm expenses, especially with a wife and 5 children, 5 servants and 10 'assigned' convicts. He eventually became the largest sheep owner before 1819.

Without proper authorisation, the new orphanage building had cost 4,000 pound to construct. The original estimate to Macquarie (HRNSW) was 500 pound. This is just another example of Macquarie's extravagance which could not be reined in, not even by Lord Bathurst. It demonstrates the deviousness that Marsden could show when he craved something badly enough.

It is questionable, as well, that the 45 orphans housed in the original buildings could consume a monthly average food bill , for meat (of 70 pound) or of flour (of over 50 pound). With meat selling at about or below 6d per lb, the supposed quantity of meat was unmanageable, in infants. It is possible that during the period, the butcher was being paid for extra sheep on the hoof going to the Marsden farm. The amount of firewood purchased was 278 pound , regardless of the available wood on the orphanage farm and the surplus labour available to the farm. Shoes and clothing, in the amount of 600 pound during the period from 1825, for the orphans suggests frequent new clothing items, whilst the monthly 'donation' to the orphanage matron of 5 pound made her the highest paid female in the Colony.

There were five ' charity' schools operating until Macquarie decided to bring them under the umbrella of the governor, leave the administration to Marsden but now using paid and supervised teachers and other staff. These schools paid over 2,000 pound in salaries to its staff plus a further 187 pound in school supplies, books during the period.

D'Arcy Wentworth's fiduciary responsibilities, as Treasurer of the Police Fund were marginally better but this is mainly due to his handling over 120,000 pound during his eight years as Treasurer. His areas of revenue raising were hotel and spirit licences, road tolls (mainly Sydney to Parramatta), auction and marketing licences, and the bulk of import duties.

Wentworth also had ample opportunity to salt some revenues away to his own use, although in the main his financial statements did not contain too many arithmetic errors. His main areas of expenditure was repair work and new work on the many streets and roads within the Sydney and Parramatta areas.

Wentworth was the Treasurer of the Police Fund as well as a Police Magistrate for the town, and the 'Commissioner' of Police, it was not surprising to find that all of his repair work was carried out by soldiers and police officers. The recapturing of escaped convicts was paid for handsomely and most of these payments was again made by Wentworth to police officers and soldiers. It may be questioned whether they were being paid more to guard to convicts or to re-catch them, after they escaped. So, if 'trading' was not the military people's forte, Wentworth remunerated them well with extra pay for services and assistance from within his bailiwick. Road repairs and minor new construction came to over 15,000 pound whilst new wharves came to 2,000 pound. His largest single item was for salaries to those many people not on the civil list. This amounted to over 53,000 pound during the period

The Funds available to Wentworth and the Governor from the Police Fund , at the end of 1818 was nearly 17,000 pound. This amount was directed (by Macquarie in 1818) to be placed on deposit in the new Bank of New South Wales.

Macquarie's policy's of improving the Colonial operations did work, as can be seen from the 'investment', from Wentworth's account, in new buildings and other contract work of over 25,000 pound.

In terms of revenue, the Colony increased its costs of living by over 173,000 pound in just 7 years. In terms of pounds per head per year, it is estimated that amount is equivalent to at an impost of nearly two pound per head per year of additional duty, tolls, fees etc.

That Macquarie's successor, Sir Thomas Brisbane, as well as Commissioner Bigge, demanded full, proper and regularised accounting of all revenue and expenditures is reflected in the transfer to the 'Blue Book' system in 1822 and the appointment of a full-time salaried financial officer, for the Colony, in the same year.

Remaining British

B. The Consequences of Transportation:

The next task must be to record some of the consequences of transportation to the Colony of New South Wales. It was during the time that convicts provided the principal source of labour for government purposes and private enterprise, that the consequences of transportation appeared to be measurable. One of the indirect consequences was the 'opportunity' cost to both Britain and the Colony of the transportation program. The Molesworth Committee in 1838, believing that their definitive opinion on the value of transported labour could only justify its continuation stated that transportation was an obstacle to continued economic growth. Some twelve years later, an advocate of transportation, (Archibald Atchison—Crime and Transportation) produced figures to show that just the opposite was true.—transportation had been of great value to the Colony.

A consequence first raised by Samuel Marsden was that adult convicts were beyond re-training but that the young people needed education. A further social consequence was that the transfer of so many male convicts led, by 1841, to 'a dearth of females', a situation named as alarming by

Ralph Mansfield 'Analytical view of the census of 1841 in New South Wales'.

Governor Phillip was the first to publicly recognise that the nature of the penal settlement required a 'peculiar form of government', but one of the goals of Commissioner Bigge was to review the legal side of Colonial administration and report on changes needed for the administration of justice. Bigge did make such a report and the recommendations were immediately adopted by Macquarie.

The Molesworth Committee report into transportation concluded that "Some persons contend that the pecuniary interests of the penal Colony require the continuation of transportation; that as the extraordinary commercial prosperity of these colonies was occasioned by the constant supply of convict labour, if that supply be cur off the colonies would be ruined, from great wealth be reduced to great poverty; and that this change in the fortune of inhabitants, especially if it were sudden, would necessarily produce the worst moral effects upon their character, and still further demoralise the already demoralised.

"The extraordinary wealth of these colonies was occasioned by the regular and increasing supply of convict labourers. The convicts were assigned to settlers as slaves, they were forced to work in combination, and raised more produce than they could consume; for this surplus produce Government provided a market, by maintaining military and convict establishments, which have cost this country above 7,000,000 pound of the public money.

"Labour is in short supply whilst capital has amazingly increased. The flocks of sheep are double the size they ought to be; a vast number perish for want of care; labour must be furnished from sources, other than convicts, if the colonies are to continue to flourish"

CHAPTER 42

THE BENEFITS TO THE UNITED KINGDOM

Although the more significant consequences of transportation of British convicts to the Colony of New South Wales may have been both economic and social, the general benefits of transportation of British convicts out of the United Kingdom are economic.

The essential question becomes—Would the United Kingdom have pursued a Colonial expansion policy if there had not been a need to transfer convicts from the Americas elsewhere?

The answer is of course, a simple—'yes'. The trade, defence and colonisation policies , in place, and under discussion, made territorial acquisition essential. The British Navy needed supplies of masts and spars to maintain its fleet in sailing condition. The British Trade tsars wanted to see further expansion, after a successful entrance into the Caribbean area, and the eyes of the East India Company were wanting to spread further across the Asian region. Terra Australis—the great south land—was an obvious desire.

Therefore, it is fair to say that the gains to Britain were enormous in economic terms, especially in terms of the opportunity cost in dealing with the housing, feeding and guarding of the great surge of prisoners between 1750 and 1850.

Some of the direct advantages to Britain include:

a. The build-up of trade by the East-India Company
b. The advantage of a secure, in-house, supply of raw wool, to keep the spinning mills occupied
c. the opportunity cost of housing, feeding and guarding prisoners
d. The use of convict labour in the new Colony

- land clearing, farming, food production
- for road construction
- public wharves
- barracks
- Public Buildings
- for Materials supply eg brick & tile production.
- as unpaid day labour for the pastoral & agricultural industry

e. We can assume that Land grants, in the Colony, to men on the military and civil list was a form of 'fringe benefits' and should be quantified as an alternative to paid remuneration for these people.
f. Even land grants to emancipists were used as an incentive to increase food production.
g. We can quantify items C, D, E and F into a 'value of direct gain to the British economy of nearly 140,000,000 pound (refer details in the attached), compared with the publicly recorded expenditure on transportation, supplies, and military personnel of 5,600,000 pound, between 1788 and 1822.

The extent of the benefits depends on the pound value attached to the opportunity cost of a prisoner housed in Britain. James Matra wrote in 1784 that the contract cost of a prisoner maintained on the Thames River hulks was 26.75 pound, probably significantly less than cost of prisoners housed in the London prisons especially Ludgate, which was probably costing close to 40.0.0 pound per head per annum. So if we assume an opportunity cost of 20 pounds in lieu of the 10 pound, our benefit rises to 180 million pound from 130 million.

The purposes of trying to quantify these benefits is to challenge to traditional concept that 'the British invested millions of pounds in the Colony of New South Wales'.

It is obviously only the case, that the British Treasury invested millions when the outlay is shown and by not accounting for the on-going benefits for over fifty years, and indeed for two hundred years. It is still arguable that the Continent of Australia is, in Captain Arthur Phillip's words ' the best investment Britain will ever make'.

What the accounts don't tell us but in hindsight we could see happening is that the short-sighted English arrogance and limited social understanding was heading in a definite direction. They had no alternative plans for the placement of convicts after the loss of the American Colonies, except the earlier consideration of Africa , which idea was scotched before Botany Bay became so attractive, but there was a move, not long after the penal colony had been commenced that the transportation program was not going to work. We noted previously the negative observations in the Molesworth Report of 1828, however, John Howard , in 1770 wrote a serious report on 'The State of the Prisons in England and Wales' and noted :

"the general prevalence and spread of wickedness in prisons, and abroad by the discharged prisoners will now be as easily accounted for, as the propagation of disease. It is often said, 'A prisoner pays no debts ;' I am sure, it may be added, that a prison mend no morals. Sir John Fielding observes, that . . . . ' a criminal discharged by the court will generally, by the next sessions, after the execution of his comrades, become the head of a gang of his own raising'. Improved, no doubt, in skill , by the company he kept in gaol: petty offenders who are committed to prison, not to hard labour, but in idleness and wicked company or are sent to county gaols, generally grow desperate, and come out fitted for any villainy."

We can conclude that this view held a lot of sway with Pitt, the Prime Minister of the day. So, this view along with the projected cost of transportation and establishing the Colony, suggested that strong opposition would be prevalent within the Commons to stop the transportation program very quickly.

That funds were short in the British Treasury is suggested by a number of events, especially the pressure on each Governor, to trim costs. It took the appointment of the Chief Justice of Jamaica , John Thomas Bigge, sent to Sydney to review progress in the Colony, to muzzle the extravagances of Macquarie, because he took little interest in the pleadings and persuasion of Colonial Secretary Bathurst, who was concerned about the expense of new exploration, the expense of the new settlements in Newcastle and elsewhere. The substantial 'investment' in new buildings as well as the new roads and bridges in this vast and empty land as well as the early emancipation , conditional discharges and early release that were being handed out to many of the convicts, along with land grants.

Further support for cutting the high cost of the transportation program was forthcoming from the Report by the Select Committee on Finance released to the Commons on 26th June, 1798.

"For the first twelve years of the transportation program, 5,858 convicts were transported at a cost of 1,037,230.6.7 ¾. This worked out at the extraordinary cost of 177 pound per head for naval expenses, supplies, civil salaries, military costs and establishment costs.

That this figure was inflated or padded by the British Treasury officials, is without doubt , as the naval cost portion of the total charge of 1,037,230 pound was 166,341 or 29 pound per head. The contracted cost for the second fleet onward was under 12 pound per head for convicts loaded in England, rather than the number unloaded in Sydney or elsewhere. This cost cutting exercise was the biggest contributor to the high loss of convict lives on route from London to Australia in the second and third fleet and was substantially due to the treatment received by the convicts from their handlers, the contractors,(whose sole goal was to complete the run at a profit) whereas Phillip lost no convicts or passengers, or military personnel during his long trip.

The Select Committee on Finance thought obliquely about the problems of making the Colony too attractive. They concluded" The more thriving the setting, the less terrible the threat. It may lose its terrors altogether, especially if by money or other means, servitude be avoidable." The original estimate of total cost, including transportation was 30 pound per head. This estimate was accompanied by a Government projection that within the first four years, 10,000 convicts would be shipped for this 30 pound per head rather than the 5,800 convicts shipped over twelve years at 177 pound per head. The Peel Plan of 1828 which had compared the original estimates with the actual results also concluded that 'should the authorities succeed in sending home to Britain the expected surplus produce, for which at the moment the Government are indebted to Powers which it would be their policy to suppress, they would effect a national good which time could not erase from the annals of British History.'

Thus the real argument was not one of not punishing the prisoners sufficiently or of releasing them before full redemption could be guaranteed, but of the cost to the British Treasury. No official in that day considered or noted the opportunity costs or the other benefits accruing to the Government, as has been analyzed above.

Summary & Conclusion

Our goal was to identify the British colonial policy, determine its economic value to the Kingdom, identify the rewards from the colonies and translate differences in various colonial acquisitions and see how Australia fared from being the last of the colonial attainments.

Probably the turning point in colonial policy – from the old to the new – was the union of Scotland and England. The Scots were great traders and entrepreneurs and had long been at the fore of economic planning (Adam Smith, amongst others), and their union not only made the kingdom a safer place for the two peoples but the political global savvy of the English offered a great match of trade, entrepreneurial ability and the political wiliness of the Westminster officials and the investment ability of the City of London.

The economic effort of both the old and new colonial system was enormous. The value of the English ships, the cargoes and the foreign investment into the colonies by the English investors was over 2 billion pound in the mid 1800s.

The giant colonial system was almost complete but the human side let the British down.

The theory of scattered colonies, full of British immigrants, attractive to growing British investment, and a growing source of British finished goods imported whilst providing raw materials for British manufacturers was sound. Even the political theory of constitutional independence and empire cohesion to the colonies and the potential for common laws and parliamentary representation caste a mould around this potential union. However the missing link was to bring the empire down – the British domination required all peoples to think and act British – there was no recognition of the ideology of independent culture, tradition or the recognition of the need for harmony between laissez-faire economies. It all had to be the British way or nothing and the collapse of British North America into a minor colonial interest (with many yet unanswered challenges – the union of Upper and Lower Canada) was an indication that parochial interests and demands were not met with the required pragmatic thinking and responses.

The British hardly acted consistently. With New Zealand colonisation was delayed for almost 75 years after Cook declared for the South Island on behalf of Britain, but circumstances led to colonisation of New South Wales only 18 years after Cook's claim for the east coast of the continent in 1770. The approach to the land grab was equally as different, for Cook claimed the Australian east coast on the basis of terra nullius whilst the British negotiated the North Island land of New Zealand by treaty with compensation (of a non-monetary kind).

Britain's financial problems didn't start with the Seven Year War, although the Napoleonic War and the War of Independence placed a further substantial burden on her Treasury resources. The balance of payments in the late 1700s was badly out of balance. 80% of British food imports came from foreign countries and amounted to over 114 million pound – the various colonies only sent 27 million pound or 19%. In reality food consumption (as measured by Sir John Caird was about 370 million of which the import content was the 114 million, so 256 million was home produced. With population rising dramatically, it could be expected that the nation's food import bill would rise annually. With the new tax on imported foodstuffs, there would be a flow-on effect, from an increase in rents, prices would be under pressure, government revenues would increase, and hunger would abound in the poorer districts, all because of the tax on food. The question became – would the colonial markets make up the difference and negate the impact of a tax on food? One of the concerns upon the repeal of the Navigation Act was that the American's would take over and dominate the sea-trade. This proved groundless as the American settlers found their potential was in growing food and raising livestock rather than being seafarers. Their food exports kept Europe, but mostly England, in food. The imposition of tax on Corn, mostly American corn, further soured relations between Britain and her former colony. The concern became that if America was driven out of food production and into manufactures then Britain industry would be at further disadvantage and unable to compete with the more efficient production from North America. Effect of economic turmoil in Britain ignored many of Adam Smith's theories. The depression in business of the early 1810s was markedly distinguished from earlier commercial recession by the fact that it affected profits far more, and more quickly than it affected employment, wages or the well-being of the working classes. The employers suffered much more than the employees.

The remaining colonies wanted unrestricted access to the British markets. Obviously the colonies would benefit enormously. Britain would enjoy a significant advantage as well. A differential tariff between the colonies and other foreign countries would assist both parties. India could export more tea if China was disadvantaged. Australia and South Africa could export more wine if France and Spain were disadvantaged. This concept of comparative advantage within the Empire would have remarkable empirical advantage. Indirectly Britain would pay less to subsidise the colonial operations whilst enjoying the advantages of cheaper foods. The Cobden led argument for an Empire Customs Union was shown to be impractical. The argument for fair trade was persuasive rather than differential duties. Only one –quarter of Britain's trade was with the colonies, so discriminatory tariffs against British and/or colonial goods hurt both markets and the consumers in each.

The point here is that the British Balance of Payments was under severe pressure and the changing colonial policy was as much guided by economic considerations as political or geographic.

The next point to ask is – Where did slavery fit into these calculations and policy considerations.

The coastal exploration of Africa and the invasion of North and South America by Europeans in the 15th century, and the subsequent colonization of the Americas during the next three centuries, provided the impetus for the modern slave trade. Portugal, lacking in agricultural workers, was the first modern European nation to meet its labour needs by importing slaves. The Portuguese began the practice in 1444; by 1460, they were annually importing 700 to 800 slaves to Portugal from trading posts and forts established on the African coast. These were African people captured by other Africans and transported to the western coast of Africa. Spain soon followed, but for more than a century Portugal virtually monopolized the African traffic. Throughout the 15th century, Arab traders in northern Africa shipped African people taken from central Africa to markets in Arabia, Iran, and India. England entered the slave trade in the latter half of the 16th century, contesting the right to supply the Spanish colonies held until then by Portugal. France, Holland, Denmark, and the American colonies themselves subsequently entered the trade as competitors. In 1713 the exclusive right to supply the Spanish colonies was granted to the British South Sea Company. As African slaves became an increasingly important element in the English colonies in America, particularly in the South where they were considered fundamental to the economy and society, the laws affecting them were modified. By the time of the American War of Independence (1775-1783), they were no longer indentured servants but slaves in the fullest sense of the term, and laws defining their legal, political, and social status with respect to their owners were specific.

Denmark was the first European country to abolish the slave trade, in 1792. Great Britain followed in 1807, and the United States followed in 1808. At the Congress of Vienna in 1814, Great Britain exerted its influence to induce other foreign powers to adopt a similar policy, and eventually nearly all the states of Europe passed laws or entered into treaties prohibiting the traffic. The Ashburton Treaty of 1842, between Great Britain and the United States, provided for the maintenance by each country of a squadron on the African coast to enforce prohibition of the trade, and in 1845 a joint cooperation of the naval forces of England and France was substituted for the mutual right of search. The limited supply of slaves led to a greater attention on the part of the owners to the condition of their slaves.

The French slaves had freedom conferred on them in 1848; the Dutch slaves in 1863. Most of the new republics of South America provided for the emancipation of slaves at the time of their establishment. In Brazil, however, slavery was not abolished until 1888.

So our question is – how close did the Aboriginals of Australia come to being enslaved – not to be shipped to other countries, but to be slave labour to meet the agricultural needs of the colony?

The facts are that Britain had been active in the slave trade for over 100 years when the First Fleet was being assembled and the British South Seas Company was both active and experienced in slave trade operations.

The South Sea Bubble was a plan devised by the English statesman Robert Harley, 1st Earl of Oxford, in 1711, for the retirement of the floating national debt of Great Britain. Under the plan, the debt was assumed by merchants to whom the government guaranteed annual payments equal to £2 million for a certain period. This sum, amounting to 6 per cent interest, was to be obtained from duties on imports. The monopoly of British trade in the South Seas and South America was given to these merchants, incorporated as the South Sea Company, and extravagant notions of the riches of South America were fostered. In the spring of 1720 the company offered to assume practically the whole national debt, at that time equal to more than £80 million.

However, a political crisis was averted through the efforts of Sir Robert Walpole, 1st Earl of Oxford, who at that time was serving as the Chancellor of the Exchequer. About one-third of the original capital was recovered for the stockholders.

Walpole had also determined to repay the losses in Britannia Incorporated, made by Scottish Speculation in Panama, prior to the Union of the two countries. The repayment of Scottish losses hastened the Union and gave Britain a launching pad for further colonization and foreign trade projects.

Another familiar name in the colonization program for Britain was that of Edward Gibbon Wakefield. His was a murky career. After the death of his first wife, he tricked an heiress into marrying him and was convicted of abduction in 1826. The marriage was dissolved by Parliament and Wakefield was imprisoned in Newgate Prison until 1830. While in prison he prepared a book on capital punishment (1831) and, in 'A Letter from Sydney' (1829). The latter book set down the basis for the theory of colonization. He later expanded into England and America (1833) and wrote 'A View of the Art of Colonization' (1849). Aware of the links between increased population, poverty, and crime, Wakefield proposed that colonies be settled by ordinary citizens, encouraged by the sale of small lots at fixed price, rather than by convicts. The land sales would also raise revenue for further colonization while social stability was maintained by a replication of the English class system. His ideas led to the founding of the South Australian Association (1834), which established the South Australian Colony in 1836. Wakefield separately formed the New Zealand Association in 1837, which became the New Zealand Company in 1841. In 1838 he was adviser to Lord Durham in Canada and influenced Durham's report on Canadian colonial policy. He encouraged the first group of settlers to emigrate to New Zealand in the following year, and thus put pressure on the British government to annex the country. After the constitution had been enacted in 1852, Wakefield joined the settlers and entered politics, becoming a member of the first assembly in 1854. That Wakefield changed the course of colonial policy is unquestioned. That the Aboriginals were given special treatment under the original colonial policy is also unquestioned.

- Phillip made suggestions to Lord Sydney on the future conduct of the settlement in 1787, included references to the natives:

  - 'I think it necessary to punish with severity men who use the native women ill

- The laws of the new settlement will be introduced and will not allow any form of slavery in a free land, and consequently no slaves.

In response and in accordance with tradition, the official Instructions to Phillip confirmed the proposed Phillip policy to the natives"

- The Instructions dated 25th April 1787, included an admonition to 'open an intercourse with the natives and to conciliate their affections, enjoining all our subjects to live in amity and kindness with them, and if any of our subjects wantonly destroy the, to punish those responsible according to the degree of the offence.

  - You will endeavour to procure an account of the numbers of the natives and report your opinion in what manner our intercourse with these people may be turned to the advantage of this colony.

Phillip wrote to Lord Sydney on May 15, 1788 and reported that he had not had any occasion to fire upon them but La Perouse, during his stay, had fired upon them and Phillip was attempting to restore the native's trust. Overall Phillip reported that the natives were friendly and welcoming of the trinkets and gifts he made available to them. Phillip expressed the opinion that the natives could have lived up to 50 miles inland from the coast – he having actually seen them at least 30 miles inland. In February 1790 Phillip reported that he had captured a native named Bennilong who he hoped to reconcile with the white people. Phillip took the first step in trying to understand Aboriginal culture by reporting on February 13th 1790, that 'the natives believe in spirits and say the bones of the dead are in the graves but the body is in the clouds!' (HRNSW)

Yarwood in 'Marsden – The Great Survivor' attributes to Marsden a double standard with regard to Aborigines.

Yarwood writes: "As Marsden was rejoicing in the improvement of his fleeces, which presaged the destruction of aboriginal culture in eastern Australia, some incidents at the Hawkesbury indicated certain elements of this incompatibility. An unspoken assumption was that the needs of the invader would prevail wherever interests clashed whether because of an initial need for a distant open-air gaol for Briton's convicted felons, or because of consequential requirements such as farming and grazing land and watercourses, from which the aborigines derived their traditional food supplies. Even for an invader of comparative goodwill, it was almost impossible to identify and preserve the basic needs of the Aborigines, for they had paid for their long blessed exemption from the Neolithic revolution with a life-style which set down no villages or farms of which incoming settlers could say 'That is clearly theirs'. Neither the basic economic need for game nor the indispensable link with their ancestors through the sacred places of the tribe made any perceptible mark on the land. Given as well the effects of a conditioning process which had gone on for many millennia, the Aborigines were unwilling to assimilate to a way of life that stressed fixity of residence, continuity of labour, and the accumulation of material possessions by individuals."

In response to his thought that 'native policy was no longer a matter for arid theoretical discussion, but one touching the very survival of outlying settlers', Macquarie recommended that he settle some adult Aborigines on land fronting the north shore of Port Jackson, where their anticipated success could not 'fail of Inviting and Encouraging other natives to settle on and Cultivate Lands' (Marsden evidence to Commissioner Bigge as reported by A.T. Yarwood)

Marsden recommended education of native youngsters and the need for reciprocal language studies, and the duty of teachers to 'prevent white children from making any improper reflexions on the Aborigines' colour, or of treating them in any other way contemptuously'. Yarwood also reveals that Marsden ceased his education program on the basis that the 'natives were beyond assistance 'of that type'.

One of the goals of this paper was to conclude whether or not the British colonial policy was consistent in its treatment of indigenous peoples.

Reynolds helps us in this regard, and makes three findings of interest:

a. Buxton, a Wilberforce associate, submitted to the 1834 Select Committee on Land Rights for Aborigines: "we have two objectives (1) to examine past relations between the British settlers and Aboriginal people and (2) to 'institute certain rules and laws on principle of justice'. In his final report as Chairman of the Committee, Buxton wrote "It might be presumed that the native inhabitants of any land have an incontrovertible right to their own soil; a plain and sacred right, which seems not to have been understood . . . . We have entered their land, and punished the natives as aggressors if they have evinced a disposition to live in their own country'.

b. Reynolds writes that ' by overlooking the commitment made by the first colonists to respect Aboriginal land rights, the later history of white-aboriginal relations can be presented in a much more favourable light than would otherwise be possible. What has been forgotten is the powerful commitment to racial equality, which ran through both the anti-slavery and Aboriginal protection movements'. This commitment was verified by the Court in the Gove Land Rights case/'The Letters Patent of 1836 guaranteed respect for land rights, and was an affirmation of a principle of benevolence' (Justice Blackburn)

c. Reynolds confirms that the British 'recognised the need to provide an equivalent 'financial compensation' for native title, as was the obligation to pay for the education, conversion and 'civilisation' of the displaced tribes. The question was first tackled in the *Imperial Crown Land Sale Act* (1842), which gave the Crown discretion to use the proceeds of land sales. – The Colonial Office had decided that 15% of land revenues should be spent on the indigenes in all new colonies. The Australian Governors were informed by despatch from London in September 1842 that they were to use an amount' not exceeding in the whole 15% of the gross proceeds of land sales for the benefit, civilisation and protection of the Aborigines'

d. Comparison with other former colonies is odious. The Canadian Supreme Court ruled "an aboriginal Indian interest in nature which is a burden on the title of the Crown and is inalienable except to the crown and extinguishable only by a legislative enactment of the Parliament of Canada. The Aboriginal title does not depend on treaty, executive order or legislative enactment but flows from the fact that the owners have from time immemorial occupied the areas and have established am pre-existing right of possession. In the absence of any indication that the sovereign intends to extinguish that right, the aboriginal title continues".

Our question, by way of conclusion should be what does all this mean for British Colonial policy and Aborigines. The British treated Canadian Indians and New Zealand Maoris differently to Australian Aborigines. By a stroke of luck and good timing the Aborigines avoided being drafted into slavery for the benefit of Agriculture, but lost their land rights in an ignominious way – as compared to the Canadian Indians who lawfully maintained their native title rights, and the New Zealand natives who bargained away their land in exchange for something of value.

In other respects the British directed a level of tolerance and respect for the Aborigines that at the official level, at least, was confirmed and implemented. Could the Crown's representative have enforced the fair treatment by settlers of the natives whose lives had been changed so radically with the arrival of the white settler? If the sins of the father cannot be visited on the coming generations, then Phillip and the following governors cannot be held responsible either for the misdeeds of the settlers.

Our conclusion must be that the British Colonial policy was a wonderful theory of world trade and political domination. It was not funded sufficiently to be fully successful and the competing demands for funds led to a certain failure of the theory. On the other hand, the British colonists were generally successful in their economic goals without relying on wars, civil unrest or depravation. That Britain took on too many colonies at the one time and ran out of supporting funds is not a crime but shortsightedness, although administratively the British Administration in the colonies was remarkably successful. The Commonwealth today is a living testimony to the success of the British colonial policies and their lasting benefits for the people who endured the changes.

We can conclude also that the changing role of colonisation and the emergence of the American interests largely influenced the political and economic changes pursued under the evolving policies. That there was a difference in approach between many colonies was a reflection of a learning process rather than a pragmatism born of greed or desire for unseemly world domination. These differences, other than respect to native title do not seem to have had any dramatic or lasting effect.

The overall success of Britain as a colonizer of merit stands out when compared to the competitors – the French, Spanish, Portuguese and Dutch. Having said that, it can be shown that the colonization program was not completely altruistic. The British received a generous return by way of interest on its invested capital, as well as a full return of capital from its investments into the colonies. This writer estimates that public investment was in excess of 60 million pound but the return to Britain, based on the 'opportunity cost' model was in excess of 180 million pound.

Could it be concluded that Britain made a 'profit' out of the colony?

CHAPTER 43

FOREIGN INVESTMENT TO THE RESCUE

EXPLAINING THE COLONIAL ECONOMIC DRIVERS 1788-1856

In order to understand the growth of the colonial economy, we must understand the economic drivers that underpinned, sustained and supported the colonial economy. There are at least six, if not seven, such economic drivers. They include the factors of (a) population growth, the (b) economic development within the colony, the (c) funding sources such as British Treasury appropriations and the (d) revenues raised from within the local economy (for example, taxes and duties on imports) and (e) foreign investment (both public and private). The traditional concept of growth within the colonial economy comes from (f) the rise of the pastoral industry. A seventh driver would be the all-important Land Board, which played such an important role within the colonial economy The Land Board played an important role in co-ordinating crown land policy, controlling land sales, squatting licenses and speculators, re-setting boundaries of location, establishing set aside lands for future townships and for church and school estates, carrying out the survey of millions of acres of land transferred by grant and sale, and offering terms sales for crown lands and being responsible for the collection of repayments, rents, license fees, quit-rents and depasturing fees. In addition the land board was vested with road reserves for hundreds of miles of unmade roads but important rights-of-way that would well into the future protect access to remote pastoral and farming properties. The main thrust of published material about the Land Board is in conjunction with crown land sales policy, but the Board had a much larger role and the overall Board policies sand performances are what are to be reviewed here.

Although an important factor it is no more important that our other five motivators of the colonial economy between 1802 and 1856. Why have I selected these two specific dates? 1802 was when Governor King first imposed an illegal, but justified and well-intentioned impost on the local free community to build a local gaol to replace one burnt to the ground through a lightening strike but which the British would not replace. The local residents thought a more solid and durable prison was a worthwhile community investment. At the other end, the year of 1856 signalled the first real representative and responsible government in the colony, and although it was not the end of the colonial era, it was certainly the end of Britain's financial support of sand for the colony and as such the colony was expected to stand on its own two feet.

These six factors will be discussed as mechanisms for 'growing the colonial economy between 1802 and 1856'

One consideration that must not be forgotten is the externally enforced pace of colonial expansion, particularly through the organised rather than the market-induced inflow of both convicts and assisted migrants. What this means is that instead of market forces requiring additional labour and human resources, extra labour and resources were imposed on the colony and there was an obligatory process of putting these people to work, in many cases by creating a public works program and pushing development ahead at an artificial pace rather than at a time and rate suited to the local economy. In much the same way, the 'assignment' system in the 1810-1830 period forced landowners to create clearing and development programs in order to utilise the labour available rather than only develop land as demand required.

1. Population growth including immigration of convicts & free settlers

The reason the colonial society did not change very much in the 1820s is that relatively few immigrants arrived. During 1823, Lord Bathurst, Colonial Secretary, sent instructions to Governor Brisbane (Macquarie's successor) altering the administration of the colony of NSW in most of the ways Commissioner Bigge had recommended in his reports.[18] One result of the Bigge Reports was that Macquarie was officially recalled to Britain even though he had canvassed his retirement before Bigge's arrival in 1819. Macquarie was distressed by the Bigge Reports and took very personally the recommendations made for change. Although there were many implied criticisms Macquarie considered that the public perception was that he had not acted properly in his role as Governor. Macquarie set to and compared the circumstances of the colony at the time of his arrival in 1810, with the great achievements he had made through 1821. In hindsight, Macquarie had accomplished much, mostly by means of arrogantly pursuing a series of policies without the pre-approval of the Secretary or the Government in London.

The arrival of only a few immigrants was because Bigge and the Colonial Office believed that only men of capital would emigrate. Labourers and the poor of England should not be encouraged and, as these people rarely had money to pay for the long passage to Sydney, few of them arrived.[19] Although the numbers were small, few of them came unassisted. In 1821 320 free immigrants arrived and this increased each year; 903 in 1826; 1005 in 1829, but slipping to 772 in 1830. Mostly they were family groups with some financial security.

---

[18] Commissioner J.T. Bigge had been sent by Bathurst to Enquire into the State and Operations of the colony of NSW in 1819; the House of Commons had demanded an inquiry into the colony and had threatened to hold one of its own; Bathurst pre-empted a difficult government situation by appointing Bigge with a very broad and wide-ranging terms of Enquiry. Bigge held two years of investigations in the colony and reported to the Commons in 1823 with the printing of three Reports.

[19] Australian History – The occupation of a Continent *Bessant* (Ed)

In 1828, the first census (as opposed to musters) of white persons in NSW was taken. 20,930 persons were classified as free and 15,668 were classified as convicts. However, of the free persons, many had arrived as convicts or were born of convicts. In fact, 70% of the population in 1828 had convict associations. However, by 1828, one quarter of the NSW population was native born; 3,500 were over 12 years of age

There was another side to this migration of unregulated souls. Shaw writes" The cost of assistance, the unsuitability of many emigrants, their ill-health, and the numbers of children and paupers that were sent – all these gave the colonists a source of grievance".[20] A large part of the problem was that the English wanted emigration – but those they wished to see emigrate were not welcomed in the colony. A growing opinion in the colony was that free migrants could not work with convicts; the convicts by themselves were too few and with growing expense; therefore transportation must stop and immigration be encouraged. However, immigrants of a good quality were not those the English wanted to send; its preference was for the paupers and the disruptive in the society. To stop transportation would be "attended with the most serious consequences unless there be previous means taken too ensure the introduction of a full supply of free labour". [21] In the next five years, the number of free immigrants increased so much that transportation could be stopped with little political backlash. Between 1835 and 1840, the colony was quite prosperous (it was a case of boom and bust—the great depression came in 1841); sales of crown land were large, and consequently the funds available for assisting immigrants were plentiful.[22]

---

[20] Shaw, A.G.L. *The economic development of Australia* p.44
[21] HRA Bourke to Colonial Secretary *Governor's despatches* 1835
[22] The British Treasury had agreed to put 50% of land sale proceeds into assisting immigrants with shipping costs; a further 15% into assisting Aborigines' and the balance was for discretionary use by the crown. These percentages changed in 1840 when all sale proceeds were spent on immigration but the land fund still ran out of funds in 1842 and no further assistance was made to immigrants other than by the colonial government borrowing funds in the London market through its own credit.

In 1838, land revenue was over £150,000 and assisted migrants numbered 7,400; in 1839, land revenue was £200,000 and assisted migrants 10,000; in 1840 revenue was over £500,000 and assisted migrants 22,500.

Between 1832 and 1842, over 50,000 assisted and 15,000 unassisted migrants arrived in NSW; or they might have arrived as convicts, and over 3,000 arrived that way each year. Thus between 1830 and 1840 the population of the whole of Australia increased from 70,000 to 190,000, with 130,000 of those in 1840 being in NSW. Of these 87000 were men and 43000 were women; 30,000 had been born in the colony; 50,000 were free settlers, 20,000 were emancipists and 30,000 were convicts.[23]

2. Foreign Private Investment

We need to make the distinction between foreign public investment, and foreign private investment. The British Treasury appropriated specific funds for infrastructure programs in the colony, such as public buildings, churches, gaols, roads etc.

One reason that local colonial taxes and duties were imposed on the colony was to give the governor the funding source for discretionary expenditures in order to improve his administration. There were many instances of expenditures which could not be covered by the British funds, such as a bounty to recapture runaway convicts, building fences around the cemeteries and whitewashing the walls of public buildings (for instance barracks) in the settlement. The British Treasury would have considered such items of expense as being unnecessary. Road repair and maintenance was intended to be covered from toll receipts but they were never sufficient to make necessary repairs. Governors Hunter and Bligh did little to improve public and community buildings, roads and bridges and by the time Macquarie arrived in the colony in 1810, there was a major backlog of building work and maintenance to be undertaken. Macquarie expanded the local revenue tax base in order to give himself more flexibility in pursuing improved conditions for the settlers and the population at large.

---

[23]   Shaw *ibid*

Although Macquarie did not specifically seek new free immigrants for the colony, word of mouth circulated that the colony was in a growth stage and worthy of being considered for either immigration or investment. Usually one accompanied the other. The first private investment came with the immigrants. Free settlers would either cash up in England or transfer their possessions to the colony, and this small level of private investment was the start of a major item of capital transfers to the colony.

However, private capital formation took many forms; the early settlers, bought or built houses, they built or bought furnishings; they had carriages and often employed water conservation.

As the system of land grants was expanded and farming was encouraged the spread of settlement required a combination of public and private investment.

The government had to provide roads and townships, and the settlers had to provide pastoral investment. This pastoral capital formation consisted of five main types of assets:

> Buildings – residence, outbuildings, wool shed or grain storage
> Fences – stockyards, posts and rails
> Water conservation – dams, tanks, wells
> Plant – cultivators, tools
> Stocks – food, clothing, household items, materials for animal care and general repairs—livestock

Stephen Roberts offers an interesting insight into the colony of 1835.[24]

"It did not need much prescience to foresee the whole of the country united by settlement – so much had it outgrown the coastal stage of Sydney town. It was a new Australia – a land of free settlement and progressive occupation – that was there, and the old convict days were ending.

Both human and monetary capital were pouring into the various colonies and transforming the nature of their population and problems. Convicts

---

[24]   Roberts, S.H *The Squatting Age in Australia 1835-1847 (published 1935)*

no longer set the tone; even autocratic governors belonged to a day that was passing, and instead, the country was in the grip of a strangely buoyant, and equally optimistic, race of free men".

As part of our private capital formation, we must remember the growth of human capital and the needs for specific labour. Capital requires labour with a specific role. The establishment and expansion of farming meant more than shepherding and ploughing. There was a considerable demand for building skills, for construction and maintenance of equipment such as drays and carts, harness making and repair, tool-making etc. It became important, in order to support and sustain capital growth and economic development to be able to employ labour with multi-skills. This was a new phenomenon for the colony, especially since Britain did not develop these types of broad skills and self-motivation in its criminal class. The Rev. J.D. Lang sought a temporary answer by specifically recruiting 'mechanics' in Scotland as immigrant for the colony.

3. British Public Funding transfers

Public Capital formation is obviously different to private capital formation. I have given an example of rural-based private capital formation elsewhere in this study and will do so again here, in order to demonstrate both types of capital investment.

Private capital formation took many forms; the early settlers, bought or built houses, they built or bought furnishings; they had carriages and often employed water conservation techniques, which included tanks or earthen dams.

As the system of land grants was expanded and farming was encouraged the spread of settlement required a combination of public and private investment.

The government had to provide roads and townships, and the settlers had to provide pastoral investment. This pastoral (rural-based) capital formation usually consisted of five main types of assets:

Buildings – residence, outbuildings, wool shed or grain storage

Fences – stockyards, posts and rails

Water conservation – dams, tanks, wells

Plant – cultivators, tools

Stocks – food, clothing, household items, materials for animal care and general repairs—livestock

Public capital on the other hand was a socio-economic based government asset, and included:

Roads, bridges, crossings, drainage, excavation and embanking, retaining walls

Hospital, storehouses, military barracks, convict barracks, Court-house, police posts, government office buildings

Market house, burial ground, Church, tollhouse, military magazines.

Obviously the list can go on and on.

Major Public Works in NSW 1817-1821

Roads
Sydney to Botany Bay
Sydney to South Head
Parramatta to Richmond
Liverpool to Bringelly, the Nepean and Appin
Buildings
Sydney
A military hospital; military barracks; convict barracks; carters barracks; Hyde Park
Toll-house; residences for the Supreme Court Judge, the Chaplain and the
Superintendent of Police; an asylum; a fort and powder magazines; stables for
Government House; a market house; a market wharf; a burial ground; St. James
Church
Parramatta
All Saint's church spire; a hospital; a parsonage; military and convict barracks; a
Factory; stables and coach-house at Government House; a reservoir

Windsor
St. Matthew's Church; military barracks; convict barracks
Liverpool
St. Luke's church; a gaol; a wharf; convict barracks

4. Economic Development

K. Dallas in an article on *Transportation and Colonial Income* writes, "The history of economic development in Australia is concerned with the transplanting of British economic life into a unique and novel environment. All colonial societies resemble each other in the problems of transplanting, but only in Australia was there no indigenous communal life vigorous enough to influence the course of future development"[25]

Dallas in the same article declares, "The economic effects of the transportation system are usually misunderstood. The real development of Australia begins with the pastoral industry and the export of wool in the 1820s. Until then, penal settlements were a base fore whalers, and made the pastoral possibilities known to English capitalist sheep farmers earlier than they would otherwise have known."[26]

Since this is such a major point on which much disagreement exists, an analysis of its merits is required. No less authority than N.G. Butlin, J.Ginswick and Pamela Statham disagree and they record in their introduction to 'The economy before 1850 "the history books are preoccupied with the pastoral expansion in NSW. It is reasonably certain from the musters that a great many complex activities developed and Sydney soon became not merely a port town but a community providing many craft products and services to the expanding settlement".[27]

The next section of this study outlines the remarkable contribution of Governor Macquarie between 1810 and 1821, most of the physical development taking place before the arrival of Commissioner J.T. Bigge in 1819. The table of infrastructure and public building development below

---

[25]   Dallas, Keith *Transportation & Colonial Income* Historical Studies ANZ Vol 3 October 1944-February 1949
[26]   Dallas *ibid*
[27]   The Australians: Statistics Chapter 7 'The economy before 1850'

confirms that the greatest period of economic development in the colonial economy took place under the Macquarie Administration and did not wait until the spread of settlement and the rise in the pastoral industry (which brought with it so many economic problems) in the late 1820s and 1830s.

IMPACT OF THE COLONIAL ISOLATION DURING THE 1800S

The question of isolation was of positive benefit to the British authorities because the concept of creating a *dumping ground for human garbage* was synonymous with finding a *penal wasteland that was out of sight and out of mind*.

However the disadvantages to the Colonial authorities were numerous

There was the tyranny of distance—the huge risks, of frightening transportation by sailing ship to a land hitherto unknown, uncharted and unexplored, promising huge risks and great loss of life.

Food preservation during the voyage and in the Colony was a challenge with no refrigeration or ice. The only preservatives being salt and pickling.

Communications between Sydney and London made exchange of correspondence, obtaining decisions and permission tiresomely long. It often occurred that the Colonial Governor wrote to a Colonial Secretary, who during the twelve months of round trip, had been replaced with another person.

Laws and justice, in the Colony, were to be based on British law, but in reality, local laws became a mix of common sense and personal philosophies eg Lt Governor Collins, as Advocate-General in the Colony desperately needed law books to practice, but they were never sent. Bligh, as Governor, ruled virtually as a despot and tyrannical dictator, knowing that a sea trip of seven months was between him and any admonishment or complaints being heard.

Factors Affecting British Investment in the Colony

A number of factors affected the level of capital investment into the colony – many were ill informed and relied on delayed newspaper reports on activity in the various settlements.

a. The offer of assisted migration
b. The failing economic conditions in Britain
c. Economic expansion for the pastoral industry due to successful exploration in the colony
d. The settlement at Port Phillip and the eventual separation of Victoria from New South Wales would promote great investment opportunities
e. The rise of the squattocracy
f. The crash of 1827-28 in the colony shakes British Investors
g. The Bigge's' Report of 1823 breathed new life into capital formation especially with Macarthur sponsoring the float of the Australian Agricultural Company
h. Further along, the good credit rating of the colonies (and there being no defaults on loans) encouraged larger investments and loans into the colonies
i. Shortage of Labour in the colony and the offer of land grants to new settlers became a useful carrot to attract small settlers bringing their own capital by way of cash or goods or livestock with them.
j. Two other steps had important consequences, one in the colony and the other in Britain. In 1827 Governor Darling began to issue grazing licenses to pastoralists, and the terms were set at 2/6d per hundred acres, with liability to quit on one month's notice. From this movement grew, writes Madgwick in Immigration into Eastern Australia, the squatting movement and the great pastoral expansion, and the idea of the earlier Governors that the colony of New South Wales should be a colony of farmers was thus abandoned. The concurrent event was the floating of the Australian Agricultural Company in London. Development by the AAC and by the free settlers brought increasing prosperity. Exports tripled between 1826 and 1831.
k. There is a connection between availability of factors of production and the level of investment. In the early days of the colony, labour

was present—bad labour, convict labour, but still labour. The governors had demanded settlers with capital to employ that labour and develop the land. They proposed to limit land grants in proportion to the means of the settler. Governor Darling declared (HRA ser 1, vol 8) that 'when I am satisfied of the character, respectability and means of the applicant settler in a rural area, he will receive the necessary authority to select a grant of land, proportionate in extent to the means he possesses.

Under Macquarie the colony had boomed with new buildings, new settlements, new investment and lots of convicts. Under Brisbane the needs for economic consolidation and new infrastructure would be addressed, together with an appeal for free settlers.

Some significant events took place during the Brisbane guardianship

The British were intent on accessing every available trading opportunity with the colony, and formed in Scotland *The Australia Company*

A road was built to connect the Windsor settlement to the new settlement at Maitland. This decision opened up the Hunter River district to new farming opportunities

The responsibility for convicts was transferred from the Superintendent of Convicts to the Colonial Secretary, although this move was to be reversed within the next decade

The first documented discovery of gold was made. It was hushed in the colony lest convicts run off to find their fortunes

In Bigge's third and final report, he recommended extra colonial import duties and less British duty on imported timber and tanning bark

The most significant event of all was the confidence placed in Bigge's favourable opinion of the potential of the colonial economy by the London Investment community and the resulting subscription of one million pound for the Australian Agricultural Company. The subscription was accompanied by a grant of one million acres of land around Port

Stephens and the allocation of 5,000 convicts, but also brought inflation to livestock prices and availability throughout the colony.

J.F. Campbell wrote about the first decade of the Australian Agricultural Company 1824-1834 in the proceedings of the 1923 RAHS.

"Soon after Commissioner Bigge's report of 1823 became available for public information, several enterprising men concerted with a view to acquire sheep-runs in the interior of this colony, for the production of fine wool.

The success which attended the efforts of John Macarthur and a few other New South Wales pastoralists, in the breeding and rearing of fine wool sheep and stock generally, as verified by Bigge, gave the incentive and led to the inauguration of proceedings which resulted in the formation of the Australian Agricultural Company.

The first formal meeting of the promoters took place at Lincoln's Inn, London, (at the offices of John Macarthur, junior).

Earl Bathurst, advised Governor Brisbane in 1824 that . . . .

His Majesty has been pleased to approve the formation of the Company, from the impression that it affords every reasonable prospect of securing to that part of His Majesty's dominions the essential advantage of the immediate introduction of large capital, and of agricultural skill, as well as the ultimate benefit of the increase of fine wool as a valuable commodity for export.

The chief proposals of the company are:

The company was to be incorporated by Act of Parliament or Letters Patent.

The capital of the company was to be 1 million pound sterling divided into 10,000 shares of 100 pound each

A grant of land of one million acres to be made to the company

That no rival joint stock company to be established in the colony for the next twenty years

That agents of the company would select the situation or the land grants.

The shepherds and labourers would consist of 1,400 convicts, thereby lessening the maintenance of such convicts by an estimated 30,800 pound or 22 pound/per head/ per annum.

The Royal Charter of 1824 forming the company provided for payment of quit-rents over a period of twenty years, or the redemption of the same by paying the capital sum of 20 times the amount of the rent so to be redeemed. These quit-rents were to be waived if the full number of convicts were maintained for a period of five years. No land was to be sold during the five-year period from the date of the grant".

Being important that the investment be seen to have the support of strong leaders in Britain, and democratic governance, the company operated with· One Governor; · 25 directors; and 365 stockholders (proprietors). The old English structure was retained, that of, Governor and his Court, with the directors being the members of the Court whilst the Governor was the Chairman of the Board or Court

Leading stockholders included

- Robert Campbell
- Chief Justice Forbes
- Son of Governor King
- Rev'd Samuel Marsden
- John MacArthur

· Each Macarthur son, John Jr, Hannibal, James, Charles, Scott & William John Oxley. The Colonial-Surveyor (Oxley) had recommended the area of Port Stephens as an eligible spot for the land grant. The local directors inspected and approved the site but John Macarthur was extremely critical of the selection, the management plan and the extravagance of the first buildings.

This venture was the first major investment into the colony and set the scene for later developments. In 1825 the Van Diemen's Land Company was chartered by the British Parliament and granted land on the northwest corner of the territory.

Both the A.A. Coy and the VDL Coy still operate today after nearly 180 years of continuous operation, a record beaten only by the operation of the Hudson Bay Company in Canada.

Sir Timothy Coghlan was the colonial statistician whilst he was involved in preparing the series 'The Wealth and Progress of New South Wales 1900-01'. He was later appointed as Agent-General in London before compiling the 4-volume set of 'Labour and Industry in Australia'.

Circumstances in Britain contributed greatly to the climate of 'greener pastures' over the seas.

Conditions were never more favourable for emigration than they were during the 1830s. The decade had opened with rioting in the agricultural districts in the south of England. This was followed by the upheavals of the Reform Bill of 1832, the Factory Act of 1833 and the Corn Laws, which kept wages low and unemployment high. The Poor Law of 1834 withdrew assistance from the poor and re-introduced the workhouse. The Irish rebellion was creating both upheaval and poverty

These conditions were met by the enthusiastic reports coming from Australia of the progress being made in agriculture, commerce and the pastoral industry. The assistance granted to emigrants as a result of Edward Gibbon Wakefield's reforms made possible the emigration of people who had previously been prevented by the expense. It is almost certain that free passage would not have been a sufficient enticement if conditions in Britain had not been unfavourable. It is significant that years of small migration coincided with good conditions in England accompanied by unfavourable reports from the colony.

4. Creating Opportunities in the Colony

Availability of land and labour to yield profit on invested capital is the constant decisive condition and test of material prosperity in any community, and becomes the keystone of an economy as well as defining its national identity.

British Government policy for the Australian colonies was formulated and modified from time to time. Policies for the export of British capital and the supply of labour (both convict and free) were adjusted according to British industrial and demographic and other social situations, as well as the capability and capacity of the various colonial settlements top contribute to solving British problems.

By the 1820s there was official encouragement of British Investment in Australia by adopting policies for large land grants to persons of capital and for the sale of land and assignment of convict labour to those investors. Then followed the reversal of the policy of setting up ex-convicts on small 30 acre plots as small proprietors. The hardship demanded by this policy usually meant these convicts and families remained on the commissary list for support (food and clothing) at a continuing cost to the government. It was much cheaper to assign these convicts to men of property and capital who would support them fully – clothe, house and feed them.

We can ask, what led directly to the crash of 1827?

a. Firstly, the float of the Australian Agricultural Company raised a large amount of capital, mostly from the City of London investment community, and this contributed to speculation and 'sheep and cattle mania instantly seized on all ranks and classes of the inhabitants' (written by Rev'd John Dunmore Lang) 'and brought many families to poverty and ruin'.

b. When capital imports cease, the wherewithal to speculate vanished; speculation perforce stopped; inflated prices fell to a more normal level, and wrote E.O. Shann in Economic History of Australia 'because those formerly too optimistic were now too despairing, and people had to sell goods at any price in order to get money;

men who had bought at high prices were ruined, and perforce their creditors fell with them'.

c.   In 1842, it was the same. The influx of capital from oversees, pastoral extension, and large-scale immigration, caused much speculation. The banks, competing for business, advanced too much credit. Loans were made on the security of land and livestock, which later became almost worthless; too much discounting was done for merchants. (Gipps, HRA Vol 23) In the huge central district on the western slopes, along the Murrumbidgee and the Riverina, the squatters triumphed, as was inevitable. He had the financial resources to buy his run – especially after the long period of drought. Four million acres of crown land was sold for nearly 2.5 million pound. The confidence of British investors was waning. A crisis in the Argentine and the near failure of the large clearinghouse of Baring's made them cautious. Stories of rural and industrial strife in the colony were not inducements to invest: and wood and metal prices were still falling Loan applications being raised in London were under-subscribed, at the same time, the banks were increasingly reluctant to lend money for land development, which was so often unsound.

5. Assisted Migration

The dual policy of selling land to people with sufficient capital to cultivate it, and keeping a careful check on the number of free grants was adopted after 1825. 'Yet the Colonial Office', says Madgwick, 'failed to administer land policy with any certainty (R.B. Madgwick 'Immigration into Eastern Australia'). There was no uniform policy adopted to encourage economic development in a systematic and rational way. The Wakefield system found new supporters. The principle had been established that the sale of land was preferred to the old system of grants. The dual system of sales and grants had failed to encourage local (colonial) purchases. They were willing to accept grants or even 'squat' rather than purchase land. Sales to absentee landlords and investors stepped up, and as can be seen from the following table, provided extensive revenue to the British Government to promote free and sponsored migration.

6. Successful exploration promotes new interest in the Colony

A period of rapid expansion followed the change in economic policy. Wool exports by 1831 were 15 times as great as they had been only 10 years earlier (in 1821). The increase in the number of sheep led to a rapid opening of new territories for grazing. It was the search for new land with economic value that underpinned most of the explorations. Settlers and sheep-men quickly followed exploration, and growth fanned out in all directions from Sydney town.

However, exploration was not the only catalyst for growth. a. The growing determination to exclude other powers from the continent stimulated official interest in long-distance exploration by sea and by land and in the opening of new settlements. For instance, J.M. Ward in his work ' The Triumph of the Pastoral Economy 1821-1851' writes that Melville and Bathurst Islands, were annexed and settled between 1824 and 1827, whilst Westernport and Albany were settled in order to clinch British claims to the whole of Australia b. When Governor Brisbane opened the settlement at Moreton Bay in 1824, it was to establish a place for punishment of unruly convicts and a step towards further economic development, and of extending the settlements for the sake of attracting new investment

7. Colonial Failures fuel loss of Confidence

The collapse of British Investment can be traced to one or two causes, or indeed both.

I. The British crisis of 1839 reflected the availability of capital for expansion by the Australian banks of that day – The Bank of Australasia and the Union Bank. These banks, three mortgage companies and the Royal Bank went into a slump due to shortage of available funds and deferred the raising of new funds until after the crisis. Stringency in the English Capital market had a serious impact on the capital raising opportunities in the colonies.

II. The second possibility is that the sharp decline was initiated by bad news of returns in the colonies, and that its role accentuated a slump with the dire consequences experienced in 1842-43. Recovery was delayed and made more difficult as there was 'no surplus labour in the colony'

It would be dangerous to imply or decide that every slump in Australia could be explained as being caused by economic events. British investment was independent then, as it is now, and so the more valid explanation of the downturn in British investment in this period is that negative reports from the colonies disappointed and discouraged investors with capital to place.

Most facts about public finance in New South Wales lead to the conclusion that it was disappointed expectations that caused the turn down in the transfer of funds. At this same time Governor Gipps (Sir George Gipps) was being pushed by bankers and merchants to withdraw government deposits from the banks and thus this action caused a contraction in lending by the banks which in turn caused a slowdown of colonial economic activity. The attached statistics of land sales, registered mortgages and liens on wool and livestock reflects the strong downturn in the agricultural economy, which naturally flowed on to the economy as a whole.